Concurrent and Distributed
Computing in Java

Concurrent and Distributed Computing in Java

Vijay K. Garg
University of Texas at Austin

IEEE PRESS

A JOHN WILEY & SONS, INC., PUBLICATION

Library of Congress Cataloging-in-Publication Data:

Garg, Vijay Kumar, 1938–
    Concurrent and distributed computing in Java / Vijay K. Garg.
      p. cm.
    Includes bibliographical references and index.
    ISBN 0-471-43230-X (cloth) $O|- | 4 - O5$
    1. Parallel processing (Electronic computers). 2. Electronic data processing—Distributed processing. 3. Java (Computer program language). I. Title.

QA76.58G35 2004
005.2'75—dc22   2003065883

Printed in the United States of America.

10 9 8 7 6 5 4 3 2 1

To
my teachers and
my students

Contents

List of Figures   xiii

Preface   xix

1   Introduction   **1**
   1.1   Introduction   1
   1.2   Distributed Systems versus Parallel Systems   3
   1.3   Overview of the Book   4
   1.4   Characteristics of Parallel and Distributed Systems   6
   1.5   Design Goals   7
   1.6   Specification of Processes and Tasks   8
       1.6.1   Runnable Interface   11
       1.6.2   Join Construct in Java   11
       1.6.3   Thread Scheduling   13
   1.7   Problems   13
   1.8   Bibliographic Remarks   15

2   Mutual Exclusion Problem   **17**
   2.1   Introduction   17
   2.2   Peterson's Algorithm   20
   2.3   Lamport's Bakery Algorithm   24
   2.4   Hardware Solutions   27
       2.4.1   Disabling Interrupts   27
       2.4.2   Instructions with Higher Atomicity   27
   2.5   Problems   28
   2.6   Bibliographic Remarks   30

3   Synchronization Primitives   **31**
   3.1   Introduction   31
   3.2   Semaphores   31

        3.2.1   The Producer-Consumer Problem   33
        3.2.2   The Reader-Writer Problem   36
        3.2.3   The Dining Philosopher Problem   36
    3.3   Monitors   42
    3.4   Other Examples   46
    3.5   Dangers of Deadlocks   49
    3.6   Problems   50
    3.7   Bibliographic Remarks   51

4 Consistency Conditions   53
    4.1   Introduction   53
    4.2   System Model   54
    4.3   Sequential Consistency   55
    4.4   Linearizability   57
    4.5   Other Consistency Conditions   60
    4.6   Problems   62
    4.7   Bibliographic Remarks   63

5 Wait-Free Synchronization   65
    5.1   Introduction   65
    5.2   Safe, Regular, and Atomic Registers   66
    5.3   Regular SRSW Register   70
    5.4   SRSW Multivalued Register   71
    5.5   MRSW Register   73
    5.6   MRMW Register   74
    5.7   Atomic Snapshots   76
    5.8   Consensus   78
    5.9   Universal Constructions   84
    5.10 Problems   87
    5.11 Bibliographic Remarks   87

6 Distributed Programming   89
    6.1   Introduction   89
    6.2   InetAddress Class   89
    6.3   Sockets based on UDP   90
        6.3.1   Datagram Sockets   90
        6.3.2   DatagramPacket Class   91
        6.3.3   Example Using Datagrams   92
    6.4   Sockets Based on TCP   94
        6.4.1   Server Sockets   96

	6.4.2	Example 1: A Name Server	96
	6.4.3	Example 2: A Linker	100
6.5	Remote Method Invocations		101
	6.5.1	Remote Objects	105
	6.5.2	Parameter Passing	107
	6.5.3	Dealing with Failures	108
	6.5.4	Client Program	108
6.6	Other Useful Classes		109
6.7	Problems		109
6.8	Bibliographic Remarks		110

7 Models and Clocks   111
7.1	Introduction		111
7.2	Model of a Distributed System		112
7.3	Model of a Distributed Computation		114
	7.3.1	Interleaving Model	114
	7.3.2	Happened-Before Model	114
7.4	Logical Clocks		115
7.5	Vector Clocks		117
7.6	Direct-Dependency Clocks		122
7.7	Matrix Clocks		125
7.8	Problems		126
7.9	Bibliographic Remarks		127

8 Resource Allocation   129
8.1	Introduction	129
8.2	Specification of the Mutual Exclusion Problem	130
8.3	Centralized Algorithm	132
8.4	Lamport's Algorithm	135
8.5	Ricart and Agrawala's Algorithm	136
8.6	Dining Philosopher Algorithm	138
8.7	Token-Based Algorithms	142
8.8	Quorum-Based Algorithms	144
8.9	Problems	146
8.10	Bibliographic Remarks	147

9 Global Snapshot   149
9.1	Introduction	149
9.2	Chandy and Lamport's Global Snapshot Algorithm	151
9.3	Global Snapshots for non-FIFO Channels	154

9.4   Channel Recording by the Sender 154
9.5   Application: Checkpointing a Distributed Application 157
9.6   Problems 161
9.7   Bibliographic Remarks 162

10 Global Properties   **163**
10.1 Introduction 163
10.2 Unstable Predicate Detection 164
10.3 Application: Distributed Debugging 169
10.4 A Token-Based Algorithm for Detecting Predicates 169
10.5 Problems 173
10.6 Bibliographic Remarks 176

11 Detecting Termination and Deadlocks   **177**
11.1 Introduction 177
11.2 Diffusing Computation 177
11.3 Dijkstra and Scholten's Algorithm 180
      11.3.1 An Optimization 181
11.4 Termination Detection without Acknowledgment Messages 182
11.5 Locally Stable Predicates 185
11.6 Application: Deadlock Detection 188
11.7 Problems . . . . , . 189
11.8 Bibliographic Remarks 189

12 Message Ordering   **191**
12.1 Introduction 191
12.2 Causal Ordering 193
      12.2.1 Application: Causal Chat 196
12.3 Synchronous Ordering 196
12.4 Total Order for Multicast Messages 203
      12.4.1 Centralized Algorithm 203
      12.4.2 Lamport's Algorithm for Total Order 204
      12.4.3 Skeen's Algorithm 204
      12.4.4 Application: Replicated State Machines 205
12.5 Problems 205
12.6 Bibliographic Remarks 207

13 Leader Election   **209**
13.1 Introduction 209
13.2 Ring-Based Algorithms 210

        13.2.1 Chang–Roberts Algorithm 210
        13.2.2 Hirschberg–Sinclair Algorithm 212
    13.3 Election on General Graphs 213
        13.3.1 Spanning Tree Construction 213
    13.4 Application: Computing Global Functions 215
    13.5 Problems 217
    13.6 Bibliographic Remarks 219

14 Synchronizers   **221**
    14.1 Introduction 221
    14.2 A Simple Synchronizer 223
        14.2.1 Application: BFS Tree Construction 225
    14.3 Synchronizer α 226
    14.4 Synchronizer β 228
    14.5 Synchronizer γ 230
    14.6 Problems 232
    14.7 Bibliographic Remarks 232

15 Agreement   **233**
    15.1 Introduction 233
    15.2 Consensus in Asynchronous Systems (Impossibility) 234
    15.3 Application: Terminating Reliable Broadcast 238
    15.4 Consensus in Synchronous Systems 239
        15.4.1 Consensus under Crash Failures 240
        15.4.2 Consensus under Byzantine Faults 243
    15.5 Knowledge and Common Knowledge 244
    15.6 Application: Two-General Problem 248
    15.7 Problems 249
    15.8 Bibliographic Remarks 250

16 Transactions   **253**
    16.1 Introduction 253
    16.2 ACID Properties 254
    16.3 Concurrency Control 255
    16.4 Dealing with Failures 256
    16.5 Distributed Commit 257
    16.6 Problems 261
    16.7 Bibliographic Remarks 262

17 Recovery   **263**
  17.1 Introduction 263
  17.2 Zigzag Relation 265
  17.3 Communication-Induced Checkpointing 267
  17.4 Optimistic Message Logging: Main Ideas 268
      17.4.1 Model 269
      17.4.2 Fault-Tolerant Vector Clock 270
      17.4.3 Version End Table 272
  17.5 An Asynchronous Recovery Protocol 272
      17.5.1 Message Receive 274
      17.5.2 On Restart after a Failure 274
      17.5.3 On Receiving a Token 274
      17.5.4 On Rollback 276
  17.6 Problems 277
  17.7 Bibliographic Remarks 278

18 Self-Stabilization   **279**
  18.1 Introduction 279
  18.2 Mutual Exclusion with K-State Machines 280
  18.3 Self-Stabilizing Spanning Tree Construction 285
  18.4 Problems 286
  18.5 Bibliographic Remarks 289

A. Various Utility Classes   **291**

Bibliography   **297**

Index   **305**

List of Figures

1.1 A parallel system 2
1.2 A distributed system 2
1.3 A process with four threads 9
1.4 HelloWorldThread.java 11
1.5 FooBar.java 12
1.6 Fibonacci.java 14

2.1 Interface for accessing the critical section 18
2.2 A program to test mutual exclusion 19
2.3 An attempt that violates mutual exclusion 20
2.4 An attempt that can deadlock 21
2.5 An attempt with strict alternation 21
2.6 Peterson's algorithm for mutual exclusion 22
2.7 Lamport's bakery algorithm 25
2.8 TestAndSet hardware instruction 27
2.9 Mutual exclusion using TestAndSet 28
2.10 Semantics of swap operation 28
2.11 Dekker.java 29

3.1 Binary semaphore 32
3.2 Counting semaphore 33
3.3 A shared buffer implemented with a circular array 34
3.4 Bounded buffer using semaphores 35
3.5 Producer-consumer algorithm using semaphores 37
3.6 Reader-writer algorithm using semaphores 38
3.7 The dining philosopher problem 39
3.8 Dining Philosopher 40
3.9 Resource Interface 41
3.10 Dining philosopher using semaphores 41
3.11 A pictorial view of a Java monitor 44

3.12 Bounded buffer monitor   45
3.13 Dining philosopher using monitors   47
3.14 Linked list   48

4.1   Concurrent histories illustrating sequential consistency   56
4.2   Sequential consistency does not satisfy locality   58
4.3   Summary of consistency conditions   62

5.1   Safe and unsafe read–write registers   67
5.2   Concurrent histories illustrating regularity   68
5.3   Atomic and nonatomic registers   69
5.4   Construction of a regular boolean register   71
5.5   Construction of a multivalued register   72
5.6   Construction of a multireader register   75
5.7   Construction of a multiwriter register   76
5.8   Lock-free atomic snapshot algorithm   77
5.9   Consensus Interface   78
5.10 Impossibility of wait-free consensus with atomic read–write registers   80
5.11 TestAndSet class   81
5.12 Consensus using TestAndSet object   82
5.13 CompSwap object   82
5.14 Consensus using CompSwap object   83
5.15 Load-Linked and Store-Conditional object   84
5.16 Sequential queue   85
5.17 Concurrent queue   86

6.1   A datagram server   93
6.2   A datagram client   95
6.3   Simple name table   97
6.4   Name server   98
6.5   A client for name server   99
6.6   Topology class 100
6.7   Connector class 102
6.8   Message class 103
6.9   Linker class 104
6.10 Remote interface 105
6.11 A name service implementation 106
6.12 A RMI client program 109

7.1   An example of topology of a distributed system 113
7.2   A simple distributed program with two processes 113

7.3   A run in the happened-before model 115
7.4   A logical clock algorithm 117
7.5   A vector clock algorithm 119
7.6   The VCLinker class that extends the Linker class 120
7.7   A sample execution of the vector clock algorithm 121
7.8   A direct-dependency clock algorithm 122
7.9   A sample execution of the direct-dependency clock algorithm. . . . 123
7.10 The matrix clock algorithm 124

8.1   Testing a lock implementation 131
8.2   ListenerThread 132
8.3   Process.java 133
8.4   A centralized mutual exclusion algorithm 134
8.5   Lamport's mutual exclusion algorithm 137
8.6   Ricart and Agrawala's algorithm 139
8.7   (a) Conflict graph; (b) an acyclic orientation with P_2 and P_4 as
      sources; (c) orientation after P_2 and P_4 finish eating 141
8.8   An algorithm for dining philosopher problem 143
8.9   A token ring algorithm for the mutual exclusion problem 145

9.1   Consistent and inconsistent cuts 151
9.2   Classification of messages 153
9.3   Chandy and Lamport's snapshot algorithm 155
9.4   Linker extended for use with SenderCamera 158
9.5   A global snapshot algorithm based on sender recording 159
9.6   Invocation of the global snapshot algorithm 160

10.1 WCP (weak conjunctive predicate) detection algorithm—checker pro-
      cess. 167
10.2 Circulating token with vector clock 170
10.3 An application that runs circulating token with a sensor 171
10.4 Monitor process algorithm at P_i 172
10.5 Token-based WCP detection algorithm. 174

11.1 A diffusing computation for the shortest path 179
11.2 Interface for a termination detection algorithm 179
11.3 Termination detection algorithm 183
11.4 A diffusing computation for the shortest path with termination . . . 184
11.5 Termination detection by token traversal. 186

12.1 A FIFO computation that is not causally ordered 191

12.2 An algorithm for causal ordering of messages at P_i 193
12.3 Structure of a causal message 194
12.4 CausalLinker for causal ordering of messages 195
12.5 A chat program 197
12.6 A computation that is synchronously ordered 198
12.7 A computation that is not synchronously ordered 198
12.8 The algorithm at P_i for synchronous ordering of messages 201
12.9 The algorithm for synchronous ordering of messages 202

13.1 The leader election algorithm 211
13.2 Configurations for the worst case (a) and the best case (b) 212
13.3 A spanning tree construction algorithm 214
13.4 A convergecast algorithm 216
13.5 A broadcast algorithm 216
13.6 Algorithm for computing a global function 218
13.7 Computing the global sum 219

14.1 Algorithm for the simple synchronizer at P_j 223
14.2 Implementation of the simple synchronizer 224
14.3 An algorithm that generates a tree on an asynchronous network . . 226
14.4 BFS tree algorithm using a synchronizer 227
14.5 Alpha synchronizer 229

15.1 (a) Commutativity of disjoint events; (b) asynchrony of messages . . 234
15.2 (a) Case 1: $proc(e) \neq proc(f)$; (b) case 2: $proc(e) = proc(f)$ 237
15.3 Algorithm at P_i for consensus under crash failures 241
15.4 Consensus in a synchronous environment 242
15.5 Consensus tester 243
15.6 An algorithm for Byzantine General Agreement 245

16.1 Algorithm for the coordinator of the two-phase commit protocol . . 259
16.2 Algorithm for the participants in the two-phase commit protocol . . 260

17.1 An example of the domino effect 264
17.2 Examples of zigzag paths 266
17.3 A distributed computation 271
17.4 Formal description of the fault-tolerant vector clock 273
17.5 Formal description of the version end-table mechanism 273
17.6 An optimistic protocol for asynchronous recovery 275

18.1 K-state self-stabilizing algorithm 280

18.2 A move by the bottom machine in the K-state algorithm 280

18.3 A move by a normal machine in the K-state algorithm 281

18.4 Self-stabilizing algorithm for mutual exclusion in a ring for the bottom machine 283

18.5 Self-stabilizing algorithm for mutual exclusion in a ring for a normal machine 284

18.6 Self-stabilizing algorithm for (BFS) spanning tree 285

18.7 Self-stabilizing spanning tree algorithm for the root 286

18.8 Self-stabilizing spanning tree algorithm for nonroot nodes 287

18.9 A Java program for spanning tree 288

A.1 Util.java 292

A.2 Symbols.java 293

A.3 Matrix.java 293

A.4 MsgList.java 294

A.5 IntLinkedList.java 294

A.6 PortAddr.java 295

Preface

This book is designed for a senior undergraduate-level course or an introductory graduate-level course on concurrent and distributed computing. This book grew out of my dissatisfaction with books on distributed systems (including books authored by me) that included pseudocode for distributed algorithms. There were two problems with pseudocode. First, pseudocode had many assumptions hidden in it making it more succinct but only at the expense of precision. Second, translating pseudocode into actual code requires effort and time, resulting in students never actually running the algorithm. Seeing the code run lends an extra level of confidence in one's understanding of the algorithms.

It must be emphasized that all of the Java code provided in this book is for educational purposes only. I have deliberately avoided error checking and other software engineering principles to keep the size of the code small. In the majority of cases, this led to Java code, that kept the concepts of the algorithm transparent.

Several examples and exercise problems are included in each chapter to facilitate classroom teaching. I have made an effort to include some programming exercises with each chapter.

I would like to thank the following people for working with me on various projects discussed in this book: Craig Chase (weak predicates), Om Damani (message logging), Eddy Fromentin (predicate detection), Joydeep Ghosh (global computation), Richard Kilgore (channel predicates), Roger Mitchell (channel predicates), Neeraj Mittal (predicate detection and control, slicing, self-stabilization, distributed shared memory), Venkat Murty (synchronous ordering), Michel Raynal (control flow properties, distributed shared memory), Alper Sen (slicing), Chakarat Skawratonand (vector clocks), Ashis Tarafdar (message logging, predicate control), Alexander Tomlinson (global time, mutual exclusion, relational predicates, control flow properties) and Brian Waldecker (weak and strong predicates). Anurag Agarwal, Arindam Chakraborty, Selma Ikiz, Neeraj Mittal, Sujatha Kashyap, Vinit Ogale, and Alper Sen reviewed parts of the book. I owe special thanks to Vinit Ogale for also helping me with figures.

I thank the Department of Electrical and Computer Engineering at The University of Texas at Austin, where I was given the opportunity to develop and teach courses on concurrent and distributed systems. Students in these courses gave me very useful feedback.

I was supported in part by many grants from the National Science Foundation over the last 14 years. Many of the results reported in this book would not have been discovered by me and my research group without that support. I also thank John Wiley & Sons, Inc. for supporting the project.

Finally, I thank my parents, wife and children. Without their love and support, this book would not have been even conceived.

There are many concurrent and distributed programs in this book. Although I have tried to ensure that there are no "bugs" in these programs, some are, no doubt, still lurking in the code. I would be grateful if any bug that is discovered is reported to me. The list of known errors and the supplementary material for the book will be maintained on my homepage:

http://www.ece.utexas.edu/~garg

Included in the Website is a program that allows animation of most of the algorithms in the book. It also includes all the source code given in the book. The reader can access the source code with the user name as **guest** and the password as **utexas**.

Vijay K. Garg
Austin, Texas

Chapter 1

Introduction

1.1 Introduction

Parallel and distributed computing systems are now widely available. A *parallel system* consists of multiple processors that communicate with each other using shared memory. As the number of transistors on a chip increases, multiprocessor chips will become fairly common. With enough parallelism available in applications, such systems will easily beat sequential systems in performance. Figure 1.1 shows a parallel system with multiple processors. These processors communicate with each other using the shared memory. Each processor may also have local memory that is not shared with other processors.

We define *distributed systems* as those computer systems that contain multiple processors connected by a communication network. In these systems processors communicate with each other using messages that are sent over the network. Such systems are increasingly available because of decrease in prices of computer processors and the high-bandwidth links to connect them. Figure 1.2 shows a distributed system. The communication network in the figure could be a local area network such as an Ethernet, or a wide area network such as the Internet.

Programming parallel and distributed systems requires a different set of tools and techniques than that required by the traditional sequential software. The focus of this book is on these techniques.

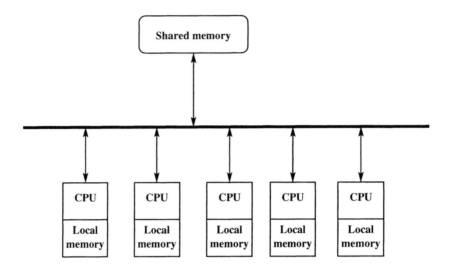

Figure 1.1: A parallel system

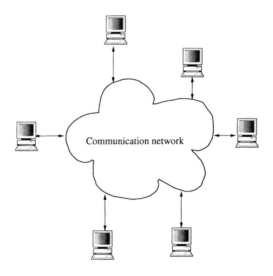

Figure 1.2: A distributed system

1.2 Distributed Systems versus Parallel Systems

In this book, we make a distinction between distributed systems and parallel systems. This distinction is only at a logical level. Given a physical system in which processors have shared memory, it is easy to simulate messages. Conversely, given a physical system in which processors are connected by a network, it is possible to simulate shared memory. Thus a parallel hardware system may run distributed software and vice versa.

This distinction raises two important questions. Should we build parallel hardware or distributed hardware? Should we write applications assuming shared memory or message passing? At the hardware level, we would expect the prevalent model to be multiprocessor workstations connected by a network. Thus the system is both parallel and distributed. Why would the system not be completely parallel? There are many reasons.

- *Scalability*: Distributed systems are inherently more scalable than parallel systems. In parallel systems shared memory becomes a bottleneck when the number of processors is increased.

- *Modularity and heterogeneity*: A distributed system is more flexible because a single processor can be added or deleted easily. Furthermore, this processor can be of a type completely different from that of the existing processors.

- *Data sharing*: Distributed systems provide data sharing as in distributed databases. Thus multiple organizations can share their data with each other.

- *Resource sharing*: Distributed systems provide resource sharing. For example, an expensive special-purpose processor can be shared by multiple organizations.

- *Geographic structure*: The geographic structure of an application may be inherently distributed. The low communication bandwidth may force local processing. This is especially true for wireless networks.

- *Reliability*: Distributed systems are more reliable than parallel systems because the failure of a single computer does not affect the availability of others.

- *Low cost*: Availability of high-bandwidth networks and inexpensive workstations also favors distributed computing for economic reasons.

Why would the system not be a purely distributed one? The reasons for keeping a parallel system at each node of a network are mainly technological in nature. With the current technology it is generally faster to update a shared memory location than

to send a message to another processor. This is especially true when the new value of
the variable must be communicated to multiple processors. Consequently, it is more
efficient to get fine-grain parallelism from a parallel system than from a distributed
system.

So far our discussion has been at the hardware level. As mentioned earlier, the
interface provided to the programmer can actually be independent of the underlying
hardware. So which model would then be used by the programmer? At the programming level, we expect that programs will be written using multithreaded distributed
objects. In this model, an application consists of multiple heavyweight processes
that communicate using messages (or remote method invocations). Each heavyweight process consists of multiple lightweight processes called *threads*. Threads
communicate through the shared memory. This software model mirrors the hardware that is (expected to be) widely available. By assuming that there is at most one
thread per process (or by ignoring the parallelism within one process), we get the
usual model of a distributed system. By restricting our attention to a single heavyweight process, we get the usual model of a parallel system. We expect the system to
have aspects of distributed objects. The main reason is the logical simplicity of the
distributed object model. A distributed program is more object-oriented because
data in a remote object can be accessed only through an explicit message (or a remote procedure call). The object orientation promotes reusability as well as design
simplicity. Furthermore, these object would be multithreaded because threads are
useful for implementing efficient objects. For many applications such as servers, it
is useful to have a large shared data structure. It is a programming burden and
inefficient to split the data structure across multiple heavyweight processes.

1.3   Overview of the Book

This book is intended for a one-semester advanced undergraduate or introductory
graduate course on concurrent and distributed systems. It can also be used as
a supplementary book in a course on operating systems or distributed operating
systems. For an undergraduate course, the instructor may skip the chapters on
consistency conditions, wait-free synchronization, synchronizers, recovery, and self-
stabilization without any loss of continuity.

Chapter 1 provides the motivation for parallel and distributed systems. It compares advantages of distributed systems with those of parallel systems. It gives the
defining characteristics of parallel and distributed systems and the fundamental difficulties in designing algorithms for such systems. It also introduces basic constructs
of starting threads in Java.

Chapters 2–5 deal with multithreaded programming. Chapter 2 discusses the mutual exclusion problem in shared memory systems. This provides motivation to students for various synchronization primitives discussed in Chapter 3. Chapter 3 exposes students to multithreaded programming. For a graduate course, Chapters 2 and 3 can be assigned for self-study. Chapter 4 describes various consistency conditions on concurrent executions that a system can provide to the programmers. Chapter 5 discusses a method of synchronization which does not use locks. Chapters 4 and 5 may be skipped in an undergraduate course.

Chapter 6 discusses distributed programming based on sockets as well as remote method invocations. It also provides a layer for distributed programming used by the programs in later chapters. This chapter is a prerequisite to understanding programs described in later chapters.

Chapter 7 provides the fundamental issues in distributed programming. It discusses models of a distributed system and a distributed computation. It describes the *interleaving model* that totally orders all the events in the system, and the *happened before model* that totally orders all the events on a single process. It also discusses mechanisms called *clocks* used to timestamp events in a distributed computation such that order information between events can be determined with these clocks. This chapter is fundamental to distributed systems and should be read before all later chapters.

Chapter 8 discusses one of the most studied problems in distributed systems— mutual exclusion. This chapter provides the interface Lock and discusses various algorithms to implement this interface. Lock is used for coordinating resources in distributed systems.

Chapter 9 discusses the abstraction called Camera that can be used to compute a consistent snapshot of a distributed system. We describe Chandy and Lamport's algorithm in which the receiver is responsible for recording the state of a channel as well as a variant of that algorithm in which the sender records the state of the channel. These algorithms can also be used for detecting stable global properties— properties that remain true once they become true.

Chapters 10 and 11 discuss the abstraction called Sensor that can be used to evaluate global properties in a distributed system. Chapter 10 describes algorithms for detecting conjunctive predicates in which the global predicate is simply a conjunction of local predicates. Chapter 11 describe algorithms for termination and deadlock detection. Although termination and deadlock can be detected using techniques described in Chapters 9 and 10, we devote a separate chapter for termination and deadlock detection because these algorithms are more efficient than those used to detect general global properties. They also illustrate techniques in designing distributed algorithms.

Chapter 12 describe methods to provide messaging layer with stronger properties than provided by the Transmission Control Protocol (TCP). We discuss the causal ordering of messages, the synchronous and the total ordering of messages.

Chapter 13 discusses two abstractions in a distributed system—`Election` and `GlobalFunction`. We discuss election in ring-based systems as well as in general graphs. Once a leader is elected, we show that a global function can be computed easily via a convergecast and a broadcast.

Chapter 14 discusses synchronizers, a method to abstract out asynchrony in the system. A synchronizer allows a synchronous algorithm to be simulated on top of an asynchronous system. We apply synchronizers to compute the breadth-first search (BFS) tree in an asynchronous network.

Chapters 1–14 assume that there are no faults in the system. The rest of the book deals with techniques for handling various kinds of faults.

Chapter 15 analyze the possibility (or impossibility) of solving problems in the presence of various types of faults. It includes the fundamental impossibility result of Fischer, Lynch, and Paterson that shows that consensus is impossible to solve in the presence of even one unannounced failure in an asynchronous system. It also shows that the consensus problem can be solved in a synchronous environment under crash and Byzantine faults. It also discusses the ability to solve problems in the absence of reliable communication. The two-generals problem shows that agreement on a bit (gaining common knowledge) is impossible in a distributed system.

Chapter 16 describes the notion of a transaction and various algorithms used in implementing transactions.

Chapter 17 discusses methods of recovering from failures. It includes both checkpointing and message-logging techniques.

Finally, Chapter 18 discusses self-stabilizing systems. We discuss solutions of the mutual exclusion problem when the state of any of the processors may change arbitrarily because of a fault. We show that it is possible to design algorithms that guarantee that the system converges to a legal state in a finite number of moves irrespective of the system execution. We also discuss self-stabilizing algorithms for maintaining a spanning tree in a network.

There are numerous starred and unstarred problems at the end of each chapter. A student is expected to solve unstarred problems with little effort. The starred problems may require the student to spend more effort and are appropriate only for graduate courses.

1.4   Characteristics of Parallel and Distributed Systems

Recall that we distinguish between parallel and distributed systems on the basis of shared memory. A distributed system is characterized by absence of shared memory. Therefore, in a distributed system it is impossible for any one processor to know the global state of the system. As a result, it is difficult to observe any global property of the system. We will later see how efficient algorithms can be developed for evaluating a suitably restricted set of global properties.

A parallel or a distributed system may be *tightly coupled* or *loosely coupled* depending on whether multiple processors work in a lock step manner. The absence of a shared clock results in a loosely coupled system. In a geographically distributed system, it is impossible to synchronize the clocks of different processors precisely because of uncertainty in communication delays between them. As a result, it is rare to use physical clocks for synchronization in distributed systems. In this book we will see how the concept of causality is used instead of time to tackle this problem. In a parallel system, although a shared clock can be simulated, designing a system based on a tightly coupled architecture is rarely a good idea, due to loss of performance because of synchronization. In this book, we will assume that systems are loosely coupled.

Distributed systems can further be classified into synchronous and asynchronous systems. A distributed system is *asynchronous* if there is no upper bound on the message communication time. Assuming asynchrony leads to most general solutions to various problems. We will see many examples in this book. However, things get difficult in asynchronous systems when processors or links can fail. In an asynchronous distributed system it is impossible to distinguish between a slow processor and a failed processor. This leads to difficulties in developing algorithms for consensus, election, and other important problems in distributed computing. We will describe these difficulties and also show algorithms that work under faults in synchronous systems.

1.5 Design Goals

The experience in large parallel and distributed software systems has shown that their design should take the following concepts into consideration [TvS02]:

- *Fault tolerance*: The software system should mask the failure of one or more components in the system, including processors, memory, and network links. This generally requires redundancy, which may be expensive depending on the degree of fault tolerance. Therefore, cost–benefit analysis is required to determine an appropriate level of fault tolerance.

- *Transparency*: The system should be as user-friendly as possible. This requires that the user not have to deal with unnecessary details. For example, in a heterogeneous distributed system the differences in the internal representation of data (such as the little endian format versus the big endian format for integers) should be hidden from the user, a concept called *access transparency*. Similarly, the use of a resource by a user should not require the user to know where it is located (*location transparency*), whether it is replicated (*replication transparency*), whether it is shared (*concurrency transparency*), or whether it is in volatile memory or hard disk (*persistence transparency*).

- *Flexibility*: The system should be able to interact with a large number of other systems and services. This requires that the system adhere to a fixed set of rules for syntax and semantics, preferably a standard, for interaction. This is often facilitated by specification of services provided by the system through an *interface definition language*. Another form of flexibility can be given to the user by a separation between *policy* and *mechanism*. For example, in the context of Web caching, the mechanism refers to the implementation for storing the Web pages locally. The policy refers to the high-level decisions such as size of the cache, which pages are to be cached, and how long those pages should remain in the cache. Such questions may be answered better by the user and therefore it is better for users to build their own caching policy on top of the caching mechanism provided. By designing the system as one monolithic component, we lose the flexibility of using different policies with different users.

- *Scalability*: If the system is not designed to be scalable, then it may have unsatisfactory performance when the number of users or the resources increase. For example, a distributed system with a single server may become overloaded when the number of clients requesting the service from the server increases. Generally, the system is either completely decentralized using distributed algorithms or partially decentralized using a hierarchy of servers.

1.6   Specification of Processes and Tasks

In this book we cover the programming concepts for shared memory-based languages and distributed languages. It should be noted that the issues of concurrency arise even on a single CPU computer where a system may be organized as a collection of cooperating processes. In fact, the issues of synchronization and deadlock have roots in the development of early operating systems. For this reason, we will refer to constructs described in this section as *concurrent* programming.

Before we embark on concurrent programming constructs, it is necessary to understand the distinction between a *program* and a *process*. A computer program is simply a set of instructions in a high-level or a machine-level language. It is only when we execute a program that we get one or more *processes*. When the program is sequential, it results in a single process, and when concurrent—multiple processes. A process can be viewed as consisting of three segments in the memory: code, data and execution stack. The *code* is the machine instructions in the memory which the process executes. The *data* consists of memory used by static global variables and runtime allocated memory (heap) used by the program. The *stack* consists of local variables and the activation records of function calls. Every process has its own stack. When processes share the address space, namely, code and data, then they are called *lightweight processes* or *threads*. Figure 1.3 shows four threads. All threads share the address space but have their own local stack. When process has its own code and data, it is called a *heavyweight process*, or simply a process. Heavyweight processes may share data through files or by sending explicit messages to each other.

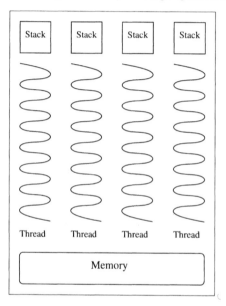

Figure 1.3: A process with four threads

Any programming language that supports concurrent programming must have a way to specify the process structure, and how various processes communicate and synchronize with each other. There are many ways a program may specify the process structure or creation of new processes. We look at the most popular ones. In UNIX, processes are organized as a tree of processes with each process identified using a unique process id (pid). UNIX provides system calls *fork* and *wait* for creation and synchronization of processes. When a process executes a *fork* call, a child process is created with a copy of the address space of the parent process. The only difference between the parent process and the child process is the value of the return code for the *fork*. The parent process gets the pid of the child process as the return code, and the child process gets the value 0 as shown in the following example.

```
pid = fork();
if (pid == 0) {
    // child process
    cout << "child process";
}
else {
    // parent process
    cout << "parent process";
}
```

The *wait* call is used for the parent process to wait for termination of the child process. A process terminates when it executes the last instruction in the code or makes an explicit call to the system call *exit*. When a child process terminates, the parent process, if waiting, is awakened and the pid of the child process is returned for the wait call. In this way, the parent process can determine which of its child processes terminated.

Frequently, the child process makes a call to the *execve* system call, which loads a binary file into memory and starts execution of that file.

Another programming construct for launching parallel tasks is *cobegin-coend* (also called *parbegin-parend*). Its syntax is given below:

$$cobegin \ S_1 \parallel S_2 \ coend$$

This construct says that S_1 and S_2 must be executed in parallel. Further, if one of them finishes earlier than the other, it should wait for the other one to finish. Combining the cobegin-coend with the sequencing, or the series operator, semicolon (;), we can create any series-parallel task structure. For example,

$$S_0; \ cobegin \ S_1 \parallel S_2 \ coend; \ S_3$$

starts off with one process that executes S_0. When S_0 is finished, we have two processes (or threads) that execute S_1 and S_2 in parallel. When both the statements are done, only then S_3 is started.

Yet another method for specification of concurrency is to explicitly create thread objects. For example, in Java there is a predefined class called Thread. One can extend the class **Thread**, override the method **run** and then call **start()** to launch the thread. For example, a thread for printing "Hello World" can be launched as shown in Figure 1.4.

```
public class HelloWorldThread extends Thread {
    public void run () {
        System.out.println ("Hello World");
    }
    public static void main(String [] args ) {
        HelloWorldThread t = new HelloWorldThread ();
        t.start ();
    }
}
```

Figure 1.4: HelloWorldThread.java

1.6.1 Runnable Interface

In the **HelloWorld** example, the class **HelloWorldThread** needed to inherit methods only from the class **Thread**. What if we wanted to extend a class, say, **Foo**, but also make the objects of the new class run as separate thread? Since Java does not have multiple inheritance, we could not simply extend both **Foo** and the **Thread** class. To solve this problem, Java provides an interface called **Runnable** with the following single method:

```
public void run()
```

To design a runnable class **FooBar** that extends **Foo**, we proceed as shown in Figure 1.5. The class **FooBar** implements the **Runnable** interface. The **main** function creates a runnable object **f1** of type **FooBar**. Now we can create a thread **t1** by passing the runnable object **f1** as an argument to the constructor for **Thread**. This thread can then be started by invoking the **start** method. The program creates two threads in this manner. Each of the threads prints out the string **getName()** inherited from the class **Foo**.

1.6.2 Join Construct in Java

We have seen that we can use **start()** to start a thread. The following example shows how a thread can wait for other thread to finish execution via the **join** mechanism. We write a program in Java to compute the nth Fibonacci number F_n

```
class Foo {
    String name;
    public Foo(String s) {
        name = s;
    }
    public void setName(String s) {
        name = s;
    }
    public String getName() {
        return name;
    }
}
class FooBar extends Foo implements Runnable {
    public FooBar(String s) {
        super(s);
    }
    public void run() {
        for (int i = 0; i < 10; i++)
            System.out.println(getName() + ": Hello World");
    }
    public static void main(String[] args) {
        FooBar f1 = new FooBar("Romeo");
        Thread t1 = new Thread(f1);
        t1.start();
        FooBar f2 = new FooBar("Juliet");
        Thread t2 = new Thread(f2);
        t2.start();
    }
}
```

Figure 1.5: FooBar.java

using the recurrence relation

$$F_n = F_{n-1} + F_{n-2}$$

for $n \geq 2$. The base cases are

$$F_0 = 1$$

and

$$F_1 = 1$$

To compute F_n, the `run` method forks two threads that compute F_{n-1} and F_{n-2} recursively. The main thread waits for these two threads to finish their computation using `join`. The complete program is shown in Figure 1.6.

1.6.3   Thread Scheduling

In the `FooBar` example, we had two threads. The same Java program will work for a single-CPU machine as well as for a multiprocessor machine. In a single-CPU machine, if both threads are runnable, which one would be picked by the system to run? The answer to this question depends on the *priority* and the *scheduling policy* of the system.

The programmer may change the priority of threads using `setPriority` and determine the current priority by `getPriority`. `MIN_PRIORITY` and `MAX_PRIORITY` are integer constants defined in the `Thread` class. The method `setPriority` can use a value only between these two constants. By default, a thread has the priority `NORM_PRIORITY`.

A Java thread that is running may block by calling *sleep*, *wait*, or any system function that is blocking (these calls will be described later). When this happens, a highest-priority runnable thread is picked for execution. When the highest-priority thread is running, it may still be suspended when its time slice is over. Another thread at the same priority level may then be allowed to run.

1.7   Problems

1.1. Give advantages and disadvantages of a parallel programming model over a distributed system (message-based) model.

1.2. Write a Java class that allows parallel search in an array of integer. It provides the following `static` method:

```
public static int parallelSearch(int x, int[] A, int numThreads)
```

```
public class Fibonacci extends Thread {
    int n;
    int result;
    public Fibonacci(int n) {
        this.n = n;
    }
    public void run() {
        if ((n == 0)||(n == 1 )) result = 1;
        else {
            Fibonacci f1 = new Fibonacci(n-1);
            Fibonacci f2 = new Fibonacci(n-2);
            f1.start();
            f2.start();
            try {
                f1.join();
                f2.join();
            } catch (InterruptedException e){};
            result = f1.getResult() + f2.getResult();
        }
    }
    public int getResult(){
        return result;
    }
    public static void main(String[] args) {
        Fibonacci f1 = new Fibonacci(Integer.parseInt(args[0]));
        f1.start();
        try {
            f1.join();
        } catch (InterruptedException e){};
        System.out.println("Answer is " + f1.getResult());
    }
}
```

Figure 1.6: Fibonacci.java

This method creates as many threads as specified by `numThreads`, divides the array `A` into that many parts, and gives each thread a part of the array to search for `x` sequentially. If any thread finds `x`, then it returns an index `i` such that `A[i]` = `x`. Otherwise, the method returns -1.

1.3. Consider the class shown below.

```
class Schedule {
    static int x = 0;
    static int y = 0;
    public static int op1(){x = 1; return y;}
    public static int op2(){y = 2; return 3*x;}
}
```

If one thread calls `op1` and the other thread calls `op2`, then what values may be returned by `op1` and `op2`?

1.4. Write a multithreaded program in Java that sorts an array using recursive merge sort. The main thread forks two threads to sort the two halves of arrays, which are then merged.

1.5. Write a program in Java that uses two threads to search for a given element in a doubly linked list. One thread traverses the list in the forward direction and the other, in the backward direction.

1.8 Bibliographic Remarks

There are many books available on distributed systems. The reader is referred to books by Attiya and Welch [AW98], Barbosa [Bar96], Chandy and Misra [CM89], Garg [Gar96, Gar02], Lynch [Lyn96], Raynal [Ray88], and Tel [Tel94] for the range of topics in distributed algorithms. Couloris, Dollimore and Kindberg [CDK94], and Chow and Johnson [CJ97] cover some other practical aspects of distributed systems such as distributed file systems, which are not covered in this book. Goscinski [Gos91] and Singhal and Shivaratri [SS94] cover concepts in distributed operating systems. The book edited by Yang and Marsland [YM94] includes many papers that deal with global time and state in distributed systems. The book edited by Mullender [SM94] covers many other topics such as protection, fault tolerance, and real-time communications.

There are many books available for concurrent computing in Java as well. The reader is referred to the books by Farley [Far98], Hartley [Har98] and Lea [Lea99] as examples. These books do not discuss distributed algorithms.

Chapter 2

Mutual Exclusion Problem

2.1 Introduction

When processes share data, it is important to synchronize their access to the data so that updates are not lost as a result of concurrent accesses and the data are not corrupted. This can be seen from the following example. Assume that the initial value of a shared variable x is 0 and that there are two processes, P_0 and P_1 such that each one of them increments x by the following statement in some high-level programming language:

$$x = x + 1$$

It is natural for the programmer to assume that the final value of x is 2 after both the processes have executed. However, this may not happen if the programmer does not ensure that $x = x + 1$ is executed atomically. The statement $x = x + 1$ may compile into the machine-level code of the form

```
LD  R, x    ; load register R from x
INC R       ; increment register R
ST  R, x    ; store register R to x
```

Now the execution of P_0 and P_1 may get interleaved as follows:

P_0: LD R, x		; load register R from x
P_0: INC R		; increment register R
	P_1: LD R, x	; load register R from x
	P_1: INC R	; increment register R
P_0: ST R,x		; store register R to x
	P_1: ST R,x	; store register R to x

Thus both processes load the value 0 into their registers and finally store 1 into x resulting in the "lost update" problem.

To avoid this problem, the statement $x = x + 1$ should be executed `atomically`. A section of the code that needs to be executed atomically is also called a *critical region* or a *critical section*. The problem of ensuring that a critical section is executed atomically is called the *mutual exclusion problem*. This is one of the most fundamental problems in concurrent computing and we will study it in detail.

The mutual exclusion problem can be abstracted as follows. We are required to implement the interface shown in Figure 2.1. A process that wants to enter the critical section (CS) makes a call to `requestCS` with its own identifier as the argument. The process or the thread that makes this call returns from this method only when it has the exclusive access to the critical section. When the process has finished accessing the critical section, it makes a call to the method `releaseCS`.

```
public interface Lock {
    public void requestCS(int pid); //may block
    public void releaseCS(int pid);
}
```

Figure 2.1: Interface for accessing the critical section

The entry protocol given by the method `requestCS` and the exit protocol given by the method `releaseCS` should be such that the mutual exclusion is not violated.

To test the Lock, we use the program shown in Figure 2.2. This program tests the Bakery algorithm that will be presented later. The user of the program may test a different algorithm for a lock implementation by invoking the constructor of that lock implementation. The program launches N threads as specified by `arg[0]`. Each thread is an object of the class `MyThread`. Let us now look at the class `MyThread`. This class has two methods, `nonCriticalSection` and `CriticalSection`, and it overrides the `run` method of the `Thread` class as follows. Each thread repeatedly enters the critical section. After exiting from the critical section it spends an undetermined amount of time in the noncritical section of the code. In our example, we simply use a random number to sleep in the critical and the noncritical sections.

```
import java.util.Random;
public class MyThread extends Thread {
    int myId;
    Lock lock;
    Random r = new Random();
    public MyThread(int id, Lock lock) {
        myId = id;
        this.lock = lock;
    }
    void nonCriticalSection() {
        System.out.println(myId + " is not in CS");
        Util.mySleep(r.nextInt(1000));
    }
    void CriticalSection() {
        System.out.println(myId + " is in CS *****");
        // critical section code
        Util.mySleep(r.nextInt(1000));
    }
    public void run() {
        while (true) {
            lock.requestCS(myId);
            CriticalSection();
            lock.releaseCS(myId);
            nonCriticalSection();
        }
    }
    public static void main(String[] args) throws Exception {
        MyThread t[];
        int N = Integer.parseInt(args[0]);
        t = new MyThread[N];
        Lock lock = new Bakery(N); //or any other mutex algorithm
        for (int i = 0; i < N; i++) {
            t[i] = new MyThread(i, lock);
            t[i].start();
        }
    }
}
```

Figure 2.2: A program to test mutual exclusion

Let us now look at some possible protocols, one may attempt, to solve the mutual exclusion problem. For simplicity we first assume that there are only two processes, P_0 and P_1.

2.2   Peterson's Algorithm

Our first attempt would be to use a shared boolean variable openDoor initialized to true. The entry protocol would be to wait for openDoor to be true. If it is true, then a process can enter the critical section after setting it to false. On exit, the process resets it to true. This algorithm is shown in Figure 2.3.

```
class  Attempt1 implements  Lock {
    boolean  openDoor = true;
    public  void  requestCS (int  i ) {
        while  (! openDoor )  ;  // busy  wait
        openDoor = false ;
    }
    public  void  releaseCS (int  i ) {
        openDoor = true;
    }
}
```

Figure 2.3: An attempt that violates mutual exclusion

This attempt does not work because the testing of openDoor and setting it to false is not done atomically. Conceivably, one process might check for the openDoor and go past the while statement in Figure 2.3. However, before that process could set openDoor to false, the other process starts executing. The other process now checks for the value of openDoor and also gets out of busy wait. Both the processes now can set openDoor to false and enter the critical section. Thus, mutual exclusion is violated.

In the attempt described above, the shared variable did not record who set the openDoor to false. One may try to fix this problem by keeping two shared variables, wantCS[0] and wantCS[1], as shown in Figure 2.4. Every process P_i first sets its own wantCS bit to true at line 4 and then waits until the wantCS for the other process is false at line 5. We have used $1 - i$ to get the process identifier of the other process when there are only two processes - P_0 and P_1. To release the critical section, P_i simply resets its wantCS bit to false. Unfortunately, this attempt also does not work. Both processes could set their wantCS to true and then indefinitely loop, waiting for the other process to set its wantCS false.

```
 1 class Attempt2 implements Lock {
 2      boolean wantCS[] = { false , false };
 3      public void requestCS(int i) {  // entry protocol
 4          wantCS[i] = true;     //declare intent
 5          while ( wantCS[1 - i]) ;  // busy wait
 6      }
 7      public void releaseCS(int i) {
 8          wantCS[i] = false;
 9      }
10 }
```

Figure 2.4: An attempt that can deadlock

Yet another attempt to fix the problem is shown in Figure 2.5. This attempt is based on evaluating the value of a variable **turn**. A process waits for its turn to enter the critical section. On exiting the critical section, it sets **turn** to **1-i**.

```
class Attempt3 implements Lock {
    int turn = 0;
    public void requestCS(int i) {
        while ( turn == 1 - i ) ;
    }
    public void releaseCS(int i) {
        turn = 1 - i;
    }
}
```

Figure 2.5: An attempt with strict alternation

This protocol does guarantee *mutual exclusion*. It also guarantees that if both processes are trying to enter the critical section, then one of them will succeed. However, it suffers from another problem. In this protocol, both processes have to alternate with each other for getting the critical section. Thus, after process P_0 exits from the critical section it cannot enter the critical section again until process P_1 has entered the critical section. If process P_1 is not interested in the critical section, then process P_0 is simply stuck waiting for process P_1. This is not desirable.

By combining the previous two approaches, however, we get Peterson's algorithm for the mutual exclusion problem in a two-process system. In this protocol, shown in Figure 2.6, we maintain two flags, wantCS[0] and wantCS[1], as in Attempt2, and the turn variable as in Attempt3. To request the critical section, process P_i sets its wantCS flag to true at line 6 and then sets the turn to the other process P_j

at line 7. After that, it waits at line 8 so long as the following condition is true:

$$(\texttt{wantCS[j]} \&\& \ (\texttt{turn} == \texttt{j}))$$

Thus a process enters the critical section only if either it is its turn to do so or if
the other process is not interested in the critical section.

To release the critical section, P_i simply resets the flag $\texttt{wantCS[i]}$ at line 11.
This allows P_j to enter the critical section by making the condition for its **while**
loop false.

```
 1 class  PetersonAlgorithm  implements  Lock  {
 2      boolean  wantCS [] = { false ,  false };
 3      int  turn  = 1;
 4      public  void  requestCS ( int  i )  {
 5          int  j  = 1 − i ;
 6          wantCS [ i ] =  true ;
 7          turn  = j ;
 8          while  ( wantCS [ j ] && ( turn  == j ))  ;
 9      }
10      public  void  releaseCS ( int  i )  {
11          wantCS [ i ] =  false ;
12      }
13 }
```

Figure 2.6: Peterson's algorithm for mutual exclusion

We show that Peterson's algorithm satisfies the following desirable properties:

1. *Mutual exclusion*: Two processes cannot be in the critical section at the same
   time.

2. *Progress*: If one or more processes are trying to enter the critical section and
   there is no process inside the critical section, then at least one of the processes
   succeeds in entering the critical section.

3. *Starvation-freedom*: If a process is trying to enter the critical section, then it
   eventually succeeds in doing so.

We first show that mutual exclusion is satisfied by Peterson's algorithm. Assume
without loss of generality that P_0 was the first one to enter the critical section. To
enter the critical section, P_0 must have either read $wantCS[1]$ as false, or $turn$ as
0. We now perform a case analysis:

Case 1: P_0 read $wantCS[1]$ as false. If $wantCS[1]$ is false, then for P_1 to enter the critical section, it would have to set $wantCS[1]$ to true. From this case, we get the following order of events: P_0 reads $wantCS[1]$ as false before P_1 sets the value of $wantCS[1]$ as true. This order of events implies that P_1 would set $turn = 0$ before checking the entry condition and after the event of P_0 reading $wantCS[1]$. On the other hand, P_0 set $turn = 1$ before reading $wantCS[1]$. Therefore, we have the following order of events in time:

- P_0 sets $turn$ to 1.

- P_0 reads $wantCS[1]$ as false.

- P_1 sets $wantCS[1]$ as true.

- P_1 sets $turn$ to 0.

- P_1 reads $turn$.

Clearly, $turn$ can be only 0 when P_1 reads it. Now let us look at the set of values of $wantCS[0]$ that P_1 can possibly read. From the program, we know that P_0 sets $wantCS[0]$ as true before reading $wantCS[1]$. Similarly, P_1 sets $wantCS[1]$ before reading $wantCS[0]$. We know that P_0 read $wantCS[1]$ as false. Therefore, P_1 sets $wantCS[1]$ as true after P_0 reads $wantCS[1]$. This implies that we have the following order of events:

- P_0 sets $wantCS[0]$ as true.

- P_0 reads $wantCS[1]$ as false.

- P_1 sets $wantCS[1]$ as true.

- P_1 reads $wantCS[0]$.

Therefore, P_1 can only read $wantCS[0]$ as true. Because P_1 reads $turn$ as 0 and $wantCS[0]$ as true, it cannot enter the critical section.

Case 2: P_0 read $turn$ as 0. This implies the following order of events: P_1 sets $turn = 0$ between P_0 setting $turn = 1$ and P_0 reading the value of $turn$. Since P_1 reads the value of $turn$ only after setting $turn = 0$, we know that it can read $turn$ only as 0. Also, $wantCS[0]$ is set before P_0 sets $turn = 1$. Therefore, P_0 sets $wantCS[0]$ before P_1 sets $turn = 0$. This implies that P_1 reads the value of $wantCS[0]$ as true. Thus, even in this case, P_1 reads $turn$ as 0 and $wantCS[0]$ as true. It follows that P_1 cannot enter the critical section.

It is easy to see that the algorithm satisfies the progress property. If both the processes are forever checking the entry protocol in the while loop, then we get

$$wantCS[2] \land (turn = 2) \land wantsCS[1] \land (turn = 1)$$

which is clearly false because $(turn = 2) \land (turn = 1)$ is false.

The proof of freedom from starvation is left as an exercise. The reader can also verify that Peterson's algorithm does not require strict alternation of the critical sections—a process can repeatedly use the critical section if the other process is not interested in it.

2.3   Lamport's Bakery Algorithm

Although Peterson's algorithm satisfies all the properties that we initially required from the protocol, it works only for two processes. Although the algorithm can be extended to N processes by repeated invocation of the entry protocol, the resulting algorithm is more complex.

We now describe Lamport's bakery algorithm, which overcomes this disadvantage. The algorithm is similar to that used by bakeries in serving customers. Each customer who arrives at the bakery receives a number. The server serves the customer with the smallest number. In a concurrent system, it is difficult to ensure that every process gets a unique number. So in case of a tie, we use process ids to choose the smaller process.

The algorithm shown in Figure 2.7 requires a process P_i to go through two main steps before it can enter the critical section. In the first step (lines 15–21), it is required to choose a number. To do that, it reads the numbers of all other processes and chooses its number as one bigger than the maximum number it read. We will call this step the *doorway*. In the second step the process P_i checks if it can enter the critical section as follows. For every other process P_j, process P_i first checks whether P_j is currently in the doorway at line 25. If P_j is in the doorway, then P_i waits for P_j to get out of the doorway. At lines 26–29, P_i waits for the $number[j]$ to be 0 or $(number[i], i) < (number[j], j)$. When P_i is successful in verifying this condition for all other processes, it can enter the critical section.

We first prove the assertion:

(A1) If a process P_i is in critical section and some other process P_k has already chosen its number, then $(number[i], i) < (number[k], k)$.

If the process P_i is in critical section, then it managed to get out of the kth iteration of the *for* loop in the second step. This implies that either $(number[k] = 0)$

```
 1 class Bakery implements Lock {
 2     int N;
 3     boolean[] choosing; // inside doorway
 4     int [] number;
 5     public Bakery(int numProc) {
 6         N = numProc;
 7         choosing = new boolean[N];
 8         number = new int [N];
 9         for ( int j = 0; j < N; j++) {
10             choosing [j] = false;
11             number[j] = 0;
12         }
13     }
14     public void requestCS(int i) {
15         // step 1: doorway: choose a number
16         choosing [i] = true;
17         for ( int j = 0; j < N; j++)
18             if ( number[j] > number[i])
19                 number[i] = number[j];
20         number[i]++;
21         choosing [i] = false;
22
23         // step 2: check if my number is the smallest
24         for ( int j = 0; j < N; j++) {
25             while ( choosing [j]) ; // process j in doorway
26             while (( number[j] != 0) &&
27                     (( number[j] < number[i]) ||
28                     (( number[j] == number[i]) && j < i )))
29                 ; // busy wait
30         }
31     }
32     public void releaseCS(int i) { // exit protocol
33         number[i] = 0;
34     }
35 }
```

Figure 2.7: Lamport's bakery algorithm

or $((number[i], i) < (number[k], k))$ at that iteration. First assume that process P_i read $number[k]$ as 0. This means that process P_k must not have finished choosing the number yet. There are two cases. Either P_k has not entered the doorway or it has entered the doorway but not exited yet. If P_k has not entered the doorway, it will read the latest value of $number[i]$ and is guaranteed to have $number[k] > number[i]$. If it had entered the doorway, then this entry must be after P_i had checked $choosing[k]$ because P_i waits for P_k to finish choosing before checking the condition $(number[k] = 0) \vee ((number[i], i) < (number[k], k))$. This again means that that P_k will read the latest value of $number[i]$ and therefore $(number[i] < number[k])$. If $((number[i], i) < (number[k], k))$ at the kth iteration, this will continue to hold because $number[i]$ does not change and $number[k]$ can only increase.

We now claim the assertion:

(A2) If a process P_i is in critical section, then $(number[i] > 0)$.

(A2) is true because it is clear from the program text that the value of any number is at least 0 and a process executes increment operation on its number at line 20 before entering the critical section.

Showing that the bakery algorithm satisfies mutual exclusion is now trivial. If two processes P_i and P_k are in critical section, then from (A2) we know that both of their numbers are nonzero. From (A1) it follows that $(number[i], i) < (number[k], k)$ and vice versa, which is a contradiction.

The bakery algorithm also satisfies starvation freedom because any process that is waiting to enter the critical section will eventually have the smallest nonzero number. This process will then succeed in entering the critical section.

It can be shown that the bakery algorithm does not make any assumptions on *atomicity* of any read or write operation. Note that the bakery algorithm does not use any variable that can be written by more than one process. Process P_i writes only on variables $number[i]$ and $choose[i]$.

There are two main disadvantages of the bakery algorithm: (1) it requires $O(N)$ work by each process to obtain the lock even if there is no contention, and (2) it requires each process to use timestamps that are unbounded in size.

2.4 Hardware Solutions

As we have seen, pure software solutions to mutual exclusion can be quite complex and expensive. However, mutual exclusion can be provided quite easily with the help of hardware. We discuss some techniques below.

2.4.1 Disabling Interrupts

In a single-CPU system, a process may disable all the interrupts before entering the critical section. This means that the process cannot be context-switched (because context switching occurs when the currently running thread receives a clock interrupt when its current timeslice is over). On exiting the critical section, the process enables interrupts. Although this method can work for a single-CPU machine, it has many undesirable features. First, it is infeasible for a multiple-CPU system in which even if interrupts are disabled in one CPU, another CPU may execute. Disabling interrupts of all CPUs is very expensive. Also, many system facilities such as clock registers are maintained using hardware interrupts. If interrupts are disabled, then these registers may not show correct values. Disabling interrupts can also lead to problems if the user process has a bug such as an infinite loop inside the critical section.

2.4.2 Instructions with Higher Atomicity

Most machines provide instructions with a higher level of atomicity than *read* or *write*. The `testAndSet` instruction provided by some machines does both read and write in one atomic instruction. This instruction reads and returns the old value of a memory location while replacing it with a new value. We can abstract the instruction as a `testAndSet` method on an object of the class `TestAndSet` as shown in Figure 2.8.

```
public class TestAndSet {
    int myValue = −1;
    public synchronized int testAndSet (int newValue) {
        int oldValue = myValue;
        myValue = newValue;
        return oldValue;
    }
}
```

Figure 2.8: TestAndSet hardware instruction

If the `testAndSet` instruction is available, then one can develop a very simple protocol for mutual exclusion as shown in Figure 2.9.

```
class HWMutex implements Lock {
    TestAndSet lockFlag ;
    public void requestCS (int  i ) {  // entry  protocol
        while ( lockFlag . testAndSet (1) == 1 ) ;
    }
    public void releaseCS (int  i ) {  // exit  protocol
        lockFlag . testAndSet (0);
    }
}
```

Figure 2.9: Mutual exclusion using TestAndSet

This algorithm satisfies the mutual exclusion and progress property. However, it does not satisfy starvation freedom. Developing such a protocol is left as an exercise.

Sometimes machines provide the instruction `swap`, which can swap two memory locations in one atomic step. Its semantics is shown in Figure 2.10. The reader is invited to design a mutual exclusion protocol using `swap`.

```
public class Synch{
    public static synchronized void swap(boolean m1,  boolean m2){
        boolean temp = m1;
        m1 = m2;
        m2 = temp;
    }
}
```

Figure 2.10: Semantics of `swap` operation

2.5   Problems

2.1. Show that any of the following modifications to Peterson's algorithm makes it incorrect:

(a) A process in Peterson's algorithm sets the *turn* variable to itself instead of setting it to the other process.

(b) A process sets the *turn* variable before setting the *wantCS* variable.

```
class Dekker implements Lock {
    boolean wantCS [] = { false , false };
    int turn = 1;
    public void requestCS (int i ) {  // entry protocol
        int j = 1 − i ;
        wantCS[ i ] = true ;
        while ( wantCS[ j ]) {
            if ( turn == j ) {
                wantCS[ i ] = false ;
                while ( turn == j ) ; // busy wait
                wantCS[ i ] = true ;
            }
        }
    }
    public void releaseCS (int i ) {  // exit protocol
        turn = 1 − i ;
        wantCS[ i ] = false ;
    }
}
```

Figure 2.11: Dekker.java

2.2. Show that Peterson's algorithm also guarantees freedom from starvation.

2.3. Show that the bakery algorithm does not work in absence of *choosing* variables.

2.4. Consider the software protocol shown in Figure 2.11 for mutual exclusion between two processes. Does this protocol satisfy (a) mutual exclusion, and (b) livelock freedom (both processes trying to enter the critical section and none of them succeeding)? Does it satisfy starvation freedom?

2.5. Modify the bakery algorithm to solve k-mutual exclusion problem, in which at most k processes can be in the critical section concurrently.

2.6. Give a mutual exclusion algorithm that uses atomic swap instruction.

2.7. Give a mutual exclusion algorithm that uses TestAndSet instruction and is free from starvation.

*2.8. Give a mutual exclusion algorithm on N processes that requires $O(1)$ time in absence of contention.

2.6   Bibliographic Remarks

The mutual exclusion problem was first introduced by Dijkstra [Dij65a]. Dekker developed the algorithm for mutual exclusion for two processes. Dijkstra [Dij65b] gave the first solution to the problem for N processes. The bakery algorithm is due to Lamport [Lam74], and Peterson's algorithm is taken from a paper by Peterson [Pet81].

Chapter 3

Synchronization Primitives

3.1 Introduction

All of our previous solutions to the mutual exclusion problem were wasteful in one regard. If a process is unable to enter the critical section, it repeatedly checks for the entry condition to be true. While a process is doing this, no useful work is accomplished. This way of waiting is called *busy wait*. Instead of checking the entry condition repeatedly, if the process checked the condition only when it could have become true, it would not waste CPU cycles. Accomplishing this requires support from the operating system.

In this chapter we introduce synchronization primitives that avoid busy wait. Synchronization primitives are used for mutual exclusion as well as to provide order between various operations by different threads. Although there are many types of synchronization constructs in various programming languages, two of them are most prevalent: semaphores and monitors. We discuss these constructs in this chapter.

3.2 Semaphores

Dijkstra proposed the concept of *semaphore* that solves the problem of busy wait. A semaphore has two fields, its `value` and a `queue` of blocked processes, and two operations associated with it — $P()$ and $V()$. The semantics of a binary semaphore is shown in Figure 3.1. The `value` of a semaphore (or a binary semaphore) can be only *false* or *true*. The `queue` of blocked processes is initially empty and a process may add itself to the queue when it makes a call to $P()$. When a process calls $P()$ and `value` is *true*, then the value of the semaphore becomes *false*. However, if

31

the value of the semaphore is *false*, then the process gets blocked at line 7 until it becomes *true*. The invocation of `Util.myWait()` at line 8 achieves this. The class `Util` is shown in the appendix, but for now simply assume that this call inserts the caller process into the queue of blocked processes.

When the value becomes *true*, the process can make it *false* at line 9 and return from $P()$. The call to $V()$ makes the value *true* and also notifies a process if the queue of processes sleeping on that semaphore is nonempty.

```
 1 public class BinarySemaphore {
 2     boolean value;
 3     BinarySemaphore(boolean initValue) {
 4         value = initValue;
 5     }
 6     public synchronized void P() {
 7         while (value == false)
 8             Util.myWait(this); // in queue of blocked processes
 9         value = false;
10     }
11     public synchronized void V() {
12         value = true;
13         notify();
14     }
15 }
```

Figure 3.1: Binary semaphore

Now, mutual exclusion is almost trivial to implement:

```
BinarySemaphore mutex = new BinarySemaphore(true);
mutex.P();
criticalSection();
mutex.V();
```

Another variant of semaphore allows it to take arbitrary integer as its value. These semaphores are called *counting semaphores*. Their semantics is shown in Figure 3.2.

Semaphores can be used to solve a wide variety of synchronization problems. Note that Java does not provide semaphores as basic language construct, but they can easily be implemented in Java using the idea of **monitors**, which we will cover later. For now we simply assume that semaphores are available to us and solve synchronization problems using them.

```
public class CountingSemaphore {
    int value;
    public CountingSemaphore(int initValue) {
        value = initValue;
    }
    public synchronized void P() {
        value--;
        if (value < 0) Util.myWait(this);
    }
    public synchronized void V() {
        value++;
        if (value <= 0) notify();
    }
}
```

Figure 3.2: Counting semaphore

3.2.1 The Producer-Consumer Problem

We first consider the producer-consumer problem. In this problem, there is a shared buffer between two processes called the *producer* and the *consumer*. The producer produces items that are *deposited* in the buffer and the consumer *fetches* items from the buffer and consumes them. For simplicity, we assume that our items are of type `double`. Since the buffer is shared, each process must access the buffer in a mutually exclusive fashion. We use an array of `double` of size `size` as our buffer. The buffer has two pointers, `inBuf` and `outBuf`, which point to the indices in the array for depositing an item and fetching an item, respectively. The variable `count` keeps track of the number of items currently in the buffer. Figure 3.3 shows the buffer as a circular array in which `inBuf` and `outBuf` are incremented modulo `size` to keep track of the slots for depositing and fetching items.

In this problem, we see that besides mutual exclusion, there are two additional synchronization constraints that need to be satisfied:

1. The consumer should not fetch any item from an empty buffer.

2. The producer should not deposit any item in the buffer if it is full. The buffer can become full if the producer is producing items at a greater rate than the rate at which the items are consumed by the consumer.

Such form of synchronization is called *conditional synchronization*. It requires a process to wait for some condition to become true (such as the buffer to become nonempty) before continuing its operations. The class `BoundedBuffer` is shown in Figure 3.4. It uses `mutex` semaphore to ensure that all shared variables are accessed

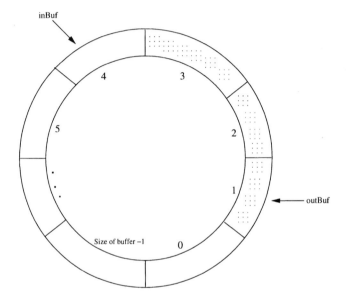

Figure 3.3: A shared buffer implemented with a circular array

in mutually exclusive fashion. The counting semaphore `isFull` is used for making a producer wait in case the buffer is full, and the semaphore `isEmpty` is used to make a consumer wait when the buffer is empty.

In the method `deposit`, line 10 checks whether the buffer is full. If it is, the process making call waits using the semaphore `isFull`. Note that this semaphore has been initialized to the value `size`, and therefore in absence of a consumer, first `size` calls to `isFull.P()` do not block. At this point, the buffer would be full and any call to `isFull.P()` will block. If the call to `isFull.P()` does not block, then we enter the critical section to access the shared buffer. The call `mutex.P()` at line 11 serves as entry to the critical section, and `mutex.V()` serves as the exit from the critical section. Once inside the critical section, we deposit the value in `buffer` using the pointer `inBuf` at line 12 (see Figure 3.4). Line 15 makes a call to `isEmpty.V()` to wake up any consumer that may be waiting because the buffer was empty. The method `fetch` is dual of the method `deposit`.

```
 1 class BoundedBuffer {
 2      final int size = 10;
 3      double[] buffer = new double[size];
 4      int inBuf = 0, outBuf = 0;
 5      BinarySemaphore mutex = new BinarySemaphore(true);
 6      CountingSemaphore isEmpty = new CountingSemaphore(0);
 7      CountingSemaphore isFull = new CountingSemaphore(size);
 8
 9      public void deposit(double value) {
10          isFull.P(); // wait if buffer is full
11          mutex.P(); // ensures mutual exclusion
12          buffer[inBuf] = value; // update the buffer
13          inBuf = (inBuf + 1) % size;
14          mutex.V();
15          isEmpty.V();   // notify any waiting consumer
16      }
17      public double fetch() {
18          double value;
19          isEmpty.P();  // wait if buffer is empty
20          mutex.P();   // ensures mutual exclusion
21          value = buffer[outBuf]; //read from buffer
22          outBuf = (outBuf + 1) % size;
23          mutex.V();
24          isFull.V(); // notify any waiting producer
25          return value;
26      }
27 }
```

Figure 3.4: Bounded buffer using semaphores

The class BoundedBuffer can be exercised through the producer-consumer program shown in Figure 3.5. This program starts a Producer thread and a Consumer thread, repeatedly making calls to deposit and fetch, respectively.

3.2.2   The Reader-Writer Problem

Next we show the solution to the reader-writer problem. This problem requires us to design a protocol to coordinate access to a shared database. The requirements are as follows:

1. *No read-write conflict:* The protocol should ensure that a reader and a writer do not access the database concurrently.

2. *No write-write conflict:* The protocol should ensure that two writers do not access the database concurrently.

Further, we would like multiple readers to be able to access the database concurrently. A solution using semaphores is shown in Figure 3.6. We assume that the readers follow the protocol that they call startRead before reading the database and call endRead after finishing the read. Writers follow a similar protocol. We use the wlock semaphore to ensure that either there is a single writer accessing the database or only readers are accessing it. To count the number of readers accessing the database, we use the variable numReaders.

The methods startWrite and endWrite are quite simple. Any writer that wants to use the database locks it using wlock.P(). If the database is not locked, this writer gets the access. Now no other reader or writer can access the database until this writer releases the lock using endWrite().

Now let us look at the startRead and the endRead methods. In startRead, a reader first increments numReaders. If it is the first reader (numReaders equals 1), then it needs to lock the database; otherwise, there are already other readers accessing the database and this reader can also start using it. In endRead, the variable numReaders is decremented and the last reader to leave the database unlocks it using the call wlock.V().

This protocol has the disadvantage that a writer may starve in the presence of continuously arriving readers. A starvation-free solution to the reader-writer problem is left as an exercise.

3.2.3   The Dining Philosopher Problem

This problem, first posed and solved by Dijkstra, is useful in bringing out issues associated with concurrent programming and symmetry. The dining problem consists of multiple philosophers who spend their time thinking and eating spaghetti.

```
import java.util.Random;
class Producer implements Runnable {
    BoundedBuffer b = null;
    public Producer(BoundedBuffer initb) {
        b = initb;
        new Thread(this).start();
    }
    public void run() {
        double item;
        Random r = new Random();
        while (true) {
            item = r.nextDouble();
            System.out.println("produced item " + item);
            b.deposit(item);
            Util.mySleep(200);
        }
    }
}
class Consumer implements Runnable {
    BoundedBuffer b = null;
    public Consumer(BoundedBuffer initb) {
        b = initb;
        new Thread(this).start();
    }
    public void run() {
        double item;
        while (true) {
            item = b.fetch();
            System.out.println("fetched item " + item);
            Util.mySleep(50);
        }
    }
}
class ProducerConsumer {
    public static void main(String[] args) {
        BoundedBuffer buffer = new BoundedBuffer();
        Producer producer = new Producer(buffer);
        Consumer consumer = new Consumer(buffer);
    }
}
```

Figure 3.5: Producer-consumer algorithm using semaphores

```
class ReaderWriter {
    int numReaders = 0;
    BinarySemaphore mutex = new BinarySemaphore(true);
    BinarySemaphore wlock = new BinarySemaphore(true);
    public void startRead() {
        mutex.P();
        numReaders++;
        if (numReaders == 1) wlock.P();
        mutex.V();
    }
    public void endRead() {
        mutex.P();
        numReaders--;
        if (numReaders == 0) wlock.V();
        mutex.V();
    }
    public void startWrite() {
        wlock.P();
    }
    public void endWrite() {
        wlock.V();
    }
}
```

Figure 3.6: Reader-writer algorithm using semaphores

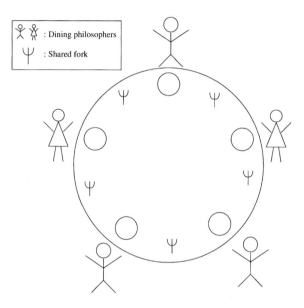

Figure 3.7: The dining philosopher problem

However, a philosopher requires shared resources, such as forks, to eat spaghetti (see Figure 3.7). We are required to devise a protocol to coordinate access to the shared resources. A computer-minded reader may substitute processes for philosophers and files for forks. The task of eating would then correspond to an operation that requires access to shared files.

```java
class Philosopher implements Runnable {
    int id = 0;
    Resource r = null;
    public Philosopher(int initId, Resource initr) {
        id = initId;
        r = initr;
        new Thread(this).start();
    }
    public void run() {
        while (true) {
            try {
                System.out.println("Phil " + id + " thinking");
                Thread.sleep(30);
                System.out.println("Phil " + id + " hungry");
                r.acquire(id);
                System.out.println("Phil " + id + " eating");
                Thread.sleep(40);
                r.release(id);
            } catch (InterruptedException e) {
                return;
            }
        }
    }
}
```

Figure 3.8: Dining Philosopher

Let us first model the process of a philosopher. The class `Philosopher` is shown in Figure 3.8. Each philosopher P_i repeatedly cycles through the following states — *thinking, hungry,* and *eating.* To eat, a philosopher requires resources (forks) for which it makes call to `acquire(i)`. Thus, the protocol to acquire resources is abstracted as an interface `Resource` shown in Figure 3.9.

The first attempt to solve this problem is shown in Figure 3.10. It uses a binary semaphore for each of the forks. To acquire the resources for eating, a philosopher i grabs the fork on its left by using `fork[i].P()` at line 12, and the fork on the right by using `fork[(i+1) % n].P()` at line 13. To release the resources, the philosopher invokes `V()` on both the forks at lines 16 and 17.

This attempt illustrates the dangers of *symmetry* in a distributed system. This

```
interface Resource {
    public void acquire(int i);
    public void release(int i);
}
```

Figure 3.9: Resource Interface

```
1  class DiningPhilosopher implements Resource {
2      int n = 0;
3      BinarySemaphore[] fork = null;
4      public DiningPhilosopher(int initN) {
5          n = initN;
6          fork = new BinarySemaphore[n];
7          for (int i = 0; i < n; i++) {
8              fork[i] = new BinarySemaphore(true);
9          }
10     }
11     public void acquire(int i) {
12         fork[i].P();
13         fork[(i + 1) % n].P();
14     }
15     public void release(int i) {
16         fork[i].V();
17         fork[(i + 1) % n].V();
18     }
19     public static void main(String[] args) {
20         DiningPhilosopher dp = new DiningPhilosopher(5);
21         for (int i = 0; i < 5; i++)
22             new Philosopher(i, dp);
23     }
24 }
```

Figure 3.10: Dining philosopher using semaphores

protocol can result in deadlock when each philosopher is able to grab its left fork and then waits for its right neighbor to release its fork.

There are many ways that one can extend the solution to ensure freedom from deadlock. For example:

1. We can introduce asymmetry by requiring one of the philosophers to grab forks in a different order (i.e., the right fork followed by the left fork instead of vice versa).

2. We can require philosophers to grab both the forks at the same time.

3. Assume that a philosopher has to stand before grabbing any fork. Allow at most four philosophers to be standing at any given time.

It is left as an exercise for the reader to design a protocol that is free from deadlocks.

The dining philosopher problem also illustrates the distinction between deadlock freedom and starvation freedom. Assume that we require a philosopher to grab both the forks at the same time. Although this eliminates deadlock, we still have the problem of a philosopher being starved because its neighbors continuously alternate in eating. The reader is invited to come up with a solution that is free from deadlock as well as starvation.

3.3 Monitors

The *Monitor* is a high-level object-oriented construct for synchronization in concurrent programming. A monitor can be viewed as a `class` that can be used in concurrent programs. As any `class`, a monitor has data variables and methods to manipulate that data. Because multiple threads can access the shared data at the same time, monitors support the notion of *entry* methods to guarantee mutual exclusion. It is guaranteed that at most one thread can be executing in any entry method at any time. Sometimes the phrase "thread t is inside the monitor" is used to denote that thread t is executing an entry method. It is clear that at most one thread can be in the monitor at any time. Thus associated with every monitor object is a queue of threads that are waiting to enter the monitor.

As we have seen before, concurrent programs also require *conditional synchronization* when a thread must wait for a certain condition to become true. To address conditional synchronization, the monitor construct supports the notion of *condition variables*. A condition variable has two operations defined on it: *wait* and *notify* (also called a *signal*). For any condition variable x, any thread, say, t_1, that makes a call to $x.wait()$ is blocked and put into a queue associated with x. When another thread, say, t_2, makes a call to $x.notify()$, if the queue associated with x

is nonempty, a thread is removed from the queue and inserted into the queue of threads that are eligible to run. Since at most one thread can be in the monitor, this immediately poses a problem: which thread should continue after the notify operation—the one that called the *notify* method or the thread that was waiting. There are two possible answers:

1. One of the threads that was waiting on the condition variable continues execution. Monitors that follow this rule are called *Hoare* monitors.

2. The thread that made the notify call continues its execution. When this thread goes out of the monitor, then other threads can enter the monitor. This is the semantics followed in Java.

One advantage of Hoare's monitor is that the thread that was notified on the condition starts its execution without intervention of any other thread. Therefore, the state in which this thread starts executing is the same as when the *notify* was issued. On waking up, it can assume that the condition is true. Therefore, using Hoare's mointor, a thread's code may be

$$\texttt{if (!B) x.wait();}$$

Assuming that t_2 notifies only when B is true, we know that t_1 can assume B on waking up. In Java-style monitor, even though t_2 issues the *notify*, it continues its execution. Therefore, when t_1 gets its turn to execute, the condition B may not be true any more. Hence, when using Java, the threads usually wait for the condition as

$$\texttt{while (!B) x.wait();}$$

The thread t_1 can take a `notify()` only as a hint that B may be true. Therefore, it explicitly needs to check for truthness of B when it wakes up. If B is actually false, it issues the `wait()` call again.

In Java, we specify an object to be a monitor by using the keyword `synchronized` with its methods. To get conditional synchronization, Java provides

1. `wait()`: which inserts the thread in the wait queue. For simplicity, we use `Util.myWait()` instead of `wait()` in Java. The only difference is that `myWait` catches the `InterruptedException`.

2. `notify()`: which wakes up a thread in the wait queue.

3. `notifyAll()`: which wakes up all the threads in the wait queue.

Java does not have condition variables. Thus, associated with each object there is a single `wait` queue for conditions. This is sufficient for most programming needs. If one needs, it is also easy to simulate condition variables in Java. A pictorial representation of a Java monitor is shown in Figure 3.11. There are two queues associated with an object—a queue of threads waiting for the lock associated with the monitor and another queue of threads waiting for some condition to become true.

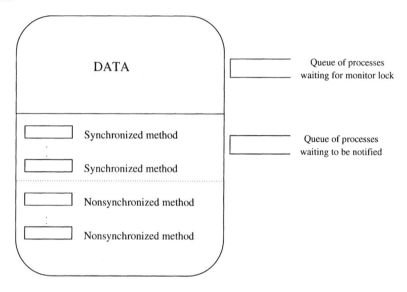

Figure 3.11: A pictorial view of a Java monitor

Let us solve some synchronization problems with Java monitors. We first look at the producer-consumer problem. The `BoundedBufferMonitor` shown in Figure 3.12 has two entry methods: `deposit` and `fetch`. This means that if a thread is executing the method `deposit` or `fetch`, then no other thread can execute `deposit` or `fetch`. The `synchronized` keyword at lines 5 and 14 allows mutual exclusion in access of shared variables and corresponds to acquiring the *monitor lock*. Let us now look at the method `deposit`. At line 6, if the buffer is full, (i.e., `count` is equal to `sizeBuf`), then the thread that called `deposit` must wait for a slot in the `buffer` to be consumed. Therefore, it invokes the method `myWait()`. When a thread waits for the condition, it goes in a *queue* waiting to be notified by some other thread. It also has to release the monitor lock so that other threads can enter the monitor and make the condition on which this thread is waiting true. When this thread is notified, it has to acquire the monitor lock again before continuing its execution.

Now assume that the condition in the while statement at line 6 is false. Then the value can be deposited in the buffer. The variable inBuf points to the tail of the circular buffer. It is advanced after the insertion at line 9 and the count of the number of items in the buffer is incremented at line 10. We are not really done yet. While designing a monitor, one also needs to ensure that if some thread may be waiting for a condition that may have become true, then that thread must be notified. In this case, a consumer thread may be waiting in the method fetch for some item to become available. Therefore, if count is 1, we notify any waiting thread at line 12.

The method fetch is very similar to deposit.

```
1 class BoundedBufferMonitor {
2     final int sizeBuf = 10;
3     double[] buffer = new double[sizeBuf];
4     int inBuf = 0, outBuf = 0, count = 0;
5     public synchronized void deposit(double value) {
6         while (count == sizeBuf) // buffer full
7             Util.myWait(this);
8         buffer[inBuf] = value;
9         inBuf = (inBuf + 1) % sizeBuf;
10        count++;
11        if (count == 1) // items available for fetch
12            notify();
13    }
14    public synchronized double fetch() {
15        double value;
16        while (count == 0) // buffer empty
17            Util.myWait(this);
18        value = buffer[outBuf];
19        outBuf = (outBuf + 1) % sizeBuf;
20        count--;
21        if (count == sizeBuf - 1) // empty slots available
22            notify();
23        return value;
24    }
25 }
```

Figure 3.12: Bounded buffer monitor

Now let us revisit the dining philosophers problem. In the solution shown in Figure 3.13, a philosopher i uses the method test at line 18 to determine if any of neighboring philosophers is eating. If not, then this philosopher can start eating. Otherwise the philosopher must wait for the condition (state[i] == eating) at line 19 to begin eating. This condition can become true when one of the neighboring philosophers finishes eating. After eating, the philosopher invokes the method `release` to check at lines 24 and 25, whether the left neighbor or the right neighbor can now eat. If any of them can eat, this philosopher wakes up all the waiting philosophers by invoking `notifyAll()` at line 32. This solution guarantees mutual exclusion of neighboring philosophers and is also free from deadlock. However, it does not guarantee freedom from starvation. The reader should devise a protocol for starvation freedom.

3.4 Other Examples

In this section we give another example of concurrent programming in Java. Figure 3.14 shows a thread-safe implementation of a queue that is based on a linked list. The class `Node` declared at line 2 contains a String as data and the reference to the next node in the linked list. To `enqueue` data, we first create a `temp` node at line 8. This node is inserted at the `tail`. If the linked list is empty, this is the only node in the linked list and both `head` and `tail` are made to point to this node at lines 11–13. To `dequeue` a node, a thread must wait at line 22 if `head` is null (the linked list is empty). Otherwise, the data in the `head` node is returned and `head` is moved to the `next` node.

As mentioned earlier, whenever a thread needs to execute a synchronized method, it needs to get the monitor lock. The keyword `synchronized` can also be used with any statement as `synchronized (expr) statement`. The expression `expr` must result in a reference to an object on evaluation. The semantics of the above construct is that the `statement` can be executed only when the thread has the lock for the object given by the `expr`. Thus a synchronized method

```
public synchronized void method() {
    body();
}
```

can simply be viewed as a short form for

```
public void method() {
  synchronized (this) {
    body();
  }
}
```

Just as nonstatic methods can be **synchronized**, so can the static methods. A **synchronized** static method results in a classwide lock.

```
1 class DiningMonitor implements Resource {
2       int n = 0;
3       int state [] = null;
4       static final int thinking = 0, hungry = 1, eating = 2;
5       public DiningMonitor ( int initN ) {
6             n = initN ;
7             state = new int [n];
8             for ( int i = 0; i < n; i++) state [i] = thinking ;
9       }
10      int left ( int i ) {
11            return ( n + i - 1) % n;
12      }
13      int right ( int i ) {
14            return ( i + 1) % n;
15      }
16      public synchronized void acquire ( int i ) {
17            state [i] = hungry ;
18            test ( i );
19            while ( state [i] != eating )
20                  Util . myWait( this );
21      }
22      public synchronized void release ( int i ) {
23            state [i] = thinking ;
24            test ( left ( i ));
25            test ( right ( i ));
26      }
27      void test ( int i ) {
28            if (( state [ left ( i )] != eating ) &&
29            ( state [i] == hungry) &&
30            ( state [ right ( i )] != eating )) {
31                  state [i] = eating ;
32                  notifyAll ();
33            }
34      }
35      public static void main( String [] args ) {
36            DiningMonitor dm = new DiningMonitor (5);
37            for ( int i = 0; i < 5; i++)
38                  new Philosopher ( i , dm);
39      }
40 }
```

Figure 3.13: Dining philosopher using monitors

```
 1 public class ListQueue {
 2     class Node {
 3         public String data;
 4         public Node next;
 5     }
 6     Node head = null, tail = null;
 7     public synchronized void enqueue(String data) {
 8         Node temp = new Node();
 9         temp.data = data;
10         temp.next = null;
11         if ( tail == null ) {
12             tail = temp;
13             head = tail;
14         } else {
15             tail.next = temp;
16             tail = temp;
17         }
18         notify();
19     }
20     public synchronized String dequeue() {
21         while ( head == null )
22             Util.myWait(this);
23         String returnval = head.data;
24         head = head.next;
25         return returnval;
26     }
27 }
```

Figure 3.14: Linked list

One also needs to be careful with inheritance. When an extended class overrides a `synchronized` method with an unsynchronized method, the method of the original class stays synchronized. Thus, any call to `super.method()` will result in synchronization.

3.5 Dangers of Deadlocks

Since every synchronized call requires a lock, a programmer who is not careful can introduce deadlocks. For example, consider the following class that allows a cell to be swapped with the other cell. An object of class `BCell` provides three methods: `getValue`, `setValue` and `swap`. Although the implementation appears correct at first glance, it suffers from deadlock. Assume that we have two objects, p and q, as instances of class `BCell`. What happens if a thread t_1 invokes `p.swap(q)` and another thread, say, t_2, invokes `q.swap(p)` concurrently? Thread t_1 acquires the lock for the monitor object p and t_2 acquires the lock for the monitor object q. Now, thread t_1 invokes `q.getValue()` as part of the `swap` method. This invocation has to wait because object q is locked by t_2. Similarly, t_2 has to wait for the lock for p, and we have a deadlock!

```
class BCell { // can result in deadlocks
    int value;
    public synchronized int getValue() {
        return value;
    }
    public synchronized void setValue(int i) {
        value = i;
    }
    public synchronized void swap(BCell x) {
        int temp = getValue();
        setValue(x.getValue());
        x.setValue(temp);
    }
}
```

The program that avoids the deadlock is given below. It employs a frequently used strategy of totally ordering all the objects in a system and then acquiring locks only in increasing order. In this program, both `p.swap(q)` and `q.swap(p)` result in either `p.doSwap(q)` or `q.doSwap(p)`, depending on the `identityHashCode` value of the objects `p` and `q`.

```java
class Cell {
    int value;
    public synchronized int getValue() {
        return value;
    }
    public synchronized void setValue(int i) {
        value = i;
    }
    protected synchronized void doSwap(Cell x) {
        int temp = getValue();
        setValue(x.getValue());
        x.setValue(temp);
    }
    public void swap(Cell x) {
        if (this == x)
            return;
        else if (System.identityHashCode(this)
                < System.identityHashCode(x))
            doSwap(x);
        else
            x.doSwap(this);
    }
}
```

Some other useful methods in Java Thread class are as follows:

1. The interrupt() method allows a thread to be interrupted. If thread t_1 calls $t_2.interrupt()$, then t_2 gets an InterruptedException.

2. The yield() method allows a thread to yield the CPU to other threads temporarily. It does not require any interaction with other threads, and a program without yield() would be functionally equivalent to yield() call. A thread may choose to yield() if it is waiting for some data to become available from say InputStream.

3. The method holdsLock(x) returns true if the current thread holds the monitor lock of the object x.

3.6   Problems

3.1. Show that if the P() and V() operations of a binary semaphore are not executed atomically, then mutual exclusion may be violated.

3.2. Show that a counting semaphore can be implemented using binary semaphores. (*Hint*: Use a shared variable of type integer and two binary semaphores)

3.3. Give a starvation-free solution to the reader-writer problem using semaphores.

3.4. The following problem is known as the *sleeping barber* problem. There is one thread called *barber*. The barber cuts the hair of any waiting *customer*. If there is no customer, the barber goes to sleep. There are multiple customer threads. A customer waits for the barber if there is any chair left in the barber room. Otherwise, the customer leaves immediately. If there is a chair available, then the customer occupies it. If the barber is sleeping, then the customer wakes the barber. Assume that there are n chairs in the barber shop. Write a Java class for SleepingBarber using semaphores that allows the following methods:

```
runBarber() // called by the barber thread; runs forever
hairCut() // called by the customer thread
```

How will you extend your algorithm to work for the barber shop with multiple barbers.

3.5. Give a deadlock-free solution to the dining philosophers problem using semaphores. Assume that one of the philosophers picks forks in a different order.

3.6. Assume that there are three threads—P, Q, and R—that repeatedly print "P", "Q", and "R" respectively. Use semaphores to coordinate the printing such that the number of "R" printed is always less than or equal to the sum of "P" and "Q" printed.

3.7. Write a monitor for the sleeping barber problem.

3.8. Show how condition variables of a monitor can be implemented in Java.

3.9. Write a monitor class `counter` that allows a process to sleep until the counter reaches a certain value. The `counter` class allows two operations: `increment()` and `sleepUntil(int x)`.

3.10. Write a Java class for `BoundedCounter` with a minimum and a maximum value. This class provides two methods: `increment()` and `decrement()`. Decrement at the minimum value and increment at the maximum value result in the calling thread waiting until the operation can be performed without violating the bounds on the counter.

3.7 Bibliographic Remarks

The semaphores were introduced by Dijkstra [Dij65a]. The monitor concept was introduced by Brinch Hansen [Han72] and the Hoare-style monitor, by Hoare [Hoa74].

Solutions to classical synchronization problems in Java are also discussed in the book by Hartley [Har98]. The example of deadlock and its resolution based on resource ordering is discussed in the book by Lea [Lea99].

Chapter 4

Consistency Conditions

4.1 Introduction

In the presence of concurrency, one needs to revisit the correctness conditions of executions, specifically, which behaviors are correct when multiple processes invoke methods concurrently on a shared object. Let us define a concurrent object as one that allows multiple processes to execute its operations concurrently. For example, a concurrent queue in a shared memory system may allow multiple processes to invoke *enqueue* and *dequeue* operations. The natural question, then, is to define which behavior of the object under concurrent operations is consistent (or correct). Consider the case when a process P enqueues x in an empty queue. Then it calls the method dequeue, while process Q concurrently enqueues y. Is the queue's behavior acceptable if process P gets y as the result of dequeue? The objective of this chapter is to clarify such questions.

The notion of consistency is also required when objects are *replicated* in a parallel or a distributed system. There are two reasons for replicating objects: fault tolerance and efficiency. If an object has multiple copies and a processor that contains one of the copies of the object goes down, the system may still be able to function correctly by using other copies. Further, accessing a remote object may incur a large overhead because of communication delays. Suppose that we knew that most accesses of the object are for *read only*. In this case, it may be better to replicate that object. A process can read the value from the replica that is closest to it in the system. Of course, when we perform a *write* on this object, we have to worry about consistency of data. This again requires us to define data consistency. Observe that any system that uses *caches*, such as a multiprocessor system, also has to grapple with similar issues.

4.2   System Model

A *concurrent system* consists of a set of *sequential processes* that communicate through *concurrent objects*. Each object has a name and a type. The type defines the set of possible values for objects of this type and the set of primitive operations that provide the only means to manipulate objects of this type. Execution of an operation takes some time; this is modeled by two events, namely, an *invocation* event and a *response* event. Let $op(arg)$ be an operation on object x issued at P; arg and *res* denote op's input and output parameters, respectively. Invocation and response events $inv(op(arg))$ *on* x *at* P and $resp(op(res))$ *from* x *at* P will be abbreviated as $inv(op)$ and $resp(op)$ when parameters, object name, and process identity are not necessary. For any operation e, we use $proc(e)$ to denote the process and $object(e)$ to denote the set of objects associated with the operation. In this chapter, we assume that all operations are applied by a single process on a single object. In the problem set, we explore generalizations to operations that span multiple objects.

A *history* is an execution of a concurrent system modeled by a directed acyclic graph $(H, <_H)$, where H is the set of operations and $<_H$ is an irreflexive transitive relation that captures the *occurred before* relation between operations. Sometimes we simply use H to denote the history when $<_H$ is clear from the context. Formally, for any two operations e and f:

$$e <_H f \quad \text{if} \quad resp(e) \text{ occurred before } inv(f) \text{ in real time.}$$

Observe that this relation includes the following relations:

Process order: $(proc(e) = proc(f)) \wedge (resp(e) \text{ occurred before } inv(f))$.

Object order: $(object(e) \cap object(f) \neq \emptyset) \wedge (resp(e) \text{ occurred before } inv(f))$.

A process subhistory $H|P$ (H at P) of a history H is a sequence of all those events e in H such that $proc(e) = P$. An object subhistory is defined in a similar way for an object x, denoted by $H|x$ (H at x). Two histories are *equivalent* if they are composed of exactly the same set of invocation and response events.

A history $(H, <_H)$ is a *sequential* history if $<_H$ is a total order. Such a history would happen if there was only one sequential process in the system. A sequential history is *legal* if it meets the sequential specification of all the objects. For example, if we are considering a read–write register x as a shared object, then a sequential history is legal if for every read operation that returns its value as v, there exists a write on that object with value v, and there does not exist another write operation on that object with a different value between the write and the read operations. For a sequential queue, if the queue is nonempty then a dequeue operation should return the item that was enqueued earliest and has not been already dequeued. If the queue is empty, then the dequeue operation should return null.

Our goal is to determine whether a given *concurrent* history is correct.

4.3 Sequential Consistency

Definition 4.1 (Sequentially Consistent) *A history* $(H, <_H)$ *is sequentially consistent if there exists a sequential history* S *equivalent to* H *such that* S *is legal and it satisfies process order.*

Thus a history is sequentially consistent if its execution is equivalent to a legal sequential execution and each process behavior is identical in the concurrent and sequential execution. In the following histories, P, Q, and R are processes operating on shared registers x, y, and z. We assume that all registers have 0 initially. The response of a read operation is denoted by $ok(v)$, where v is the value returned, and the response of a write operation is denoted by $ok()$. The histories are shown graphically in Figure 4.1.

1. $H_1 = P \ write(x, 1), \ Q \ read(x), \ Q \ ok(0), \ P \ ok()$.

   Note that H_1 is a concurrent history. Q invokes the $read(x)$ operation before the $write(x, 1)$ operation is finished. Thus $write(x, 1)$ and $read(x)$ are concurrent operations in H_1. H_1 is sequentially consistent because it is equivalent to the following legal sequential history.
   $S = Q \ read(x), \ Q \ ok(0), \ P \ write(x, 1), \ P \ ok()$.

   To see the equivalence, note that
   $H_1|P = S|P = P \ write(x, 1), \ P \ ok()$.
   $H_1|Q = S|Q = Q \ read(x), \ Q \ ok(0)$.

2. $H_2 = P \ write(x, 1), \ P \ ok(), \ Q \ read(x), \ Q \ ok(0)$.

   Somewhat surprisingly, H_2 is also sequentially consistent. Even though P got the response of its write before Q, it is okay for Q to have read an old value. Note that H_2 is a sequential history but not legal. However, it is equivalent to the following legal sequential history:
   $Q \ read(x), \ Q \ ok(0), \ P \ write(x, 1), \ P \ ok()$.

3. $H_3 = P \ write(x, 1), \ Q \ read(x), \ P \ ok(), \ Q \ ok(0), \ P \ read(x), \ P \ ok(0)$.

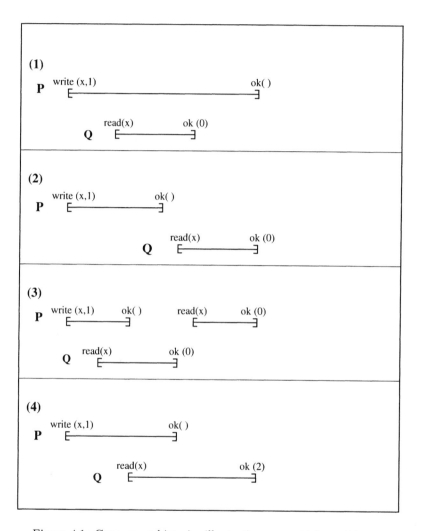

Figure 4.1: Concurrent histories illustrating sequential consistency

H_3 is not sequentially consistent. Any sequential history equivalent to H_3 must preserve process order. Thus the *read* operation by P must come after the *write* operation. This implies that the *read* cannot return 0.

4. $H_4 = P\ write(x,1),\ Q\ read(x),\ P\ ok(),\ Q\ ok(2)$.

H_4 is also not sequentially consistent. There is no *legal* sequential history equivalent to H_4 because the read by Q returns 2, which was never written on the register (and was not the initial value).

4.4 Linearizability

Linearizability is a stronger consistency condition than sequential consistency. Intuitively, an execution of a concurrent system is linearizable if it could appear to an external observer as a sequence composed of the operations invoked by processes that respect object specifications and real-time precedence ordering on operations. So, linearizability provides the illusion that each operation on shared objects issued by concurrent processes takes effect instantaneously at some point between the beginning and the end of its execution. Formally, this is stated as follows.

Definition 4.2 (Linearizable) *A history* $(H, <_H)$ *is linearizable if there exists a sequential history* $(S, <)$ *equivalent to* H *such that* S *is legal and it preserves* $<_H$.

Since $<_H$ includes process order, it follows that a linearizable history is always sequentially consistent. Let us reexamine some histories that we saw earlier.

1. $H_1 = P\ write(x,1),\ Q\ read(x),\ Q\ ok(0),\ P\ ok()$.

   H_1 is linearizable because the following legal sequential history,
   $$Q\ read(x),\ Q\ ok(0),\ P\ write(x,1),\ P\ ok()$$
   preserves $<_H$.

2. $H_2 = P\ write(x,1),\ P\ ok(),\ Q\ read(x),\ Q\ ok(0)$.

   H_2 is sequentially consistent but not linearizable. The legal sequential history used for showing sequential consistency does not preserve $<_H$.

A key advantage of linearizability is that it is a local property, that is, if for all objects x, $H|x$ is linearizable, then H is linearizable. Sequential consistency does not have this property. For example, consider two concurrent queues, s and t. Process P enqueues x in s and t. Process Q enqueues y in t and then in s. Now P gets y from deq on s and Q get x when it does deq on t.

58 CHAPTER 4. CONSISTENCY CONDITIONS

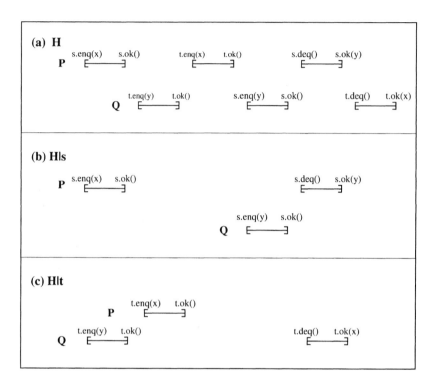

Figure 4.2: Sequential consistency does not satisfy locality

Consider the following histories shown in Figure 4.2:

$H =$
> $P\ s.enq(x), P\ s.ok(),$
> $Q\ t.enq(y),\ Q\ t.ok(),$
> $P\ t.enq(x),\ P\ t.ok(),$
> $Q\ s.enq(y),\ Q\ s.ok(),$
> $P\ s.deq(),\ P\ s.ok(y),$
> $Q\ t.deq(),\ Q\ t.ok(x)$

$H|s =$
> $P\ s.enq(x), P\ s.ok(),$
> $Q\ s.enq(y),\ Q\ s.ok(),$
> $P\ s.deq(),\ P\ s.ok(y).$

$H|t =$
> $Q\ t.enq(y),\ Q\ t.ok(),$
> $P\ t.enq(x),\ P\ t.ok(),$
> $Q\ t.deq(),\ Q\ t.ok(x)$

Both $H|s$ and $H|t$ are sequentially consistent but H is not.

To see that the linearizability is a local property, assume that $(S_x, <_x)$ is a linearization of $H|x$, that is, $(S_x, <_x)$ is a sequential history that is equivalent to $H|x$. We construct an acyclic graph that orders all operations on any object and also preserves occurred before order $<_H$. Any sort of this graph will then serve as a linearization of H. The graph is constructed as follows. The vertices are all the operations. The edges are all the edges given by union of all $<_x$ and $<_H$. This graph totally orders all operations on any object. Moreover, it preserves $<_H$. The only thing that remains to be shown is that it is acyclic. Since $<_x$ are acyclic, it follows that any cycle, if it exists, must involve at least two objects.

We will show that cycle in this graph implies a cycle in $<_H$. If any two consecutive edges in the cycle are due to just $<_x$ or just $<_H$, then they can be combined due to transitivity. Note that $e <_x f <_y g$ for distinct objects x and y is not possible because all operations are unary ($e <_x f <_y g$ implies that f operates on both x and y). Now consider any sequence of edges such that $e <_H f <_x g <_H h$.

> $e <_H f$ implies $res(e)$ precedes $inv(f)$ { definition of $<_H$ }
> $f <_x g$ implies $inv(f)$ precedes $res(g)$ { $<_x$ is a total order }
> $g <_H h$ implies $res(g)$ precedes $inv(h)$ { definition of $<_H$ }.

These relations can be combined to give that $res(e)$ precedes $inv(h)$. Therefore, $e <_H h$. Thus any cycle in the graph can be reduced to a cycle in $<_H$, a contradiction because $<_H$ is irreflexive.

So far we have only looked at consistency conditions for complete histories, that is, histories in which every *invocation* operation has a corresponding *response* operation. We can generalize the consistency conditions for partial histories as follows. A partial history H is linearizable if there exists a way of completing the history by appending response events such that the complete history is linearizable. For example, consider the following history:

$$H_3 = P \; write(x,1), \; Q \; read(x), \; Q \; ok(0)$$

H_3 is linearizable because

$$P \; write(x,1), \; Q \; read(x), \; Q \; ok(0), P \; ok()$$

is linearizable. This generalization allows us to deal with systems in which some processes may fail and consequently some response operations may be missing.

4.5 Other Consistency Conditions

Although we have focused on sequential consistency and linearizability, there are many consistency conditions that are weaker than sequential consistency. A weaker consistency condition allows more efficient implementation at the expense of increased work by the programmer, who has to ensure that the application works correctly despite weaker consistency conditions.

Consider a program consisting of two processes, P and Q, with two shared variables x and y. Assume that the initial values of x and y are both 0. P writes 1 in x and then reads the value of y; Q writes 1 in y and then reads the value of x. Strong consistency conditions such as sequential consistency or linearizability prohibit the results of both reads from being 0. However, if we assume that the minimum possible time to read plus the minimum possible time to write is less than the communication latency, then both reads must return 0. The latency is the information delivery time, and each processor cannot possibly know of the events that have transpired at the other processor. So, no matter what the protocol is, if it implements sequential consistency, it must be slow.

Causal consistency is weaker than sequential consistency. Causal consistency allows for implementation of read and write operations in a distributed environment that do not always incur communication delay; that is, causal consistency allows for cheap read and write operations.

With sequential consistency, all processes agree on the same legal sequential history S. The agreement defined by causal consistency is weaker. Given a history H, it is not required that two processes P and Q agree on the same ordering for the write operations, which are not ordered in H. The reads are, however, required to be legal. Each process considers only those operations that can affect it, that is, its own operations and only write operations from other processes. Formally, for read–write objects causal consistency can be defined as follows.

Definition 4.3 (Causally Consistent) *A history* $(H, <_H)$ *is causally consistent if for each process* P_i, *there is a legal sequential history* $(S_i, <_{S_i})$ *where* S_i *is the set of all operations of* P_i *and all write operations in* H, *and* $<_{S_i}$ *respects the following order:*

> `Process order`*: If* P_i *performs operation* e *before* f, *then* e *is ordered before* f *in* S_i.

> `Object order`*: If any process* P *performs a write on an object* x *with value* v *and another process* Q *reads that value* v, *then the write by* P *is ordered before read by* Q *in* S_i.

Intuitively, causal consistency requires that causally related writes be seen by all processes in the same order. The concurrent writes may be seen in different order by different processes.

It can be proved that sequential consistency implies causal consistency but the converse does not hold. As an example, consider history H_1 in which P_1 does $w_1(x, 1)$, $r_1(x, 2)$ and P_2 does $w_2(x, 2)$, $r_2(x, 1)$.

The history is causally consistent because the following serializations exist:

$$S_1 = w_1(x, 1), w_2(x, 2), r_1(x, 2)$$
$$S_2 = w_2(x, 2), w_1(x, 1), r_2(x, 1)$$

Thus we require only that there is a legal sequential history for every process and not one for the entire system. P_1 orders w_1 before w_2 in S_1 and P_2 orders w_2 before w_1 but that is considered causally consistent because w_1 and w_2 are concurrent writes. It can be easily proved that history H_1 is not sequentially consistent.

The following history is not even causally consistent. Assume that the initial value of x is 0. The history at process P is

$$H|P = P \ r(x, 4), P \ w(x, 3).$$

The history at process Q is

$$H|Q = Q \ r(x, 3), Q \ w(x, 4).$$

Since Q reads the value 3 and then writes the value of x, the write by Q should be ordered after the write by P. P's read is ordered before its write; therefore, it cannot return 4 in a causally consistent history.

The table in Figure 4.3 summarizes the requirements of all consistency conditions considered in this chapter. The second column tells us whether the equivalent legal

Consistency	Legal History	Order Preserved
Linearizability	Global	Occurred before order
Sequential	Global	Process order
Causal	Per process	Process, object order
FIFO (Problem 4.4)	Per process	Process order

Figure 4.3: Summary of consistency conditions

history required for the consistency condition is global. The third column tells us the requirement on the legal history in terms of the order preserved. For example, linearizability requires that there be a single equivalent legal history that preserves the occurred before order.

4.6   Problems

4.1. Consider a concurrent stack. Which of the following histories are linearizable? Which of the them are sequentially consistent? Justify your answer.
(a) $P\ push(x), P\ ok(), Q\ push(y), Q\ ok(), P\ pop(), P\ ok(x)$
(b) $P\ push(x), Q\ push(y), P\ ok(), Q\ ok(), Q\ pop(), Q\ ok(x)$

4.2. Assume that all processors in the system maintain a cache of a subset of objects accessed by that processor. Give an algorithm that guarantees sequential consistency of reads and writes of the objects.

4.3. Assume that you have an implementation of a concurrent system that guarantees causal consistency. Show that if you ensure that the system does not have any concurrent writes, then the system also ensures sequential consistency.

4.4. FIFO consistency requires that the writes done by the same process be seen in the same order. Writes done by different processes may be seen in different order. Show a history that is FIFO-consistent but not causally consistent.

4.5. Given a poset $(H, <_H)$ denoting a system execution, we define a relation $\rightarrow_H$ as the transitive closure of union of process and object order. We call $(H, <_H)$ *normal* if there exists an equivalent sequential history that preserves $\rightarrow_H$. Show that when all operations are unary, a history is linearizable iff it is normal.

4.6. Consider the following history of six events in which operations span multiple objects, assuming that A and B are initialized to 0:

$$
\begin{array}{lllll}
ev_1 = & inv(write(1)) & on & A & at & P_1 \\
ev_2 = & inv(sum()) & on & A, B & at & P_2 \\
ev_3 = & resp(write()) & from & A & at & P_1 \\
ev_4 = & inv(write(2)) & on & B & at & P_3 \\
ev_5 = & resp(write()) & from & B & at & P_3 \\
ev_6 = & resp(sum(2)) & from & A, B & at & P_2 \\
\end{array}
$$

Show that this history is not linearizable but normal.

*4.7. Assume that every message delay is in the range $[d-u, d]$ for $0 < u < d$. Show that in any system that ensures sequential consistency of read–write objects, the sum of delays for a read operation and a write operation is at least d.

*4.8. (due to Taylor [Tay83]) Show that the problem of determining whether $(H, <_H$) is sequentially consistent for read–write registers is NP-complete.

*4.9. (due to Mittal and Garg [MG98]) Generalize the definition of sequential consistency and linearizability for the model in which operations span multiple objects. Give distributed algorithms to ensure sequential consistency and linearizability in this model.

4.7 Bibliographic Remarks

Sequential consistency was first proposed by Lamport [Lam79]. The notion of linearizability for read/write registers was also introduced by Lamport [Lam86] under the name of *atomicity*. The concept was generalized to arbitrary data types and termed as linearizability by Herlihy and Wing [HW90]. Causal consistency was introduced by Hutto and Ahamad [HA90].

Chapter 5

Wait-Free Synchronization

5.1 Introduction

The synchronization mechanisms that we have discussed so far are based on locking data structures during concurrent accesses. The lock-based synchronization mechanisms are inappropriate in fault tolerance and real-time applications. When we use lock-based synchronization, if a process fails inside the critical section, then all other processes cannot perform their own operations. Even if no process ever fails, lock-based synchronization is bad for real-time systems. Consider a thread serving a request with a short deadline. If another thread is inside the critical section and is slow, then this thread may have to wait and therefore miss its deadline. Using locks also require the programmer to worry about deadlocks. In this chapter, we introduce synchronization mechanisms that do not use locks and are therefore called *lock-free*. If lock-free synchronization also guarantees that each operation finishes in a bounded number of steps, then it is called *wait-free*.

To illustrate lock-free synchronization, we will implement various concurrent objects. The implementation of a concurrent object may use other simpler concurrent objects. One dimension of simplicity of an object is based on whether it allows multiple readers or writers. We use SR, MR, SW, and MW to denote single reader, multiple reader, single writer, and multiple writer, respectively. The other dimension is the consistency condition satisfied by the register. For a single-writer register, Lamport has defined the notions of safe, regular, and atomic registers.

In this chapter, we discuss these notions and show various lock-free and wait-free constructions of concurrent objects.

5.2   Safe, Regular, and Atomic Registers

A register is *safe* if a read that does not overlap with the write returns the most recent value. If the read overlaps with the write, then it can return any value.

For an example of safe and unsafe register histories, consider the histories shown in Figure 5.1. History (a) is unsafe because the read returns the value 4 but the most recent value written to the register is 3, which had completed before the read started. History (b) is also unsafe. Even though read returns a value that had been written before, it is not the most recent value. History (c) is safe because $W(x, 3)$ and $W(x, 4)$ are concurrent and therefore $W(x, 4)$ could have taken effect before $W(x, 3)$. Histories (d) and (e) are safe because the read operation overlaps a write operation and therefore can return any value.

A register is *regular* if it is safe and when the read overlaps with one or more writes, it returns either the value of the most recent write that preceded the read or the value of one of the overlapping writes. Consider histories shown in Figure 5.2. History (a) is regular because the read operation returns the value 3, which is the most recent write that preceded the read operation. History (b) is also regular because the read operation returns the value 4, which is the value written by a concurrent write operation. History (c) is not regular (although it is safe) because the value it returns does not match either the most recent completed write or a concurrent write. History (d) is also regular. It illustrates that there may be more than one concurrent writes with the read operation.

A register is *atomic* if its histories are linearizable. Clearly, atomicity implies regularity, which in turn implies safety. Consider the histories shown in Figure 5.3. History (a) is regular but not atomic. It is regular because both the reads are valid. It is not atomic because the second read returns a value older than the one returned by the first read. History (b) is atomic. It corresponds to the linearization in which the $W(x, 3)$ operation took effect after the first $R(x)$ operation. History (c) is atomic. It corresponds to the linearization in which the $W(x, 3)$ operation took effect after the $W(x, 4)$ operation, and the read operation by the third process occurred after $W(x, 4)$ and before $W(x, 3)$. History (d) is not atomic. Since the first read returned 3, $W(x, 3)$ happens before $W(x, 4)$ in any linearization. Since the second read is after both of the writes have finished, it can return only 4.

Surprisingly, it is possible to build a multiple-reader multiple-writer (MRMW) atomic multivalued register from single-reader single-writer (SRSW) safe boolean registers. This can be achieved by the following chain of constructions:

1. SRSW safe boolean register to SRSW regular boolean register

2. SRSW regular boolean register to SRSW regular multivalued register

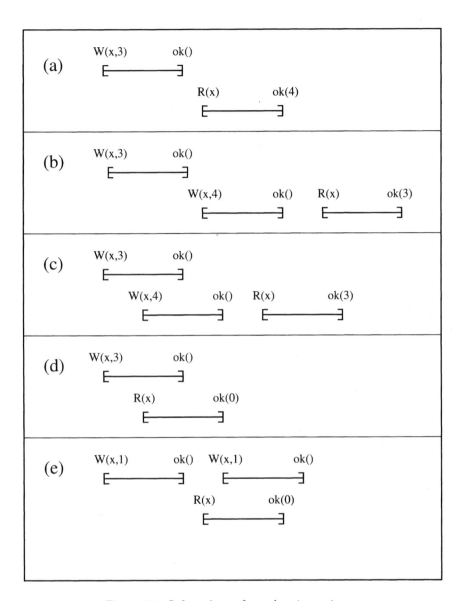

Figure 5.1: Safe and unsafe read–write registers

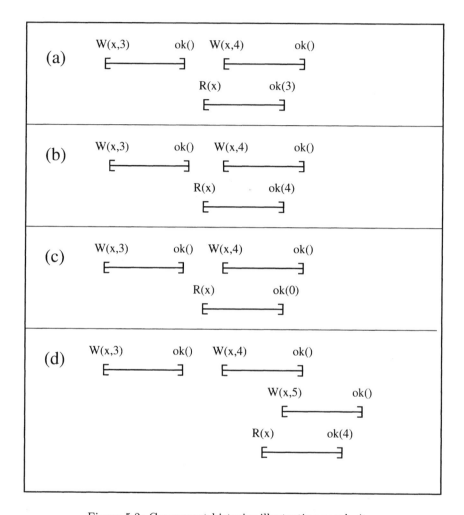

Figure 5.2: Concurrent histories illustrating regularity

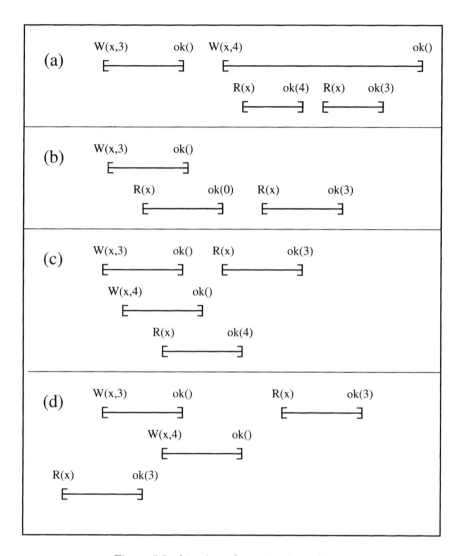

Figure 5.3: Atomic and nonatomic registers

3. SRSW regular register to SRSW atomic register

4. SRSW atomic register to MRSW atomic register

5. MRSW atomic register to MRMW atomic register

We show some of these constructions next.

5.3   Regular SRSW Register

We abstract a register as an object of a class with two methods, getValue and
setValue, used for reading and writing, respectively. Assume that we have a safe
single-reader single-writer boolean register. Since we have a single reader and a
single writer, we need to worry about the semantics of getValue and setValue
only when they overlap. In the presence of concurrency, we require that the value
that is *written* not become corrupted. The value that is read can be arbitrary. If
another getValue is performed after the write has finished, and there is no other
setValue in progress, then the value returned should be the value written by the
last setValue. We will use the following Java code as an abstraction for a SRSW
safe boolean register.

```
class SafeBoolean {
    boolean value;
    public boolean getValue() {
        return value;
    }
    public void setValue(boolean b) {
        value = b;
    }
}
```

Note that this register is not regular exactly for one scenario—if setValue and
getValue are invoked concurrently, the value being written is the same as the previous value and getValue returns a different value. This scenario is shown in Figure
5.1(e).

To make our register regular, we avoid accessing the shared register when the
previous value of the register is the same as the new value that is being written.
The construction of a regular SRSW register from a safe SRSW register in given in
Figure 5.4.

Line 8 ensures that the writer does not access value if the previous value prev
is the same as the value being written, b. Thus an overlapping read will return
the correct value. If the new value is different, then the read can return arbitrary

```
 1  class RegularBoolean {
 2      boolean prev; // not shared
 3      SafeBoolean value;
 4      public boolean getValue() {
 5          return value.getValue();
 6      }
 7      public void setValue(boolean b) {
 8          if (prev != b) {
 9              value.setValue(b);
10              prev = b;
11          }
12      }
13  }
```

Figure 5.4: Construction of a regular boolean register

value from {`true`, `false`}, but that is still acceptable because one of them is the previous value and the other is the new value. This construction exploits the fact that the value is binary and will not work for multivalued registers.

5.4 SRSW Multivalued Register

We skip the construction from a SRSW regular boolean register to a SRSW atomic (linearizable) boolean register. Now assume that we have a SRSW atomic boolean register. This register maintains a single bit and guarantees that in spite of concurrent accesses by a single reader and a single writer, it will result only in linearizable concurrent histories. We now show that, using such registers, we can implement a multivalued SRSW register. The implementation shown in Figure 5.5 is useful only when `maxVal` is small because it uses an array of `maxVal` SRSW boolean registers to allow values in the range 0...`maxVal-1`.

The idea is that the reader should return the index of the first true bit. The straightforward solution of the writer updating the array in the forward direction until it reaches the required index and the reader also scanning in the forward direction for the first true bit does not work. It can happen that the reader does not find any true bit. Come up with an execution to show this! So the first idea we will use is that the writer will first set the required bit to true and then traverse the array in the *backward* direction, setting all previous bits to false. We now describe the `setValue` method in Figure 5.5. To write the value x, the writer makes the xth bit true at line 19 and then makes all the previous values *false* at lines 20–21. The reader scans for the true bit in the forward direction at line 12. With this strategy,

```
 1 class  MultiValued {
 2     int  n = 0;
 3     boolean  A[] = null;
 4     public  MultiValued(int  maxVal, int  initVal) {
 5         n = maxVal;
 6         A = new boolean[n];
 7         for (int  i = 0; i < n; i++) A[i] = false;
 8         A[initVal] = true;
 9     }
10     public  int  getValue() {
11         int  j = 0;
12         while (!A[j]) j++; // forward  scan
13         int  v = j;
14         for (int  i = j - 1; i >= 0; i--) // backward  scan
15             if (A[i]) v = i;
16         return v;
17     }
18     public  void  setValue(int  x) {
19         A[x] = true;
20         for (int  i = x - 1; i >= 0; i--)
21             A[i] = false;
22     }
23 }
```

Figure 5.5: Construction of a multivalued register

the reader is guaranteed to find at least one bit to be true. Further, this bit would correspond to the most recent write before the read or one of the concurrent writes. Therefore, this will result in at least a *regular* register.

However, a single scan by the reader does not result in a linearizable implementation. To see this, assume that the initial value of the register is 5 and the writer first writes the value 1 and then the value 4. These steps will result in

1. Writer sets $A[1]$ to true.
2. Writer sets $A[4]$ to true.
3. Writer sets $A[1]$ to false.

Now assume that concurrent with these two writes, a reader performs two read operations. Since the initial value of $A[1]$ is false, the first read may read $A[4]$ as the first bit to be true. This can happen as follows. The reader reads $A[1]$, $A[2]$, and $A[3]$ as false. Before the reader reads $A[4]$, the writer sets $A[1]$ to true and subsequently $A[4]$ to true. The reader now reads $A[4]$ as true. The second read may happen between steps 2 and 3, resulting in the second read returning 1. The resulting concurrent history is not linearizable because there is an inversion of old and new values. If the first read returned the value 4 then the second read cannot return an older value 1.

In our implementation, the reader first does a forward scan and then does a backward scan at line 14 to find the first bit that is true. Two scans are sufficient to guarantee linearizability.

5.5 MRSW Register

We now build a MRSW register from SRSW registers. Assume that there are n readers and one writer. The simplest strategy would be to have an array of n SRSW registers, $V[n]$, one for each of the readers. The writer would write to all n registers, and the reader r can read from its own register $V[r]$. This does not result in a linearizable implementation. Assume that initially all registers are 5, the initial value of the MRSW register, and that the writer is writing the value 3. Concurrent to this write, two reads occur one after another. Assume that the first read is by the reader i and the second read is by the reader j, where i is less than j. It is then possible for the first read to get the new value 3 because the writer had updated $V[i]$ and the second read to get the old value 5 because the writer had not updated $V[j]$ by then. This contradicts linearizability.

To solve this problem, we require a reader to read not only the value written by the writer but also all the values read by other readers so far to ensure that a reader returns the most recent value. How does the reader determine the most recent value? We use a sequence number associated with each value. The writer maintains the sequence number and writes this sequence number with any value that it writes. Thus we view our SRSW register as consisting of two fields: the value and ts (for timestamp).

Now that our values are timestamped, we can build a MRSW register from SRSW registers using the algorithm shown in Figure 5.6.

Since we can only use SRSW objects, we are forced to keep $O(n^2)$ Comm registers for informing readers what other readers have read. Comm[i][j] is used by the reader i to inform the value it read to the reader j.

The reader simply reads its own register and also what other readers have read and returns the latest value. It reads its own register at line 18 in the local variable tsv (timestamped value). It compares the timestamp of this value with the timestamps of values read by other readers at line 22. After line 23, the reader has the latest value that is read by any reader. It informs other readers of this value at lines 26–28.

The writer simply increments the sequence number at line 33 and writes the value in all n registers at lines 34–35.

5.6   MRMW Register

The construction of an MRMW register from MRSW registers is simpler than the previous construction. We use n MRSW registers for n writers. Each writer writes in its own register. The only problem for the reader to solve is which of the write it should choose for reading. We use the idea of sequence numbers as in the previous implementation. The reader chooses the value with the highest sequence number. There is only one problem with this approach. Previously, there was a single writer and therefore we could guarantee that all writes had different sequence numbers. Now we have multiple writers choosing their numbers possibly concurrently. How do we assign unique sequence number to each write? We use the approach of the Bakery algorithm. The algorithm is shown in Figure 5.7. In the method setValue, we require a writer to read all the sequence numbers and then choose its sequence number to be larger than the maximum sequence number it read. Then, to avoid the problem of two concurrent writers coming up with the same sequence number, we attach the process identifier w with the sequence number. Now two writes with the same sequence number can be ordered on the basis of process ids. Furthermore, we have the following guarantee: If one write completely precedes another write, then the sequence number associated with the first write will be smaller than that with the second write. The reader reads all the values written by various writers

```
 1  class MRSW {
 2      int n = 0;
 3      SRSW V[] = null; // value written for reader i
 4      SRSW Comm[][] = null; // communication between readers
 5      int seqNo = 0;
 6      public MRSW(int readers, int initVal) {
 7          n = readers;
 8          V = new SRSW[n];
 9          for (int i = 0; i < n; i++)
10              V[i].setValue(initVal, 0);
11          Comm = new SRSW[n][n];
12          for (int i = 0; i < n; i++)
13              for (int j = 0; j < n; j++)
14                  Comm[i][j].setValue(initVal, 0);
15      }
16      public int getValue(int r) { //reader r reads
17          //read your own register
18          SRSW tsv = V[r]; // tsv is local
19
20          // find the value with the largest timestamp
21          for (int i = 0; i < n; i++)
22              if (Comm[i][r].getTS() > tsv.getTS())
23                  tsv = Comm[i][r];
24
25          // inform other readers
26          for (int i = 0; i < n; i++) {
27              Comm[r][i].setValue(tsv);
28          }
29          return tsv.getValue();
30      }
31      public void setValue(int x) { // accessed by the writer
32          // write the value with a larger timestamp
33          seqNo++;
34          for (int i = 0; i < n; i++)
35              V[i].setValue(x, seqNo);
36      }
37 }
```

Figure 5.6: Construction of a multireader register

and chooses the one with the largest timestamp.

```
class MultiWriter {
    int n = 0;
    MRSW V[] = null; // value written by the writer i
    public MultiWriter(int writers, int initVal) {
        n = writers;
        V = new MRSW[n];
        for (int i = 0; i < n; i++)
            V[i].setValue(initVal, 0, i);
    }
    public int getValue() {
        MRSW tsv = V[0]; // tsv is local
        for (int i = 1; i < n; i++)
            if ((tsv.ts < V[i].ts) ||
                ((tsv.ts == V[i].ts) && (tsv.pid < V[i].pid)))
                tsv = V[i];
        return tsv.val;
    }
    public void setValue(int w, int x) { // writer w
        int maxseq = V[0].ts;
        for (int i = 1; i < n; i++)
            if (maxseq < V[i].ts) maxseq = V[i].ts;
        V[w].setValue(x, maxseq + 1, w);
    }
}
```

Figure 5.7: Construction of a multiwriter register

5.7   Atomic Snapshots

All our algorithms so far handled single values. Consider an array of values that we want to read in an atomic fashion using an operation `readArray`. We will assume that there is a single reader and a single writer but while the array is being read, the writes to individual locations may be going on concurrently. Intuitively, we would like our `readArray` operation to behave as if it took place instantaneously.

A simple scan of the array does not work. Assume that the array has three locations initially all with value 0 and that a `readArray` operation and concurrently two writes take place one after the other. The first write updates the first location to 1 and the second write updates the second location to 1. A simple scan may return the value of array as $[0, 1, 0]$. However, the array went through the transitions $[0, 0, 0]$ to $[1, 0, 0]$, and then to $[1, 1, 0]$. Thus, the value returned by `readArray` is not consistent with linearizability. A construction that provides a `readArray` operation with consistent values in spite of concurrent writes with it is called an *atomic snapshot* operation. Such an operation can be used in getting a checkpoint for fault-tolerance applications.

We first present a *lock-free* construction of atomic snapshots shown in Figure 5.8. This construction is extremely simple. First, to determine whether a location in the array has changed, we append each value with the sequence number. Now, the `readArray` operation reads the array twice. If none of the sequence numbers changed, then we know that there exists a time interval in which the array did not change. Hence the copy read is consistent. This construction is not wait-free because if a conflict is detected, the `readArray` operation has to start all over again. There is no upper bound on the number of times this may have to be done.

```
public class LockFreeSnapshot {
    int n = 0;
    SRSW[] V;
    public void LockFreeSnapshot(int initN) {
        n = initN;
        V = new SRSW[n];
    }
    public void writeLoc(int k, int x) {
        int seq = V[k].ts;
        V[k].setValue(x, seq + 1);
    }
    public SRSW[] readArray() {
        SRSW[] W = new SRSW[n]; // W is local
        boolean done = false;
        while (!done) {
            for (int i = 0; i < n; i++) // copy V to W
                W[i].setValue(V[i].value, V[i].ts);
            done = true;
            // check if V has changed
            for (int i = 0; i < n; i++)
                if (W[i].ts != V[i].ts) {
                    done = false;
                    break;
                }
        }
        return W;
    }
}
```

Figure 5.8: Lock-free atomic snapshot algorithm

This construction is not wait-free because a `readArray` operation may be "starved" by the update operation. We do not go into detail here, but this and many other lock-free constructions can be turned into wait-free constructions by using the notion of "helping" moves. The main idea is that a thread tries to help pending operations. For example, if the thread wanting to perform an *update* operation helps another concurrent thread that is trying to do a `readArray` operation, then we call it a "helping" move. Thus one of the ingredients in constructing a wait-free atomic snapshot would require the update operation to also scan the array.

5.8   Consensus

So far we have given many wait-free (or lock-free) constructions of a concurrent object using other simpler concurrent objects. The question that naturally arises is whether it is always possible to build a concurrent object from simpler concurrent objects. We mentioned that it is possible to construct a wait-free algorithm for an `atomicSnapshot` object that allows atomic reads of multiple locations in an array and atomic write to a single location. What if we wanted to build an object that allowed both reads and writes to multiple locations in an atomic manner? Such a construction is not possible using atomic read–write registers. Another question that arises concerns the existence of *universal* objects, that is, whether there are concurrent objects powerful enough to implement all other concurrent objects.

It turns out that *consensus* is a fundamental problem useful for analyzing such problems. The consensus problem requires a given set of processes to agree on an input value. For example, in a concurrent linked list if multiple threads attempt to insert a node, then all the processes have to agree on which node is inserted first.

The consensus problem is abstracted as follows. Each process has a value input to it that it can propose. For simplicity, we will restrict the range of input values to a single bit. The processes are required to run a protocol so that they decide on a common value. Thus, any object that implements consensus supports the interface shown in Figure 5.9.

```
public interface Consensus {
    public void propose(int pid, int value);
    public int decide(int pid);
}
```

Figure 5.9: Consensus Interface

The requirements on any object implementing consensus are as follows:

- *Agreement*: Two correct processes cannot decide different values.

- *Validity*: The value decided by a correct process must be one of the proposed values.

- *Wait-free*: Each correct process decides the value after a finite number of steps. This should be true without any assumption on relative speeds of processes.

A concurrent object O is defined to have a *consensus number* equal to the largest number of processes that can use O to solve the consensus problem. If O can be used to solve consensus for any number of processes, then its consensus number is ∞ and the object O is called the *universal object*.

Now if we could show that some concurrent object O has consensus number m and another concurrent object has consensus number $m' > m$, then it is clear that there can be no wait-free implementation of O' using O. Surprisingly, the converse is true as well: If O' has consensus number $m' \leq m$, then O' can be implemented using O.

We begin by showing that linearizable (or atomic) registers have consensus number 1. Clearly, an atomic register can be used to solve the consensus problem for a single process. The process simply decides its own value. Therefore, the consensus number is at least 1. Now we show that there does not exist any protocol to solve the consensus using atomic registers.

The argument for nonexistence of a consensus protocol hinges on the concepts of a bivalent state and a critical state. A protocol is in a *bivalent state* if both the values are possible as decision values starting from that global state. A bivalent state is a *critical state* if all possible moves from that state result in nonbivalent states. Any initial state in which processes have different proposed values is bivalent because there exist at least two runs from that state that result in different decision values. In the first run, the process with input 0 gets to execute and all other processes are very slow. Because of wait freedom, this process must decide, and it can decide only on 0 to ensure validity. A similar run exists for a process with its input as 1.

Starting from a bivalent initial state, and letting any process move that keeps the state as bivalent, we must hit a critical state; otherwise, the protocol can run forever. We show that even in a two-process system, atomic registers cannot be used to go to nonbivalent states in a consistent manner. We perform a case analysis of events that can be done by two processes, say, P and Q in a critical state S.

Let e be the event at P and event f be at Q be such that $e(S)$ has a decision value different from that of $f(S)$. We now do a case analysis (shown in Figure 5.10):

- *Case 1: e and f are on different registers.* In this case, both ef and fe are possible in the critical state S. Further, the state $ef(S)$ is identical to $fe(S)$ and therefore cannot have different decision values. But we assumed that

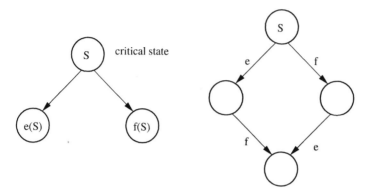

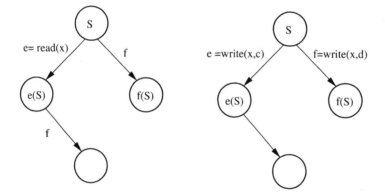

Figure 5.10: Impossibility of wait-free consensus with atomic read–write registers

$f(S)$ and $e(S)$ have different decision values, which implies that $e(f(S))$ and $f(e(S))$ have different decision values because decision values cannot change.

- *Case 2:* Either e or f is a read. Assume that e is a read. Then the state of Q does not change when P does e. Therefore, the decision value for Q from $f(S)$ and $e(S)$, if it ran alone, would be the same; a contradiction.

- *Case 3:* Both e and f are writes on the same register. Again the states $f(S)$ and $f(e(S))$ are identical for Q and should result in the same decision value.

This implies that there is no consensus protocol for two processes that uses just atomic registers. Therefore, the consensus number for atomic registers is 1.

Now let us look at a concurrent object that can do both read and write in one operation. Let us define a `TestAndSet` object as one that provides the test and set instruction discussed in Chapter 2. The semantics of the object is shown in Figure 5.11.

```
public class TestAndSet {
    int myValue = -1;
    public synchronized int testAndSet(int newValue) {
        int oldValue = myValue;
        myValue = newValue;
        return oldValue;
    }
}
```

Figure 5.11: TestAndSet class

We now show that two threads can indeed use this object to achieve consensus. The algorithm is given in Figure 5.12.

By analyzing the `testAndSet` operations on the critical state, one can show that the TestAndSet registers cannot be used to solve the consensus problem on three processes (see Problem 5.1).

Finally, we show universal objects. One such universal object is `CompSwap` (Compare and Swap). The semantics of this object is shown in Figure 5.13. Note that such objects are generally provided by the hardware and we have shown the Java code only to specify how the object behaves. Their actual implementation does no use any locks. Therefore, `CompSwap` can be used for wait-free synchronization. An object of type `CompSwap` can hold a value `myValue`. It supports a single operation `compSwapOp` that takes two arguments: `prevValue` and `newValue`. It replaces the value of the object only if the old value of the object matches the `preValue`.

```
class TestSetConsensus implements Consensus {
    TestAndSet x;
    int proposed[] = {0, 0};
    // assumes pid is 0 or 1
    public void propose(int pid, int v) {
        proposed[pid] = v;
    }
    public int decide(int pid) {
        if (x.testAndSet(pid) == -1)
            return proposed[pid];
        else
            return proposed[1 - pid];
    }
}
```

Figure 5.12: Consensus using TestAndSet object

```
public class CompSwap {
    int myValue = 0;
    public CompSwap(int initValue) {
        myValue = initValue;
    }
    public synchronized int compSwapOp(int prevValue, int newValue) {
        int oldValue = myValue;
        if (myValue == prevValue)
            myValue = newValue;
        return oldValue;
    }
}
```

Figure 5.13: CompSwap object

Processes use a `CompSwap` object x for consensus as follows. It is assumed to have the initial value of -1. Each process tries to update x with its own `pid`. They use the initial value -1 as `prevValue`. It is clear that only the first process will have the right `prevValue`. All other processes will get the `pid` of the first process when they perform this operation. The program to implement consensus is shown in Figure 5.14.

```
public class CompSwapConsensus implements Consensus {
    CompSwap x = new CompSwap(-1);
    int proposed [];
    public CompSwapConsensus(int n) {
        proposed = new int[n];
    }
    public void propose(int pid, int v) {
        proposed[pid] = v;
    }
    public int decide(int pid) {
        int j = x.compSwapOp(-1, pid);
        if (j == -1)
            return proposed[pid];
        else
            return proposed[j];
    }
}
```

Figure 5.14: Consensus using CompSwap object

We now describe another universal object called the load-linked and store-conditional (LLSC) register. An LLSC object contains an object pointer `p` of the following type.

```
public class ObjPointer {
    public Object obj;
    public int version;
}
```

It provides two atomic operations. The `load-linked` operation allows a thread to load the value of a pointer to an object. The `store-conditional` operation allows the pointer to an object to be updated if the pointer has not changed since the last load-linked operation. Thus the semantics of LLSC are shown in Figure 5.15. With each object, we also keep its version number. The method `load_linked` reads the value of the pointer `p` in the variable `local`. The method `store_conditional` takes an object `newObj` and a pointer `local` as its parameters. It updates LLSC object only if the pointer `local` is identical to `p`.

The program for implementing consensus using LLSC is left as an exercise.

```
public class LLSC {
    ObjPointer p;
    public LLSC( Object x) {
        p.obj = x;
        p.version = 0;
    }
    public synchronized void load_linked (ObjPointer local) {
        local.obj = p.obj;
        local.version = p.version;
    }
    public synchronized boolean
    store_conditional (ObjPointer local, Object newObj) {
        if ((p.obj == local.obj) && (p.version == local.version )) {
            p.obj = newObj;
            p.version++;
            return true;
        }
        return false;
    }
}
```

Figure 5.15: Load-Linked and Store-Conditional object

5.9   Universal Constructions

Now that we have seen universal objects, let us show that they can indeed be used to build all other concurrent objects. We first show a construction for a concurrent queue that allows multiple processes to enqueue and dequeue concurrently. Our construction will almost be mechanical. We first begin with a sequential implementation of a queue shown in Figure 5.16.

Now we use LLSC to implement a concurrent queue using a *pointer-swinging* technique. In the object pointer swinging technique any thread that wishes to perform an operation on an object goes through the following steps:

1. The thread makes a copy of that object.

2. It performs its operation on the copy of the object instead of the original object.

```
public class SeqQueue {
    class Element {
        public String data;
        public Element next;
        public Element(String s, Element e) {
            data = s;
            next = e;
        }
    }
    public Element head, tail;
    public SeqQueue() {
        head = null;
        tail = null;
    }
    public SeqQueue(SeqQueue copy) {
        Element node;
        head = copy.head;
        tail = copy.tail;
        for (Element i = head; i != null; i = i.next)
            node = new Element(i.data, i.next);
    }
    public void Enqueue(String data) {
        Element temp = new Element(data, null);
        if (tail == null) {
            tail = temp;
            head = tail;
        } else {
            tail.next = temp;
            tail = temp;
        }
    }
    public String Dequeue() {
        if (head == null) return null;
        String returnval = head.data;
        head = head.next;
        return returnval;
    }
}
```

Figure 5.16: Sequential queue

3. It swings the pointer of the object to the copy if the original pointer has not changed. This is done atomically.

4. If the original pointer has changed, then some other thread has succeeded in performing its operation. This thread starts all over again.

Using these ideas, we can now implement a concurrent queue class as shown in Figure 5.17. To Enqueue an item (of type string), we first save the pointer to the queue x in the variable local at line 10. Line 11 makes a local copy new_queue of the queue x accessed using local pointer. It then inserts data in new_queue at line 12. Line 13 returns true if no other thread has changed x. If store_conditional returns false, then this thread tries again by going to the line 9. The method Dequeue is similar.

```
 1 public class  CQueue {
 2     private LLSC x;
 3     public  CQueue() {
 4         x = new LLSC(new SeqQueue());
 5     }
 6     public void Enqueue(String data) {
 7         SeqQueue new_queue;
 8         ObjPointer local = new ObjPointer();
 9         while (true) {
10             x.load_linked(local);
11             new_queue = new SeqQueue((SeqQueue) local.obj);
12             new_queue.Enqueue(data);
13             if (x.store_conditional(local, new_queue))
14                 return;
15         }
16     }
17     public String Dequeue() {
18         SeqQueue new_queue;
19         ObjPointer local = new ObjPointer();
20         String returnval;
21         while (true) {
22             x.load_linked(local);
23             new_queue = new SeqQueue((SeqQueue) local.obj);
24             returnval = new_queue.Dequeue();
25             if (x.store_conditional(local, new_queue))
26                 return returnval;
27         }
28     }
29 }
```

Figure 5.17: Concurrent queue

While the above mentioned technique can be applied for lock-free construction of any concurrent object, it may be inefficient in practice for large objects because every operation requires a copy. There are more efficient algorithms for large concurrent objects. However, these algorithms are different for different data structures and will not be covered in this book.

5.10 Problems

5.1. Show that `TestAndSet` cannot be used to solve the consensus problem for three processes. (*Hint*: Show that TestAndSet by two processes in any order results in the same state and the third process cannot distinguish between the two cases.)

5.2. Consider a concurrent FIFO queue class that allows two threads to concurrently dequeue. Show that the consensus number of such an object is 2. (Hint: Assume that queue is initialized with two values 0 and 1. Whichever process dequeues 0 wins.)

5.3. Consider a concurrent object of type `Swap` that holds an integer. It supports a single method `swapOp(int v)` that sets the value with v and returns the old value. Show that `Swap` has consensus number 2.

5.4. Show that LLSC is a universal object.

*5.5. Give a lock-free construction of queue that does not make a copy of the entire queue for enqueue and dequeue.

5.11 Bibliographic Remarks

The notion of *safe*, *regular*, and *atomic* registers was first proposed by Lamport [Lam86] who also gave many of the constructions provided here. The notions of consensus number and universal objects are due to Herlihy [Her88]. The reader should also consult [AW98] (chapters 10 and 15).

Chapter 6

Distributed Programming

6.1 Introduction

In this chapter, we will learn primitives provided in the Java programming language for building distributed applications. We will see primarily two programming styles: sockets and remote method invocations. Sockets provide a lower-level interface for building distributed programs but are more efficient and flexible. Remote method invocations (RMI) are easier to use.

In this chapter we first describe the class `InetAddress`, which is useful for network programming no matter which style of primitives are used. Then we discuss primitives for programming using sockets. These sockets may use either the Universal Datagram Protocol (UDP), or the Transmission Control Protocol (TCP). We give an example of an echo server using sockets based on the UDP protocol and a simple name server using sockets based on the TCP protocol. Finally, we discuss programming using remote method invocations.

6.2 InetAddress Class

For any kind of distributed application, we need the notion of an Internet address. Any computer connected to the Internet (called a *host*) can be uniquely identified by an address called an *IP address*. Since addresses are difficult to remember, each host also has a hostname. It is the task of a domain name system (DNS) server to provide the mapping from a hostname to its address. Java provides a class `Java.net.Inetaddress`, which can be used for this translation. The relevant methods for the class InetAddress are given below:

```
public byte[] getAddress()
  Returns the raw IP address of this InetAddress object.
public static InetAddress getByName(String)
  Determines the IP address of a host, given the host's name.
public String getHostAddress()
  Returns the IP address string "%d.%d.%d.%d"
public String getHostName()
  Returns the fully qualified host name for this address.
public static InetAddress getLocalHost()
  Returns the local host.
```

6.3   Sockets based on UDP

Sockets are useful in writing programs based on communication using messages. A Socket is an object that can be used to send and receive messages. There are primarily two protocols used for sending and receiving messages: Universal Datagram Protocol (UDP) and Transmission Control Protocol (TCP). The UDP provides a low-level connectionless protocol. This means that packets sent using UDP are not guaranteed to be received in the order sent. In fact, the UDP protocol does not even guarantee reliability, that is, packets may get lost. The protocol does not use any handshaking mechanisms (such as acknowledgments) to detect loss of packets. Why is UDP useful, then? Because, even though UDP may lose packets, in practice, this is rarely the case. Since there are no overheads associated with error checking, UDP is an extremely efficient protocol.

The TCP protocol is a reliable connection-oriented protocol. It also guarantees ordered delivery of packets. Needless to say, TCP is not as efficient as UDP.

6.3.1   Datagram Sockets

The first class that we use is `DatagramSocket` which is based on the UDP protocol. This class represents a socket for sending and receiving datagram packets. A *datagram socket* is the sending or receiving point for a connectionless packet delivery service. Each packet sent or received on a datagram socket is individually addressed and routed. Multiple packets sent from a machine to another may be routed differently, and may arrive in any order. This class provides a very low level interface for sending and receiving messages. There are few guarantees associated with datagram sockets. An advantage of datagram sockets is that it allows fast data transmission.

The details for the methods in this class are given below. To construct a DatagramSocket, we can use one of the following constructors:

```
public DatagramSocket()
public DatagramSocket(int port)
public DatagramSocket(int port, InetAddress laddr)
```

The first constructor constructs a datagram socket and binds it to any available port on the local host machine. Optionally, a port may be specified as in the second constructor. The last constructor creates a datagram socket, bound to the specified local address. These constructors throw **SocketException** if the socket could not be opened, or if the socket could not bind the specified local port.

The other important methods of this class are as follows:

1. `public void close()`: This method closes a datagram socket.

2. `public int getLocalPort()`: To get the information about the socket, one can use this method, which returns the port number on the local host to which this socket is bound.

3. `public InetAddress getLocalAddress()`: This method gets the local address to which the socket is bound.

4. `public void receive(DatagramPacket p)`: This method `receive` receives a datagram packet from this socket. When this method returns, the DatagramPacket's buffer is filled with the data received. The datagram packet also contains the sender's IP address and the port number on the sender's machine. Note that this method blocks until a datagram is received. The length field of the datagram packet object contains the length of the received message. If the message is longer than the buffer length, the message is truncated. It throws IOException if an I/O error occurs. The blocking can be avoided by setting the timeout.

5. `public void send(DatagramPacket p)`: This method sends a datagram packet from this socket. The DatagramPacket includes information indicating the data to be sent, its length, the IP address of the remote host, and the port number on the remote host.

6.3.2 DatagramPacket Class

The `DatagramSocket` class required data to be sent as datagram packets. The class `java.net.DatagramPacket` is used for that. Its definition is given below.

```
public  final  class  java.net.DatagramPacket
    extends  java.lang.Object {
    public DatagramPacket(byte  ibuf[], int  ilength);
```

```
      public DatagramPacket(byte  ibuf[], int  ilength,
                            InetAddress  iaddr, int iport);
      public InetAddress getAddress();
      public byte[] getData();
      public int getLength();
      public int getPort();
      public void setAddress(InetAddress)
      public void setData(byte[])
      public void setLength(int)
      public void setPort(int)
}
```

The first constructor

```
public DatagramPacket(byte ibuf[], int ilength)
```

constructs a DatagramPacket for receiving packets of length `ilength`. The parameter `ibuf` is the buffer for holding the incoming datagram, and `ilength` is the number of bytes to read.

The constructor for creating a packet to be sent is

```
public DatagramPacket(byte ibuf[], int ilength, InetAddress iaddr, int
iport)
```

It constructs a DatagramPacket for sending packets of length `ilength` to the specified port number on the specified host. The parameters `iaddr` and `iport` are used for the destination address and the destination port number, respectively. The method `getAddress` returns the IP address of the machine to which this datagram is being sent, or from which the datagram was received. The method `getData` returns the data received, or the data to be sent. The method `getLength` returns the length of the data to be sent, or the length of the data received. Similarly, the method `getPort` returns the port number on the remote host to which this datagram is being sent, or from which the datagram was received. The `set` methods are used to set the IP address, port number, and other elements appropriately.

6.3.3 Example Using Datagrams

We give a simple example of a program that uses datagrams. This example consists of two processes—a server and a client. The client reads input from the user and sends it to the server. The server receives the datagram packet and then echoes back the same data. The program for the server is given in Figure 6.1.

```java
import java.net.*;
import java.io.*;
public class DatagramServer {
    public static void main(String [] args) {
        DatagramPacket datapacket, returnpacket;
        int port = 2018;
        int len = 1024;
        try {
            DatagramSocket datasocket = new DatagramSocket(port);
            byte[] buf = new byte[len];

            while (true) {
                try {
                    datapacket = new DatagramPacket(buf, buf.length);
                    datasocket.receive(datapacket);
                    returnpacket = new DatagramPacket(
                    datapacket.getData(),
                    datapacket.getLength(),
                    datapacket.getAddress(),
                    datapacket.getPort());
                    datasocket.send(returnpacket);
                } catch (IOException e) {
                    System.err.println(e);
                }
            }
        } catch (SocketException se) {
            System.err.println(se);
        }
    }
}
```

Figure 6.1: A datagram server

The client process reads a line of input from `System.in`. It then creates a datagram packet and sends it to the server. On receiving a response from the server it displays the message received. The program for the client is given in Figure 6.2.

6.4 Sockets Based on TCP

The second style of interprocess communication is based on the notion of streams. In this style, a connection is set up between the sender and the receiver. This style allows better error recovery and guarantees on the delivery of packets. Thus, in a stream the packets are received in the order they are sent.

The `socket` class in Java extends the `Object` class. We will give only a subset of constructors and methods available for `Socket`.

The constructor `public Socket(String host, int port)` creates a stream socket and connects it to the specified port number on the named host. It throws `UnknownHostException`, and `IOException`.

Here we have used the name of the host. Alternatively, IP address can be used in the form of the class InetAddress as below:

```
public Socket(InetAddress address, int port)
```

The methods for the socket are

- `public InetAddress getInetAddress()`, which returns the remote IP address to which this socket is connected.

- `public InetAddress getLocalAddress()`, which returns the local address to which the socket is bound.

- `public int getPort()`, which returns the remote port to which this socket is connected.

- `public InputStream getInputStream()`, which returns an input stream for reading bytes from this socket.

- `public OutputStream getOutputStream()`, which returns an output stream for writing bytes to this socket.

- `public synchronized void close()`, which closes this socket.

Note that many of these methods throw `IOException` if an I/O error occurs when applying the method to the socket.

```java
import java.net.*;
import java.io.*;
public class DatagramClient {
    public static void main(String[] args) {
        String hostname;
        int port = 2018;
        int len = 1024;
        DatagramPacket sPacket, rPacket;
        if (args.length > 0)
            hostname = args[0];
        else
            hostname = "localhost";
        try {
            InetAddress ia = InetAddress.getByName(hostname);
            DatagramSocket datasocket = new DatagramSocket();
            BufferedReader stdinp = new BufferedReader(
            new InputStreamReader(System.in));
            while (true) {
                try {
                    String echoline = stdinp.readLine();
                    if (echoline.equals("done")) break;
                    byte[] buffer = new byte[echoline.length()];
                    buffer = echoline.getBytes();
                    sPacket = new DatagramPacket(buffer,
                                        buffer.length, ia, port);
                    datasocket.send(sPacket);
                    byte[] rbuffer = new byte[len];
                    rPacket = new DatagramPacket(rbuffer, rbuffer.length);
                    datasocket.receive(rPacket);
                    String retstring = new String(rPacket.getData(), 0,
                    rPacket.getLength());
                    System.out.println(retstring);
                } catch (IOException e) {
                    System.err.println(e);
                }
            } // while
        } catch (UnknownHostException e) {
            System.err.println(e);
        } catch (SocketException se) {
            System.err.println(se);
        }
    } // end main
}
```

Figure 6.2: A datagram client

6.4.1   Server Sockets

On the server side the class that is used is called `ServerSocket`. A way to create a
server socket is `public ServerSocket(int port)`
This call creates a server socket on a specified port. Various methods on a server
socket are as follows:

- `public InetAddress getInetAddress()`, which returns the address to which
  this socket is connected, or null if the socket is not yet connected.

- `public int getLocalPort()`, which returns the port on which this socket is
  listening.

- `public Socket accept()`, which listens for a connection to be made to this
  socket and accepts it. The method blocks until a connection is made.

- `public void close()`, which closes this socket.

6.4.2   Example 1: A Name Server

We now give a simple name server implemented using server sockets. The name
server maintains a table of (`name`, `hostName`, `portNumber`) to give a mapping
from a process `name` to the host and the port number. For simplicity, we assume
that the maximum size of the table is 100 and that there are only two operations on
the table: `insert` and `search`. This table is kept by the object `NameTable` shown
in Figure 6.3.

Now let us look at the name server. The name server creates a server socket
with the specified port. It then listens to any incoming connections by the method
`accept`. The `accept` method returns the socket whenever a connection is made. It
then handles the request that arrives on that socket by the method `handleclient`.
We call `getInputStream` and `getOutputStream` to get input and output streams
associated with the socket. Now we can simply use all methods associated for reading
and writing input streams to read and write data from the socket.

In our implementation of the name server shown in Figure 6.4, at most one client
is handled at a time. Once a request is handled, the main loop of the name server
accepts another connection. For many applications this may be unacceptable if the
procedure to handle a request takes a long time. For these applications, it is quite
common for the server to be multithreaded. The server accepts a connection and
then spawns a thread to handle the request. However, it must be observed that since
the data for the server is shared among multiple threads, it is the responsibility of
the programmer to ensure that the data is accessed in a safe manner (for example,
by using `synchronized` methods).

The client program in Figure 6.5 can be used to test this name server.

```
import java.util.*;
public class NameTable {
    final int maxSize = 100;
    private String[] names = new String[maxSize];
    private String[] hosts = new String[maxSize];
    private int[] ports = new int[maxSize];
    private int dirsize = 0;
    int search(String s) {
        for (int i = 0; i < dirsize; i++)
            if (names[i].equals(s)) return i;
        return -1;
    }
    int insert(String s, String hostName, int portNumber) {
        int oldIndex = search(s); // is it already there
        if ((oldIndex == -1) && (dirsize < maxSize)) {
            names[dirsize] = s;
            hosts[dirsize] = hostName;
            ports[dirsize] = portNumber;
            dirsize++;
            return 1;
        } else // already there, or table full
            return 0;
    }
    int getPort(int index) {
        return ports[index];
    }
    String getHostName(int index) {
        return hosts[index];
    }
}
```

Figure 6.3: Simple name table

```java
import java.net.*;
import java.io.*;
import java.util.*;
public class NameServer {
    NameTable table;
    public NameServer() {
        table = new NameTable();
    }
    void handleclient(Socket theClient) {
        try {
            BufferedReader din = new BufferedReader
            (new InputStreamReader(theClient.getInputStream()));
            PrintWriter pout = new PrintWriter(theClient.getOutputStream());
            String getline = din.readLine();
            StringTokenizer st = new StringTokenizer(getline);
            String tag = st.nextToken();
            if (tag.equals("search")) {
                int index = table.search(st.nextToken());
                if (index == -1) // not found
                    pout.println(-1 + " " + "nullhost");
                else
                    pout.println(table.getPort(index) + " "
                    + table.getHostName(index));
            } else if (tag.equals("insert")) {
                String name = st.nextToken();
                String hostName = st.nextToken();
                int port = Integer.parseInt(st.nextToken());
                int retValue = table.insert(name, hostName, port);
                pout.println(retValue);
            }
            pout.flush();
        } catch (IOException e) {
            System.err.println(e);
        }
    }
    public static void main(String[] args) {
        NameServer ns = new NameServer();
        System.out.println("NameServer started:");
        try {
            ServerSocket listener = new ServerSocket(Symbols.ServerPort);
            while (true) {
                Socket aClient = listener.accept();
                ns.handleclient(aClient);
                aClient.close();
            }
        } catch (IOException e) {
            System.err.println("Server aborted:" + e);
        }
    }
}
```

Figure 6.4: Name server

```
import java.lang.*; import java.util.*;
import java.net.*; import java.io.*;
public class Name {
    BufferedReader din;
    PrintStream pout;
    public void getSocket() throws IOException {
        Socket server = new Socket(Symbols.nameServer,
                                            Symbols.ServerPort);
        din = new BufferedReader(
                    new InputStreamReader(server.getInputStream()));
        pout = new PrintStream(server.getOutputStream());
    }
    public int insertName(String name, String hname, int portnum)
            throws IOException {
        getSocket();
        pout.println("insert " + name + " " + hname + " " + portnum);
        pout.flush();
        return Integer.parseInt(din.readLine());
    }
    public PortAddr searchName(String name) throws IOException {
        getSocket();
        pout.println("search " + name);
        pout.flush();
        String result = din.readLine();
        StringTokenizer st = new StringTokenizer(result);
        int portnum = Integer.parseInt(st.nextToken());
        String hname = st.nextToken();
        return new PortAddr(hname, portnum);
    }
    public static void main(String[] args) {
        Name myClient = new Name();
        try {
            myClient.insertName("hello1", "oak.ece.utexas.edu", 1000);
            PortAddr pa = myClient.searchName("hello1");
            System.out.println(pa.getHostName() + ":" + pa.getPort());
        } catch (Exception e) {
            System.err.println("Server aborted:" + e);
        }
    }
}
```

Figure 6.5: A client for name server

6.4.3 Example 2: A Linker

We now show a java class `Linker` that allows us to link a given set of processes with each other. Assume that we want to start n processes $P_1, P_2, \ldots, P_n$ in a distributed system and establish connections between them such that any of the process can send and receive messages with any other process. We would like to support direct naming to send and receive messages; that is, processes are unaware of the host addresses and port numbers. They simply use process identifiers $\{1 \ldots n\}$ to send and receive messages.

We first read the topology of the underlying network. This is done by the method `readNeighbors` in the class `Topology` shown in Figure 6.6. The list of neighbors of P_i are assumed to be enumerated in the file "topology$i$." If such a file is not found, then it is assumed that all other processes are neighbors.

```
import java.io.*;
import java.util.*;
public class Topology {
    public static void readNeighbors(int myId, int N,
                                     IntLinkedList neighbors) {
        Util.println("Reading topology");
        try {
            BufferedReader dIn = new BufferedReader(
                          new FileReader("topology" + myId));
            StringTokenizer st = new StringTokenizer(dIn.readLine());
            while (st.hasMoreTokens()) {
                int neighbor = Integer.parseInt(st.nextToken());
                neighbors.add(neighbor);
            }
        } catch (FileNotFoundException e) {
            for (int j = 0; j < N; j++)
                if (j != myId) neighbors.add(j);
        } catch (IOException e) {
            System.err.println(e);
        }
        Util.println(neighbors.toString());
    }
}
```

Figure 6.6: Topology class

Now we discuss the `Connecter` class, which establishes connections between processes. Since processes may start at different times and at different locations, we use the `NameServer` to help processes locate each other. Any process P_i that starts up first creates a `ServerSocket` for itself. It uses the `ServerSocket` to listen for incoming requests for communication with all small numbered processes. It then contacts the `NameServer` and inserts its entry in that table. All the smaller numbered processes wait for the entry of P_i to appear in the `NameServer`. When they get the port number from the `NameServer`, they use it to connect it to P_i. Once P_i has established a TCP connection with all smaller number processes, it tries to connect with higher-number processes. This class is shown in Figure 6.7. For simplicity, it is assumed that the underlying topology is completely connected.

Once all the connections are established, the `Linker` provides methods to send and receive messages from process P_i to P_j. We will require each message to contain at least four fields: source identifier, destination identifier, message type (or the message tag), and actual message. We implement this in the Java class shown in Figure 6.8.

The Linker class is shown in Figure 6.9. It provides methods to send and receive messages based on process identifiers. Different `send` methods have been provided to facilitate sending messages of different types. Every message is assumed to have a field `tag` that corresponds to the message tag (or the message type).

6.5   Remote Method Invocations

A popular way of developing distributed applications is based on the concept of remote procedure calls (RPCs) or remote method invocations (RMIs). Here the main idea is that a process can make calls to methods of a remote object as if it were on the same machine. The process making the call is called a *client* and the process that serves the request is called the *server*. In RMI, the client may not even know the location of the remote object. This provides *location transparency* to the client. In Java, for example, the remote object may be located using `rmiregistry`. Alternatively, references to remote objects may be passed around by the application as references to local objects.

A call to a method may have some arguments, and the execution of the method may return some value. The arguments to the method when the object is remote are sent via a message. Similarly, the return value is transmitted to the caller via a message. All this message passing is hidden from the programmer, and therefore RMI can be viewed as a higher-level programming construct than sending or receiving of messages.

Although the idea behind RMI is quite simple, certain issues need to be tackled in implementing and using RMI. Since we are passing arguments to the method, we have to understand the semantics of the parameter passing. Another issue is that of a failure. What happens when the messages get lost? We will look at such issues in this section.

```
import java.util.*; import java.net.*; import java.io.*;
public class Connector {
    ServerSocket listener;   Socket [] link;
    public void Connect(String basename, int myId, int numProc,
    BufferedReader [] dataIn, PrintWriter [] dataOut) throws Exception {
        Name myNameclient = new Name();
        link = new Socket [numProc];
        int localport = getLocalPort(myId);
        listener = new ServerSocket(localport);

        /* register in the name server */
        myNameclient.insertName(basename + myId,
        (InetAddress.getLocalHost()).getHostName(), localport);

        /* accept connections from all the smaller processes */
        for (int i = 0; i < myId; i++) {
            Socket s = listener.accept();
            BufferedReader dIn = new BufferedReader(
                    new InputStreamReader(s.getInputStream()));
            String getline = dIn.readLine();
            StringTokenizer st = new StringTokenizer(getline);
            int hisId = Integer.parseInt(st.nextToken());
            int destId = Integer.parseInt(st.nextToken());
            String tag = st.nextToken();
            if (tag.equals("hello")) {
                link[hisId] = s;
                dataIn[hisId] = dIn;
                dataOut[hisId] = new PrintWriter(s.getOutputStream());
            }
        }
        /* contact all the bigger processes */
        for (int i = myId + 1; i < numProc; i++) {
            PortAddr addr;
            do {
                addr = myNameclient.searchName(basename + i);
                Thread.sleep(100);
            } while (addr.getPort() == -1);
            link[i] = new Socket(addr.getHostName(), addr.getPort());
            dataOut[i] = new PrintWriter(link[i].getOutputStream());
            dataIn[i] = new BufferedReader(new
            InputStreamReader(link[i].getInputStream()));
            /* send a hello message to P_i */
            dataOut[i].println(myId +" "+ i +" "+ "hello" + " " + "null");
            dataOut[i].flush();
        }
    }
    int getLocalPort(int id) { return Symbols.ServerPort + 10 + id; }
    public void closeSockets(){
        try {
            listener.close();
            for (int i=0;i<link.length; i++) link[i].close();
        } catch (Exception e) { System.err.println(e);}
    }
}
```

Figure 6.7: Connector class

```java
import java.util.*;
public class Msg {
    int srcId, destId;
    String tag;
    String msgBuf;
    public Msg(int s, int t, String msgType, String buf) {
        this.srcId = s;
        destId = t;
        tag = msgType;
        msgBuf = buf;
    }
    public int getSrcId() {
        return srcId;
    }
    public int getDestId() {
        return destId;
    }
    public String getTag() {
        return tag;
    }
    public String getMessage() {
        return msgBuf;
    }
    public int getMessageInt() {
        StringTokenizer st = new StringTokenizer(msgBuf);
        return Integer.parseInt(st.nextToken());
    }
    public static Msg parseMsg(StringTokenizer st){
        int srcId = Integer.parseInt(st.nextToken());
        int destId = Integer.parseInt(st.nextToken());
        String tag = st.nextToken();
        String buf = st.nextToken("#");
        return new Msg(srcId, destId, tag, buf);
    }
    public String toString(){
        String s = String.valueOf(srcId)+" " +
                   String.valueOf(destId)+ " " +
                   tag + " " + msgBuf + "#";
        return s;
    }
}
```

Figure 6.8: Message class

```java
import java.util.*;
import java.io.*;
public class Linker {
    PrintWriter [] dataOut;
    BufferedReader [] dataIn;
    BufferedReader dIn;
    int myId, N;
    Connector connector;
    public IntLinkedList neighbors = new IntLinkedList ();
    public Linker (String basename, int id, int numProc) throws Exception {
        myId = id;
        N = numProc;
        dataIn = new BufferedReader [numProc];
        dataOut = new PrintWriter [numProc];
        Topology.readNeighbors (myId, N, neighbors);
        connector = new Connector ();
        connector.Connect (basename, myId, numProc, dataIn, dataOut);
    }
    public void sendMsg (int destId, String tag, String msg) {
        dataOut [destId].println (myId + " " + destId + " " +
                                         tag + " " + msg + "#");
        dataOut [destId].flush ();
    }
    public void sendMsg (int destId, String tag) {
        sendMsg (destId, tag, " 0 ");
    }
    public void multicast (IntLinkedList destIds, String tag, String msg){
        for (int i=0; i<destIds.size (); i++) {
            sendMsg (destIds.getEntry (i), tag, msg);
        }
    }
    public Msg receiveMsg (int fromId) throws IOException   {
        String getline = dataIn [fromId].readLine ();
        Util.println (" received message " + getline);
        StringTokenizer st = new StringTokenizer (getline);
        int srcId = Integer.parseInt (st.nextToken ());
        int destId = Integer.parseInt (st.nextToken ());
        String tag = st.nextToken ();
        String msg = st.nextToken ("#");
        return new Msg( srcId, destId, tag, msg);
    }
    public int getMyId () { return myId; }
    public int getNumProc () { return N; }
    public void close () { connector.closeSockets ();}
}
```

Figure 6.9: Linker class

An RMI is implemented as follows. With each remote object there is an associated object at the client side and an object at the server side. An invocation to a method to a remote object is managed by using a local surrogate object at the client called the *stub* object. An invocation of a method results in packing the method name and the arguments in a message and shipping it to the server side. This is called *parameter marshaling*. This message is received on the server side by the server skeleton object. The skeleton object is responsible for receiving the message, reconstructing the arguments, and then finally calling the method. Note that a RMI class requires compilation by a RMI compiler to generate the stub and the skeleton routines.

6.5.1 Remote Objects

An object is called *remote object* if its methods can be invoked from another Java virtual machine running on the same host or a different host. Such an object is described using a `remote` interface. An interface is remote if it extends java.rmi.Remote. The remote interface serves to identify all remote objects. Any object that is a remote object must directly or indirectly implement this interface. Only those methods specified in a remote interface are available remotely. Figure 6.10 gives a remote interface for a name service.

```
import java.rmi.*;
public interface NameService extends Remote {
    public int search(String s) throws RemoteException;
    public int insert(String s, String hostName, int portNumber)
        throws RemoteException;
    public int getPort(int index) throws RemoteException;
    public String getHostName(int index) throws RemoteException;
}
```

Figure 6.10: Remote interface

Any object that implements a remote interface and extends `UnicastRemoteObject` is a remote object. Remote method invocation corresponds to invocation of one of the methods on a remote object. We can now provide a class that implements the `NameService` as shown in Figure 6.11.

To install our server, we first compile the file `NameServiceImpl.java`. Then, we need to invoke the RMI compiler to generate the stub and skeleton associated with the server. On a UNIX machine, one may use the following commands to carry out these steps:

```
import java.rmi.*;
import java.rmi.server.UnicastRemoteObject;
public class NameServiceImpl extends UnicastRemoteObject
        implements NameService {
    final int maxSize = 100;
    private String [] names = new String[maxSize];
    private String [] hosts = new String[maxSize];
    private int [] ports = new int[maxSize];
    private int dirsize = 0;
    public NameServiceImpl() throws RemoteException {
    }
    public int search(String s) throws RemoteException {
        for (int i = 0; i < dirsize; i++)
            if (names[i].equals(s)) return i;
        return -1;
    }
    public int insert(String s, String hostName, int portNumber)
            throws RemoteException {
        int oldIndex = search(s); // is it already there
        if ((oldIndex == -1) && (dirsize < maxSize)) {
            names[dirsize] = s;
            hosts[dirsize] = hostName;
            ports[dirsize] = portNumber;
            dirsize++;
            return 1;
        } else
            return 0;
    }
    public int getPort(int index) throws RemoteException {
        return ports[index];
    }
    public String getHostName(int index) throws RemoteException {
        return hosts[index];
    }
    public static void main(String args[]) {
        // create security manager
        System.setSecurityManager(new RMISecurityManager());
        try {
            NameServiceImpl obj = new NameServiceImpl();
            Naming.rebind("MyNameServer", obj);
            System.out.println("MyNameServer bound in registry");
        } catch (Exception e) {
            System.out.println("NameServiceImpl err: " + e.getMessage());
        }
    }
}
```

Figure 6.11: A name service implementation

```
> javac NameServiceImpl.java
> rmic NameServiceImpl
> rmiregistry &
```

Now assuming that the `rmiregistry` service is running on the machine, we can start our server. There is just one last thing that we need to take care of: security. We need to specify who can connect to the server. This specification is done by a security policy file. For example, consider a file called `policy` as follows:

```
grant {
permission java.net.SocketPermission "*:1024-65535",
"connect,accept";
permission java.net.SocketPermission "*:80", "connect";
};
```

This policy allows downloaded code, from any code base, to do two things: (1) connect to or accept connections on unprivileged ports (ports greater than 1024) on any host, or (2) connect to port 80 [the port for HTTP(Hypertext Transfer Protocol)].

Now we can start the NameServiceImpl server as follows:

```
> java -Djava.security.policy=policy NameServiceImpl
```

6.5.2 Parameter Passing

If a local object is passed as an argument to a *local* method on a local object, then in Java we simply pass the reference to the object. However, if the method is to a remote object, then reference to a local object is useless at the other side. Therefore, arguments to remote methods are handled differently.

There are three ways of passing arguments (and returning results) in remote method invocations. The primitive types in Java (e.g., `int` and `boolean`) are passed by values.

Objects that are not remote are passed by value using *object serialization*, which refers to the process of converting the object state into a stream of bytes. Any object that implements the interface `Serializable` can be communicated over the Internet using serialization. The object is written into a stream of bytes at one end ("serialized") and at the other end it is reconstructed from the stream of bytes received ("deserialized"). An interesting question is what happens if the object has references to other objects. In this case, those objects also need to be serialized; otherwise references will be meaningless at the other side. Thus, all objects that are reachable from that object get serialized. The same mechanism works when a nonremote object is returned from a remote method invocation. Java supports referential integrity, that is, if multiple references to the same object are passed from one Java Virtual Machine (JVM) to the other, then those references will refer to a single copy of the object in the receiving JVM.

Finally, references to objects that implement `remote` interface are passed as remote references. In this case, the stub for the remote object is passed.

6.5.3 Dealing with Failures

One difference between invoking a local method and a remote method is that more things can go wrong when a remote method is invoked. The machine that contains the remote object may be down, the connection to that machine be down, or the message sent may get corrupted or lost. In spite of all these possible problems, Java system guarantees *at-most-once* semantics for a remote method invocation: any invocation will result in execution of the remote method at most once.

6.5.4 Client Program

The client program first needs to obtain a reference for the remote object. The `java.rmi.Naming` class provides methods to do so. It is a mechanism for obtaining references to remote objects based on Uniform Resource Locator (URL) syntax. The URL for a remote object is specified using the usual host, port, and name:

`rmi://host:port/name`

where `host` is the host name of registry (defaults to current host), `port` is the port number of registry (defaults to the registry port number), and `name` is the name for the remote object.

The key methods in this class are

```
bind(String, Remote)
  Binds the name to the specified remote object.
list(String)
  Returns an array of strings of the URLs in the registry.
lookup(String)
  Returns the remote object for the URL.
rebind(String, Remote)
  Rebind the name to a new object; replaces any existing binding.
unbind(String)
  Unbind the name.
```

We now show how a client can use `lookup` to get a reference of the remote object and then invoke methods on it (see the program in Figure 6.12).

```
import java.rmi.*;
public class NameRmiClient {
    public static void main(String args[]) {
        try {
            NameService r = (NameService)
                            Naming.lookup("rmi://linux02/MyNameServer");
            int i = r.insert("p1", "tick.ece", 2058);
            int j = r.search("p1");
            if (j != -1)
                System.out.println(r.getHostName(j) +":" + r.getPort(j));
        } catch (Exception e) {
            System.out.println(e);
        }
    }
}
```

Figure 6.12: A RMI client program

6.6 Other Useful Classes

In this chapter, we have focused on classes that allow you to write distributed programs. For cases when a process simply needs data from a remote location, Java provides the Uniform Resource Locator (URL) class. A URL consists of six parts: protocol, hostname, port, path, filename, and document section. An example of a URL is

> http://www.ece.utexas.edu:80/classes.html#distributed

The java.net.URL class allows the programmer to read data from a URL by methods such as

> public final InputStream openStream()

This method returns a InputStream from which one can read the data. For different types of data such as images and audio clips there are methods such as
public Image getImage(URL u, String filename)
and
public void play(URL u).
We will not concern ourselves with these classes and methods.

6.7 Problems

6.1. Make the NameServer class fault-tolerant by keeping two copies of the server process at all times. Assume that the client chooses a server at random.

If that server is down (i.e., after the timeout), the client contacts the other server. You may assume that at most one server goes down. When the server comes up again, it would need to synchronize with the other server to ensure consistency.

6.2. Message passing can also be employed for communication and synchronization among threads. Implement a Java monitor library that provides message passing primitives for threads in a single Java Virtual Machine (JVM).

6.3. Develop a `Linker` class that provides *synchronous* messages. A message is synchronous if the sender of the message blocks until the message is received by the receiver.

6.4. Give advantages and disadvantages of using synchronous messages (see Problem 6.3) over asynchronous messages for developing distributed applications.

6.5. Write a Java program to maintain a large linked list on multiple computers connected by a message passing system. Each computer maintains a part of the linked list.

6.6. List all the differences between a local method invocation and a remote method invocation.

6.7. How will you provide semaphores in a distributed environment?

6.8. Solve the producer consumer problem discussed in Chapter 3 using messages.

6.9. Give advantages and disadvantages of using RMI over TCP sockets for developing distributed applications.

6.8   Bibliographic Remarks

Details on the Transmission Control Protocol can be found in the book by Comer [Com00]. Remote procedure calls were first implemented by Birrell and Nelson [BN84].

Chapter 7

Models and Clocks

7.1 Introduction

Distributed software requires a set of tools and techniques different from that required by the traditional sequential software. One of the most important issues in reasoning about a distributed program is the model used for a *distributed computation*. It is clear that when a distributed program is executed, at the most abstract level, a set of events is generated. Some examples of events are the beginning and the end of the execution of a function, and the sending and receiving of a message. This set alone does not characterize the behavior. We also impose an ordering relation on this set. The first relation is based on the physical time model. Assuming that all events are instantaneous, that no two events are simultaneous, and that a shared physical clock is available, we can totally order all the events in the system. This is called the *interleaving* model of computation. If there is no shared physical clock, then we can observe a total order among events on a single processor but only a partial order between events on different processors. The order for events on different processors is determined on the basis of the information flow from one processor to another. This is the *happened-before* model of a distributed computation. We describe these two models in this chapter.

In this chapter we also discuss mechanisms called *clocks* that can be used for tracking the order relation on the set of events. The first relation we discussed on events imposes a total order on all events. Because this total order cannot be observed, we describe a mechanism to generate a total order that could have happened in the system (rather than the one that actually happened in the system). This mechanism is called a *logical clock*. The second relation, happened-before,

111

can be accurately tracked by a *vector clock*. A vector clock assigns timestamps to states (and events) such that the happened-before relationship between states can be determined by using the timestamps.

7.2   Model of a Distributed System

We take the following characteristics as the defining ones for distributed systems:

- *Absence of a shared clock*: In a distributed system, it is impossible to synchronize the clocks of different processors precisely due to uncertainty in communication delays between them. As a result, it is rare to use physical clocks for synchronization in distributed systems. In this book we will see how the concept of causality is used instead of time to tackle this problem.

- *Absence of shared memory*: In a distributed system, it is impossible for any one processor to know the global state of the system. As a result, it is difficult to observe any global property of the system. In this book we will see how efficient algorithms can be developed for evaluating a suitably restricted set of global properties.

- *Absence of accurate failure detection*: In an asynchronous distributed system (a distributed system is asynchronous if there is no upper bound on message delays), it is impossible to distinguish between a slow processor and a failed processor. This leads to many difficulties in developing algorithms for consensus, election, and so on. In this book we will see these problems, and their solutions when synchrony is assumed.

Our model for a distributed system is based on message passing, and all of our algorithms are based around that concept. Our algorithms do not assume any upper bound on the message delays. Thus we assume asynchronous systems. An advantage is that all the algorithms developed in this model are also applicable to synchronous systems.

We model a distributed system as an asynchronous message-passing system without any shared memory or a global clock. A *distributed program* consists of a set of N processes denoted by $\{P_1, P_2, ..., P_N\}$ and a set of unidirectional channels. A channel connects two processes. Thus the topology of a distributed system can be viewed as a directed graph in which vertices represent the processes and the edges represent the channels. Figure 7.1 shows the topology of a distributed system with three processes and four channels. Observe that a bidirectional channel can simply be modeled as two unidirectional channels.

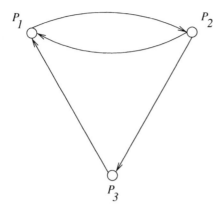

Figure 7.1: An example of topology of a distributed system

A channel is assumed to have infinite buffer and to be error-free. We do not make any assumptions on the ordering of messages. Any message sent on the channel may experience arbitrary but finite delay. The state of the channel at any point is defined to be the sequence of messages sent along that channel but not received.

A process is defined as a set of states, an initial condition (i.e., a subset of states), and a set of events. Each event may change the state of the process and the state of at most one channel incident on that process. The behavior of a process with finite states can be described visually with state transition diagrams. Figure 7.2 shows the state transition diagram for two processes. The first process P_1 sends a token to P_2 and then receives a token from P_2. Process P_2 first receives a token from P_1 and then sends it back to P_1. The state s_1 is the initial state for P_1, and the state t_1 is the initial state for P_2.

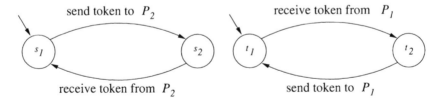

Figure 7.2: A simple distributed program with two processes

7.3 Model of a Distributed Computation

In this section, we describe the interleaving and the happened-before models for capturing behavior of a distributed system.

7.3.1 Interleaving Model

In this model, a *distributed computation* or a *run* is simply a global sequence of events. Thus all events in a run are interleaved. For example, consider a system with two processes: a bank server and a bank customer. The program of the bank customer process sends two request messages to the bank server querying the savings and the checking accounts. On receiving the response, it adds up the total balance. In the interleaving model, a run may be given as follows:

> P_1 sends "what is my checking balance" to P_2
> P_1 sends "what is my savings balance" to P_2
> P_2 receives "what is my checking balance" from P_1
> P_1 sets total to 0
> P_2 receives "what is my savings balance" from P_1
> P_2 sends "checking balance = 40" to P_1
> P_1 receives "checking balance = 40" from P_2
> P_1 sets total to 40 (total + checking balance)
> P_2 sends "savings balance = 70" to P_1
> P_1 receives "savings balance = 70" from P_2
> P_1 sets total to 110 (total + savings balance)

7.3.2 Happened-Before Model

In the interleaving model, there is a total order defined on the set of events. Lamport has argued that in a true distributed system only a partial order, called a happened-before relation, can be determined between events. In this section we define this relation formally.

As before, we will be concerned with a single computation of a distributed program. Each process P_i in that computation generates a sequence of *events*. It is clear how to order events within a single process. If event e occurred before f in the process, then e is ordered before f. How do we order events across processes? If e is the send event of a message and f is the receive event of the same message, then we can order e before f. Combining these two ideas, we obtain the following definition.

Definition 7.1 (Happened Before Relation) *The happened-before relation ($\rightarrow$) is the smallest relation that satisfies*

1. *If e occurred before f in the same process, then e → f.*

2. *If e is the send event of a message and f is the receive event of the same message, then e → f.*

3. *If there exists an event g such that (e → g) and (g → f), then (e → f).*

In Figure 7.3, $e_2 \to e_4$, $e_3 \to f_3$, and $e_1 \to g_4$.

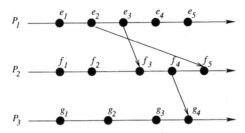

Figure 7.3: A run in the happened-before model

A *run* or a *computation* in the happened-before model is defined as a tuple $(E, \to)$ where E is the set of all events and $\to$ is a partial order on events in E such that all events within a single process are totally ordered. Figure 7.3 illustrates a run. Such figures are usually called *space-time diagrams*, *process-time diagrams*, or *happened-before diagrams*. In a process-time diagram, $e \to f$ iff it contains a directed path from the event e to event f. Intuitively, this relation captures the order that can be determined between events. The important thing here is that the happened-before relation is only a partial order on the set of events. Thus two events e and f may not be related by the happened-before relation. We say that e and f are *concurrent* (denoted by $e||f$) if $\neg(e \to f) \land \neg(f \to e)$. In Figure 7.3, $e_2||f_2$, and $e_1||g_3$.

Instead of focusing on the set of events, one can also define a computation based on the the set of states of processes that occur in a computation, say S. The happened-before relation on S can be defined in the manner similar to the happened-before relation on E.

7.4   Logical Clocks

We have defined two relations between events based on the global total order of events, and the happened-before order. We now discuss mechanisms called *clocks* that can be used for tracking these relations.

When the behavior of a distributed computation is viewed as a total order, it is impossible to determine the actual order of events in the absence of accurately synchronized physical clocks. If the system has a shared clock (or equivalently, precisely synchronized clocks), then timestamping the event with the clock would be sufficient to determine the order. Because in the absence of a shared clock the total order between events cannot be determined, we will develop a mechanism that gives a total order that *could have* happened instead of the total order that did happen.

The purpose of our clock is only to give us an order between events and not any other property associated with clocks. For example, on the basis of our clocks one could not determine the time elapsed between two events. In fact, the number we associate with each event will have no relationship with the time we have on our watches.

As we have seen before, only two kinds of order information can be determined in a distributed system—the order of events on a single process and the order between the send and the receive events of a message. On the basis of these considerations, we get the following definition.

A *logical clock* C is a map from the set of events E to $\mathcal{N}$ (the set of natural numbers) with the following constraint:

$$\forall e, f \in E : e \rightarrow f \Rightarrow C(e) < C(f)$$

Sometimes it is more convenient to timestamp states on processes rather than events. The logical clock C also satisfies

$$\forall s, t \in S : s \rightarrow t \Rightarrow C(s) < C(t)$$

The constraint for logical clocks models the sequential nature of execution at each process and the physical requirement that any message transmission requires a nonzero amount of time.

Availability of a logical clock during distributed computation makes it easier to solve many distributed problems. An accurate physical clock clearly satisfies the above mentioned condition and therefore is also a logical clock. However, by definition of a distributed system there is no shared clock in the system. Figure 7.4 shows an implementation of a logical clock that does not use any shared physical clock or shared memory.

It is not required that message communication be ordered or reliable. The algorithm is described by the initial conditions and the actions taken for each event type. The algorithm uses the variable c to assign the logical clock. The notation $s.c$ denotes the value of c in the state s. Let $s.p$ denote the process to which state s belongs.

For any send event, the value of the clock is sent with the message and then incremented at line 14. On receiving a message, a process takes the maximum of its own clock value and the value received with the message at line 17. After taking the maximum, the process increments the clock value. On an internal event, a process simply increments its clock at line 10.

```
 1 public class LamportClock {
 2      int c;
 3      public LamportClock () {
 4          c = 1;
 5      }
 6      public int getValue () {
 7          return c;
 8      }
 9      public void tick () { // on internal events
10          c = c + 1;
11      }
12      public void sendAction () {
13          // include c in message
14          c = c + 1;
15      }
16      public void receiveAction (int src , int sentValue ) {
17          c = Util.max(c, sentValue ) + 1;
18      }
19 }
```

Figure 7.4: A logical clock algorithm

The following claim is easy to verify.

$$\forall s, t \in S : s \rightarrow t \Rightarrow s.c < t.c$$

In some applications it is required that all events in the system be ordered totally. If we extend the logical clock with the process number, then we get a total ordering on events. Recall that for any state s, $s.p$ indicates the identity of the process to which it belongs. Thus the timestamp of any event is a tuple $(s.c, s.p)$ and the total order $<$ is obtained as

$$(s.c, s.p) < (t.c, t.p) \stackrel{\text{def}}{=} (s.c < t.c) \vee ((s.c = t.c) \wedge (s.p < t.p)).$$

7.5   Vector Clocks

We saw that logical clocks satisfy the following property:

$$s \rightarrow t \Rightarrow s.c < t.c.$$

However, the converse is not true; $s.c < t.c$ does not imply that $s \rightarrow t$. The computation $(S, \rightarrow)$ is a partial order, but the domain of logical clock values (the set of natural numbers) is a total order with respect to $<$. Thus logical clocks do not provide complete information about the *happened-before* relation. In this section, we describe a mechanism called a *vector clock* that allows us to infer the happened-before relation completely.

Definition 7.2 (Vector Clock) *A vector clock v is a map from S to $\mathcal{N}^k$ (vectors of natural numbers) with the following constraint*

$$\forall s, t : s \rightarrow t \Leftrightarrow s.v < t.v.$$

where $s.v$ is the vector assigned to the state s.

Because $\rightarrow$ is a partial order, it is clear that the timestamping mechanism should also result in a partial order. Thus the range of the timestamping function cannot be a total order like the set of natural numbers used for logical clocks. Instead, we use vectors of natural numbers. Given two vectors x and y of dimension N, we compare them as follows:

$$
\begin{aligned}
x < y \ &= \ (\forall k : 1 \le k \le N : x[k] \le y[k]) \ \wedge \\
&\quad\ (\exists j : 1 \le j \le N : x[j] < y[j]) \\
x \le y \ &= \ (x < y) \vee (x = y)
\end{aligned}
$$

It is clear that this order is only partial for $N \ge 2$. For example, the vectors $(2, 3, 0)$ and $(0, 4, 1)$ are incomparable. A vector clock timestamps each event with a vector of natural numbers.

Our implementation of vector clocks uses vectors of size N, the number of processes in the system. The algorithm presented in Figure 7.5 is described by the initial conditions and the actions taken for each event type. A process increments its own component of the vector clock after each event. Furthermore, it includes a copy of its vector clock in every outgoing message. On receiving a message, it updates its vector clock by taking a componentwise maximum with the vector clock included in the message. This is shown in the method `receiveAction`. It is not required that message communication be ordered or reliable. A sample execution of the algorithm is given in Figure 7.7.

Figure 7.6 extends the `Linker` class (defined in Chapter 6) to automatically include the vector clock in all outgoing messages and to take the `receiveAction` when a message is received. The method `sendMsg` prefixes the message with the tag "vector" and the vector clock. The method `simpleSendMsg` is useful for application messages that do not use vector clocks. The method `receiveMsg` determines

```
 1 public class VectorClock {
 2     public int [] v;
 3     int myId;
 4     int N;
 5     public VectorClock (int numProc , int id ) {
 6         myId = id ;
 7         N = numProc;
 8         v = new int [numProc ];
 9         for ( int i = 0; i < N; i++) v[i ] = 0;
10         v[myId] = 1;
11     }
12     public void tick () {
13         v[myId]++;
14     }
15     public void sendAction () {
16         //include the vector in the message
17         v[myId]++;
18     }
19     public void receiveAction (int [] sentValue ) {
20         for ( int i = 0; i < N; i++)
21             v[i ] = Util .max(v[i ], sentValue [i ]);
22         v[myId]++;
23     }
24     public int getValue (int i ) {
25         return v[i ];
26     }
27     public String toString (){
28         return Util . writeArray (v);
29     }
30 }
```

Figure 7.5: A vector clock algorithm

```java
public class VCLinker extends Linker {
    public VectorClock vc;
    int receiveTag[] = null;
    public VCLinker(String basename, int id, int N) throws Exception {
        super(basename, id, N);
        vc = new VectorClock(N, id);
        receiveTag = new int[N];
    }
    public void sendMsg(int destId, String tag, String msg) {
        super.sendMsg(destId, "vector", vc.toString());
        super.sendMsg(destId, tag, msg);
        vc.sendAction();
    }
    public void simpleSendMsg(int destId, String tag, String msg) {
        super.sendMsg(destId, tag, msg);
    }
    public Msg receiveMsg(int fromId) throws java.io.IOException {
        Msg ml = super.receiveMsg(fromId);
        if (ml.getTag().equals("vector")) {
            Util.readArray(ml.getMessage(), receiveTag);
            vc.receiveAction(receiveTag);
            Msg m = super.receiveMsg(fromId); //app message
            return m;
        }
        else return ml;
    }
}
```

Figure 7.6: The VCLinker class that extends the Linker class

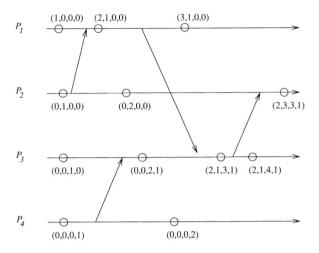

Figure 7.7: A sample execution of the vector clock algorithm

whether the message has a vector clock in it. If it does, the method removes the vector clock, invokes `receiveAction`, and then returns the application message.

We now show that $s \rightarrow t$ iff $s.v < t.v$. We first claim that if $s \neq t$, then

$$s \not\rightarrow t \Rightarrow t.v[s.p] < s.v[s.p] \qquad (7.1)$$

If $t.p = s.p$, then it follows that t occurs before s. Because the local component of the vector clock is increased after each event, $t.v[s.p] < s.v[s.p]$. So, we assume that $s.p \neq t.p$. Since $s.v[s.p]$ is the local clock of $P_{s.p}$ and $P_{t.p}$ could not have seen this value as $s \not\rightarrow t$, it follows that $t.v[s.p] < s.v[s.p]$. Therefore, we have that $(s \not\rightarrow t)$ implies $\neg(s.v < t.v)$.

Now we show that $(s \rightarrow t)$ implies $(s.v < t.v)$. If $s \rightarrow t$, then there is a message path from s to t. Since every process updates its vector on receipt of a message and this update is done by taking the componentwise maximum, we know that the following holds:

$$\forall k : s.v[k] \leq t.v[k].$$

Furthermore, since $t \not\rightarrow s$, from Equation (7.1), we know that $s.v[t.p]$ is strictly less than $t.v[t.p]$. Hence, $(s \rightarrow t) \Rightarrow (s.v < t.v)$.

It is left as an exercise to show that if we know the processes the vectors came from, the comparison between two states can be made in constant time:

$$s \rightarrow t \Leftrightarrow (s.v[s.p] \leq t.v[s.p]) \wedge (s.v[t.p] < t.v[t.p])$$

7.6   Direct-Dependency Clocks

One drawback with the vector clock algorithm is that it requires $O(N)$ integers to be sent with every message. For many applications, a weaker version of the clock suffices. We now describe a clock algorithm that is used by many algorithms in distributed systems. These clocks require only one integer to be appended to each message. We call these clocks *direct-dependency clocks*.

The algorithm shown in Figure 7.8 is described by the initial conditions and the actions taken for each event type. On a send event, the process sends only its local component in the message. It also increments its component as in vector clocks. The action for internal events is the same as that for vector clocks. When a process receives a message, it updates two components—one for itself, and the other for the process from which it received the message. It updates its own component in a manner identical to that for logical clocks. It also updates the component for the sender by taking the maximum with the previous value.

```
public class DirectClock {
    public int [] clock ;
    int myId;
    public DirectClock (int numProc, int id ) {
        myId = id ;
        clock = new int [numProc];
        for ( int i = 0; i < numProc; i++) clock [ i ] = 0;
        clock [myId] = 1;
    }
    public int getValue (int i ) {
        return clock [ i ];
    }
    public void tick () {
        clock [myId]++;
    }
    public void sendAction () {
        // sentValue = clock [myId];
        tick ();
    }
    public void receiveAction (int sender , int sentValue ) {
        clock [sender ] = Util . max( clock [ sender ], sentValue );
        clock [myId] = Util . max( clock [myId], sentValue ) + 1;
    }
}
```

Figure 7.8: A direct-dependency clock algorithm

An example of a distributed computation and its associated direct-dependency

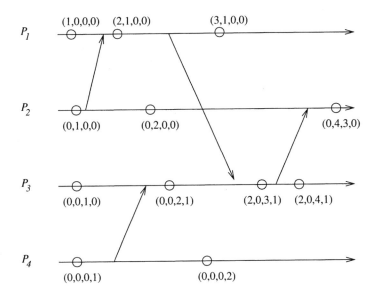

Figure 7.9: A sample execution of the direct-dependency clock algorithm.

clock is given in Figure 7.9.

We first observe that if we retain only the ith component for the ith process, then the algorithm above is identical to the logical clock algorithm. However, our interest in a direct-dependency clock is not due to its logical clock property (Lamport's logical clock is sufficient for that), but to its ability to capture the notion of direct dependency. We first define a relation, *directly precedes* ($\rightarrow_d$), a subset of $\rightarrow$, as follows: $s \rightarrow_d t$ iff there is a path from s to t that uses at most one message in the happened-before diagram of the computation. The following property makes direct-dependency clocks useful for many applications:

$$\forall s, t : s.p \neq t.p : (s \rightarrow_d t) \Leftrightarrow (s.v[s.p] \leq t.v[s.p])$$

The proof of this property is left as an exercise. The reader will see an application of direct-dependency clock in Lamport's mutual exclusion algorithm discussed in Chapter 8.

```
public class MatrixClock {
    int [][]  M;
    int myId;
    int N;
    public MatrixClock (int numProc, int id ) {
        myId = id ;
        N = numProc;
        M = new int [N][N];
        for ( int i = 0; i < N; i++)
            for ( int j = 0; j < N; j++)
                M[ i ][ j ] = 0;
        M[ myId ][ myId ] = 1;
    }
    public void tick () {
        M[ myId ][ myId]++;
    }
    public void sendAction () {
        //include the matrix in the message
        M[ myId ][ myId]++;
    }
    public void receiveAction (int [][] W, int srcId ) {
        // component−wise maximum of matrices
        for ( int i = 0; i < N; i++)
            if ( i != myId) {
                for ( int j = 0; j < N; j++)
                    M[ i ][ j ] = Util .max(M[ i ][ j ], W[ i ][ j ]);
            }

        // update the vector for this process
        for ( int j = 0; j < N; j++)
            M[ myId ][ j ] = Util .max(M[ myId ][ j ], W[ srcId ][ j ]);

        M[ myId ][ myId]++;
    }
    public int getValue (int i, int j ) {
        return M[ i ][ j ];
    }
}
```

Figure 7.10: The matrix clock algorithm

7.7   Matrix Clocks

It is natural to ask whether using higher-dimensional clocks can give processes additional knowledge. The answer is "yes." A vector clock can be viewed as a knowledge vector. In this interpretation, $s.v[i]$ denotes what process $s.p$ knows about process i in the local state s. In some applications it may be important for the process to have a still higher level of knowledge. The value $s.v[i, j]$ could represent what process $s.p$ knows about what process i knows about process j. For example, if $s.v[i, s.p] > k$ for all i, then process $s.p$ can conclude that everybody knows that its state is strictly greater than k.

Next, we discuss the matrix clock that encodes a higher level of knowledge than a vector clock. The matrix clock algorithm is presented in Figure 7.10. The following description applies to an $N \times N$ matrix clock in a system with N processes. The algorithm is easier to understand by noticing the vector clock algorithm embedded within it. If we focus only on row $myId$ for process P_{myId}, the algorithm presented above reduces to the vector clock algorithm. Consider the update of the matrix in the algorithm in Figure 7.10 when a message is received. The first step affects only rows different from $myId$ and can be ignored. When a matrix is received from process $srcId$, then we use only the row given by the index $srcId$ of the matrix W for updating row $myId$ of P_{myId}. Thus, from our discussion of vector clock algorithms, it is clear that

$$\forall s, t : s.p \neq t.p : s \rightarrow t \equiv s.M[s.p, \cdot] < t.M[t.p, \cdot]$$

The other rows of the matrix M keep the vector clocks of other processes. Note that initially M contains 0 vector for other processes. When it receives a matrix in W, it updates its information about the vector clock by taking componentwise maximum.

We now show an application of matrix clocks in garbage collection. Assume that a process P_i generated some information when its matrix clock value for $M[i][i]$ equals k. P_i sends this information directly (or indirectly) to all processes and wants to delete this information when it is known to all processes. We claim that P_i can delete the information when the following condition is true for the matrix M:

$$\forall j : M[j][i] \geq k$$

This condition implies that the vector clock of all other processes j have ith component at least k. Thus, if the information is propagated through messages, P_i knows that all other processes have received the information that P_i had when $M[i][i]$ was k.

We will later see another application of a variant of matrix clock in enforcing causal ordering of messages discussed in Chapter 12.

7.8   Problems

7.1. Give advantages and disadvantages of a parallel programming model over a distributed system (message based) model.

7.2. Show that "concurrent with" is not a transitive relation.

7.3. Write a program that takes as input a distributed computation in the happened-before model and outputs all interleavings of events that are compatible with the happened-before model.

7.4. We discussed a method by which we can totally order all events within a system. If two events have the same logical time, we broke the tie using process identifiers. This scheme always favors processes with smaller identifiers. Suggest a scheme that does not have this disadvantage. (*Hint*: Use the value of the logical clock in determining the priority.)

7.5. Prove the following for vector clocks: $s \rightarrow t$ iff

$$(s.v[s.p] \leq t.v[s.p]) \wedge (s.v[t.p] < t.v[t.p]).$$

7.6. Suppose that the underlying communication system guarantees FIFO ordering of messages. How will you exploit this feature to reduce the communication complexity of the vector clock algorithm? Give an expression for overhead savings if your scheme is used instead of the traditional vector clock algorithm. Assume that any process can send at most m messages.

7.7. Assume that you have implemented the vector clock algorithm. However, some application needs Lamport's logical clock. Write a function *convert* that takes as input a vector timestamp and outputs a logical clock timestamp.

7.8. Give a distributed algorithm to maintain clocks for a distributed program that has a dynamic number of processes. Assume that there are the following events in the life of any process: start-process, internal, send, receive, fork, join processid, terminate. It should be possible to infer the *happened-before relation* using your clocks.

7.9. Prove the following for direct-dependency clocks:

$$\forall s, t : s.p \neq t.p : (s \rightarrow_d t) \Leftrightarrow (s.v[s.p] \leq t.v[s.p])$$

7.10. Show that for matrix clocks, the row corresponding to the index $s.p$ is bigger than any other row in the matrix $s.M$ for any state s.

7.9 Bibliographic Remarks

The idea of logical clocks is from Lamport [Lam78]. The idea of vector clocks in pure form first appeared in papers by Fidge and Mattern [Fid89, Mat89]. However, vectors had been used before in some earlier papers (e.g., [SY85]). Direct-dependency clocks have been used in mutual exclusion algorithms (e.g., [Lam78]), global property detection (e.g., [Gar96]), and recovery in distributed systems. Matrix clocks have been used for discarding obsolete information [SL87] and for detecting relational global predicates [TG93].

Chapter 8

Resource Allocation

8.1 Introduction

In a distributed system mutual exclusion is often necessary for accessing shared resources such as data. For example, consider a table that is replicated on multiple sites. Assume that operations on the table can be issued concurrently. For their correctness, we require that all operations appear *atomic* in the sense that the effect of the operations must appear indivisible to the user. For example, if an update operation requires changes to two fields, x and y, then another operation should not read the old value of x and the new value of y. Observe that in a distributed system, there is no shared memory and therefore one could not use shared objects such as semaphores to implement the mutual exclusion.

Mutual exclusion is one of the most studied topics in distributed systems. It reveals many important issues in distributed algorithms such as safety and liveness properties. We will study three classes of algorithms—timestamp-based algorithms, token-based algorithms and quorum-based algorithms. The timestamp-based algorithms resolve conflict in use of resources based on timestamps assigned to requests of resources. The token-based algorithms use auxiliary resources such as tokens to resolve the conflicts. The quorum-based algorithms use a subset of processes to get permission for accessing the shared resource. All algorithms in this chapter assume that there are no faults in the distributed system, that is, that processors and communication links are reliable.

8.2   Specification of the Mutual Exclusion Problem

Let a system consist of a fixed number of processes and a shared resource called
the *critical section*. An example of a critical section is the operation performed on
the replicated table introduced earlier. The algorithm to coordinate access to the
critical section must satisfy the following properties:

Safety: Two processes should not have permission to use the critical section simultaneously.

Liveness: Every request for the critical section is eventually granted.

Fairness: Different requests must be granted in the order they are made.

We can abstract this problem as implementation of a lock in a distributed environment. The interface Lock is as follows:

```
public interface Lock extends MsgHandler {
    public void requestCS ();  //may block
    public void releaseCS ();
}
```

Any lock implementation in a distributed environment will also have to handle
messages that are used by the algorithm for locking. For this we use the interface
MsgHandler shown below.

```
import java.io.*;
public interface MsgHandler {
    public void handleMsg(Msg m, int srcId, String tag);
    public Msg receiveMsg(int fromId) throws IOException;
}
```

Any implementation of the lock can be exercised by the program shown in Figure
8.1. Line 8 creates a Linker that links all the processes in the system. After instan-
tiating a lock implementation at lines 10–17, we start separate threads to listen for
messages from all the other processes at lines 18–20. The class ListenerThread is
shown in Figure 8.2. A ListenerThread is passed a MsgHandler on its construction.
It makes a blocking receiveMsg call at line 12, and on receiving a message gives it
to the MsgHandler at line 13.

Most of our distributed programs in this book will extend the class Process
shown in Figure 8.3. This will allow processes to have access to its identifier myId,
the total number of processes N, and simple send and receive routines. The method
handleMsg is empty, and any class that extends Process is expected to override
this method.

```
 1 public class LockTester {
 2     public static void main(String [] args) throws Exception {
 3         Linker comm = null;
 4         try {
 5             String baseName = args [0];
 6             int myId = Integer.parseInt (args [1]);
 7             int numProc = Integer.parseInt (args [2]);
 8             comm = new Linker (baseName, myId, numProc);
 9             Lock lock = null;
10             if ( args [3]. equals ("Lamport"))
11                 lock = new LamportMutex (comm);
12             if ( args [3]. equals ("RicartAgrawala"))
13                 lock = new RAMutex(comm);
14             if ( args [3]. equals ("DiningPhil"))
15                 lock = new DinMutex (comm);
16             if ( args [3]. equals ("CircToken"))
17                 lock = new CircToken (comm,0);
18             for ( int i = 0; i < numProc; i++)
19                 if ( i != myId)
20                     (new ListenerThread (i, ( MsgHandler) lock )). start ();
21             while ( true) {
22                 System.out.println (myId + " is not in CS");
23                 Util.mySleep (2000);
24                 lock.requestCS ();
25                 Util.mySleep (2000);
26                 System.out.println (myId + " is in CS *****");
27                 lock.releaseCS ();
28             }
29         }
30         catch ( InterruptedException e) {
31             if (comm != null) comm.close ();
32         }
33         catch ( Exception e) {
34             System.out.println (e);
35             e.printStackTrace ();
36         }
37     }
38 }
```

Figure 8.1: Testing a lock implementation

```
 1 import java.io.*;
 2 public class ListenerThread extends Thread {
 3     int channel;
 4     MsgHandler process;
 5     public ListenerThread(int channel, MsgHandler process) {
 6         this.channel = channel;
 7         this.process = process;
 8     }
 9     public void run() {
10         while (true) {
11             try {
12                 Msg m = process.receiveMsg(channel);
13                 process.handleMsg(m, m.getSrcId(), m.getTag());
14             } catch (IOException e) {
15                 System.err.println(e);
16             }
17         }
18     }
19 }
```

Figure 8.2: ListenerThread

8.3   Centralized Algorithm

There are many algorithms for mutual exclusion in a distributed system. However, the least expensive algorithm for the mutual exclusion is the centralized algorithm shown in Figure 8.4. If we are required to satisfy just the safety and liveness properties, then this simple queue-based algorithm works. One of the processes is designated as the leader (or the coordinator) for the critical section. The variable haveToken is true for the process that has access to the critical section. Any process that wants to enter the critical section sends a *request* message to the leader. The leader simply puts these requests in the pendingQ in the order it receives them. It also grants permission to the process that is at the head of the queue by sending an *okay* message. When a process has finished executing its critical section, it sends the *release* message to the leader. On receiving a *release* message, the leader sends the *okay* message to the next process in its pendingQ if the queue is nonempty. Otherwise, the leader sets haveToken to true.

The centralized algorithm does not satisfy the notion of fairness, which says that requests should be granted in the order they are made and not in the order they are received. Assume that the process P_i makes a request for the shared resource to the leader process P_k. After making the request, P_i sends a message to the process P_j. Now, P_j sends a request to P_k that reaches P_k earlier than the request made by the

```
import java.io.*; import java.lang.*;
public class Process implements MsgHandler {
    int N, myId;
    Linker comm;
    public Process(Linker initComm) {
        comm = initComm;
        myId = comm.getMyId();
        N = comm.getNumProc();
    }
    public synchronized void handleMsg(Msg m, int src, String tag) {
    }
    public void sendMsg(int destId, String tag, String msg) {
        Util.println("Sending msg to " + destId + ":" +tag + " " + msg);
        comm.sendMsg(destId, tag, msg);
    }
    public void sendMsg(int destId, String tag, int msg) {
        sendMsg(destId, tag, String.valueOf(msg)+" ");
    }
    public void sendMsg(int destId, String tag, int msg1, int msg2) {
        sendMsg(destId,tag,String.valueOf(msg1)
        +" "+String.valueOf(msg2)+" ");
    }
    public void sendMsg(int destId, String tag) {
        sendMsg(destId, tag, " 0 ");
    }
    public void broadcastMsg(String tag, int msg) {
        for (int i = 0; i < N; i++)
            if (i != myId) sendMsg(i, tag, msg);
    }
    public void sendToNeighbors(String tag, int msg) {
        for (int i = 0; i < N; i++)
            if (isNeighbor(i)) sendMsg(i, tag, msg);
    }
    public boolean isNeighbor(int i) {
        if (comm.neighbors.contains(i)) return true;
        else return false;
    }
    public Msg receiveMsg(int fromId) {
        try {
            return comm.receiveMsg(fromId);
        } catch (IOException e){
            System.out.println(e);
            comm.close();
            return null;
        }
    }
    public synchronized void myWait() {
        try {
            wait();
        } catch (InterruptedException e) {System.err.println(e);
        }
    }
}
```

Figure 8.3: Process.java

```java
public class CentMutex extends Process implements Lock {
    // assumes that P_0 coordinates and does not request locks.
    boolean haveToken;
    final int leader = 0;
    IntLinkedList pendingQ = new IntLinkedList ();
    public CentMutex(Linker initComm) {
        super(initComm);
        haveToken = (myId == leader);
    }
    public synchronized void requestCS () {
        sendMsg(leader, "request");
        while (!haveToken) myWait();
    }
    public synchronized void releaseCS () {
        sendMsg(leader, "release");
        haveToken = false;
    }
    public synchronized void handleMsg(Msg m, int src, String tag) {
        if (tag.equals("request")) {
            if (haveToken){
                sendMsg(src, "okay");
                haveToken = false;
            }
            else
                pendingQ.add(src);
        } else if (tag.equals("release")) {
            if (!pendingQ.isEmpty()) {
                int pid = pendingQ.removeHead();
                sendMsg(pid, "okay");
            } else
                haveToken = true;
        } else if (tag.equals("okay")) {
            haveToken = true;
            notify();
        }
    }
}
```

Figure 8.4: A centralized mutual exclusion algorithm

process P_i. This example shows that it is possible for the order in which requests are received by the leader process to be different from the order in which they are made. The modification of the algorithm to ensure fairness is left as an exercise (see Problem 8.1).

8.4 Lamport's Algorithm

In Lamport's algorithm each process maintains a logical clock (used for timestamps) and a queue (used for storing requests for the critical section). The algorithm ensures that processes enter the critical section in the order of timestamps of their requests. It assumes FIFO ordering of messages. The rules of the algorithm are as follows:

- To request the critical section, a process sends a timestamped message to all other processes and adds a timestamped request to the queue.

- On receiving a request message, the request and its timestamp are stored in the queue and a timestamped acknowledgment is sent back.

- To release the critical section, a process sends a release message to all other processes.

- On receiving a release message, the corresponding request is deleted from the queue.

- A process determines that it can access the critical section if and only if (1) it has a request in the queue with timestamp t, (2) t is less than all other requests in the queue, and (3) it has received a message from every other process with timestamp greater than t (the request acknowledgments ensure this).

Figure 8.5 gives an implementation of this algorithm in Java. In this version, every process maintains two vectors. These two vectors simulate the queue used in the informal description given earlier. These vectors are interpreted at process P_i as follows:

$q[j]$: the timestamp of the request by process P_j. The value `Symbols.infinity` signifies that P_i does not have any record of outstanding request by process P_j.

$v[j]$: the timestamp of the last message seen from P_j if $j \neq i$. The component $s.v[i]$ represents the value of the logical clock in state s. Thus the vector v is simply the direct-dependency clock.

To request the critical section (method `requestCS`), P_i simply records its clock in $q[i]$. Because all other processes also maintain this information, "request" messages are sent to all processes indicating the new value of $q[i]$. It then simply waits for the condition `okayCS` to become true.

To release the critical section (method `releaseCS`), P_i simply resets $q[i]$ to ∞ and sends "release" messages to all processes. Finally, we also require processes to acknowledge any request message as shown in the method `handleMsg`. Note that every message is timestamped and when it is received, the vector v is updated according to the direct-dependency clock rules as discussed in Chapter 7.

Process P_i has permission to access the critical section when there is a request from P_i with its timestamp less than all other requests and P_i has received a message from every other process with a timestamp greater than the timestamp of its own request. Since two requests may have identical timestamps, we extend the set of timestamps to a total order using process identifiers as discussed in Chapter 7. Thus, if two requests have the same timestamp, then the request by the process with the smaller process number is considered smaller. Formally, P_i can enter the critical section if

$$\forall j : j \neq i : (q[i], i) < (v[j], j) \ \wedge \ (q[i], i) < (q[j], j)$$

This condition is checked in the method `okayCS`.

Lamport's algorithm requires $3(N - 1)$ messages per invocation of the critical section: $N - 1$ request messages, $N - 1$ acknowledgment messages, and $N - 1$ release messages. There is a time delay of two serial messages to get permission for the critical section—a request message followed by an acknowledgment. The space overhead per process is the vectors q and v which is $O(N \log m)$, where m is the maximum number of times any process enters the critical section.

8.5   Ricart and Agrawala's Algorithm

Ricart and Agrawala's algorithm uses only $2(N - 1)$ messages per invocation of the critical section. It does so by combining the functionality of acknowledgment and release messages. In this algorithm, a process does not always send back an acknowledgment on receiving a request. It may defer the reply for a later time. Another advantage of Ricart and Agrawala's algorithm is that it does not require FIFO ordering of messages.

The algorithm is stated by the following rules:

- To request a resource, the process sends a timestamped message to all processes.

```
public class LamportMutex extends Process implements Lock {
    DirectClock v;
    int [] q; // request queue
    public LamportMutex(Linker initComm) {
        super(initComm);
        v = new DirectClock(N, myId);
        q = new int [N];
        for (int j = 0; j < N; j++)
            q[j] = Symbols.Infinity;
    }
    public synchronized void requestCS() {
        v.tick();
        q[myId] = v.getValue(myId);
        broadcastMsg("request", q[myId]);
        while (!okayCS())
            myWait();
    }
    public synchronized void releaseCS() {
        q[myId] = Symbols.Infinity;
        broadcastMsg("release", v.getValue(myId));
    }
    boolean okayCS() {
        for (int j = 0; j < N; j++){
            if (isGreater(q[myId], myId, q[j], j))
                return false;
            if (isGreater(q[myId], myId, v.getValue(j), j))
                return false;
        }
        return true;
    }
    boolean isGreater(int entry1, int pid1, int entry2, int pid2) {
        if (entry2 == Symbols.Infinity) return false;
        return ((entry1 > entry2)
                || ((entry1 == entry2) && (pid1 > pid2)));
    }
    public synchronized void handleMsg(Msg m, int src, String tag) {
        int timeStamp = m.getMessageInt();
        v.receiveAction(src, timeStamp);
        if (tag.equals("request")) {
            q[src] = timeStamp;
            sendMsg(src, "ack", v.getValue(myId));
        } else if (tag.equals("release"))
            q[src] = Symbols.Infinity;
        notify(); // okayCS() may be true now
    }
}
```

Figure 8.5: Lamport's mutual exclusion algorithm

- On receiving a request from any other process, the process sends an *okay* message if either the process is not interested in the critical section or its own request has a higher timestamp value. Otherwise, that process is kept in a pending queue.

- To release a resource, the process sends *okay* to all the processes in the pending queue.

- The process is granted the resource when it has requested the resource and it has received the *okay* message from every other process in response to its *request* message.

The algorithm is presented formally in Figure 8.6. There are two kinds of messages in the system—*request* messages and *okay* messages. Each process maintains the logical time of its request in the variable *myts*. In the method `requestCS`, a process simply broadcasts a *request* message with its timestamp. The variable *numOkay* counts the number of *okay* messages received since the request was made. On receiving any request with a timestamp lower than its own, it replies immediately with *okay*. Otherwise, it adds that process to *pendingQ*.

The algorithm presented above satisfies safety, liveness, and fairness properties of mutual exclusion. To see the safety property, assume that P_i and P_j are in the critical section concurrently and P_i has the smaller value of the timestamp for its request. P_j can enter the critical section only if it received *okay* for its request. The request made by P_j can reach P_i only after P_i has made its request; otherwise, the timestamp of P_i's request would have been greater because of the rules of the logical clock. From the algorithm, P_i cannot send *okay* unless it has exited from the critical section contradicting our earlier assumption that P_j received *okay* from P_i. Thus the safety property is not violated. The process with the least timestamp for its request can never be deferred by any other process, and therefore the algorithm also satisfies liveness. Because processes enter the critical section in the order of the timestamps of the requests, the fairness is also true.

It is easy to see that every critical section execution requires $N - 1$ *request* messages and $N - 1$ *okay* messages.

8.6   Dining Philosopher Algorithm

In the previous algorithm, every critical section invocation requires $2(N - 1)$ messages. We now show an algorithm in which $2(N - 1)$ messages are required only in the worst case. Consider a large distributed system in which even though N is large, the number of processes that request the critical section, say, n, is small. In

```java
import java.util.*;
public class RAMutex extends Process implements Lock {
    int myts;
    LamportClock c = new LamportClock();
    IntLinkedList pendingQ = new IntLinkedList();
    int numOkay = 0;
    public RAMutex(Linker initComm) {
        super(initComm);
        myts = Symbols.Infinity;
    }
    public synchronized void requestCS() {
        c.tick();
        myts = c.getValue();
        broadcastMsg("request", myts);
        numOkay = 0;
        while (numOkay < N-1)
            myWait();
    }
    public synchronized void releaseCS() {
        myts = Symbols.Infinity;
        while (!pendingQ.isEmpty()) {
            int pid = pendingQ.removeHead();
            sendMsg(pid, "okay", c.getValue());
        }
    }
    public synchronized void handleMsg(Msg m, int src, String tag) {
        int timeStamp = m.getMessageInt();
        c.receiveAction(src, timeStamp);
        if (tag.equals("request")) {
            if ((myts == Symbols.Infinity)  // not interested in CS
                    || (timeStamp < myts)
                    || ((timeStamp == myts) && (src < myId)))
                sendMsg(src, "okay", c.getValue());
            else
                pendingQ.add(src);
        } else if (tag.equals("okay")) {
            numOkay++;
            if (numOkay == N - 1)
                notify(); // okayCS() may be true now
        }
    }
}
```

Figure 8.6: Ricart and Agrawala's algorithm

our next algorithm, processes that are not interested in the critical section will not be required to send messages eventually.

The next algorithm will also solve a more general problem, the dining philosopher problem, where a resource may not be shared by all the processes. The dining philosopher problem, as discussed in Chapter 3, consists of multiple philosophers who spend their time thinking and eating spaghetti. However, a philosopher requires shared resources, such as forks, to eat spaghetti. We are required to devise a protocol to coordinate access to the shared resources.

There are two requirements on the solution of the dining philosopher problem: (1) we require mutually exclusive use of shared resources, that is, a shared resource should not be used by more than one process at a time; and (2) we want freedom from starvation. Every philosopher (process) should be able to eat (perform its operation) infinitely often.

The crucial problem in resource allocation is that of resolving conflicts. If a set of processes require a resource and only one of them can use it at a time, then there is a conflict that must be resolved in favor of one of these processes. We have already studied one conflict resolution method via logical clocks in Lamport's and Ricart and Agrawala's mutual exclusion algorithms. The processes used logical clocks to resolve access to mutual exclusion. If two requests had the same logical clock value, then process identity was used to break ties. Now we study another mechanism that resolves conflicts based on location of auxiliary resources. The auxiliary resources are used only for conflict resolution and are not actual resources.

We model the problem as an undirected graph called a *conflict graph*, in which each node represents a process and an edge between process P_i and P_j denotes that one or more resources are shared between P_i and P_j. Figure 8.7(a) shows the conflict graph for five philosophers. If a process needs all the shared resources for performing its operation, then only one of any two adjacent nodes can perform its operation in any step. The conflict graph for a simple mutual exclusion algorithm is a complete graph.

Now consider the problem of five dining philosophers sitting around a table such that two adjacent philosophers share a fork. The conflict graph of this problem is a ring on five nodes.

An *orientation* of an undirected graph consists of providing direction to all edges. The edge between P_i and P_j points from P_i to P_j if P_i has precedence over P_j. We say that an orientation is acyclic if the directed graph that results from the orientation is acyclic. Figure 8.7(b) shows an acyclic orientation of the conflict graph. In a directed graph, we call a node *source* if it does not have any incoming edge. Any finite-directed acyclic graph must have at least one source (see Problem 8.5). In Figure 8.7, processes P_2 and P_4 are sources.

To maintain orientation of an edge, we use the notion of an auxiliary resource, a

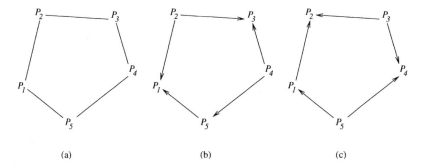

Figure 8.7: (a) Conflict graph; (b) an acyclic orientation with P_2 and P_4 as sources; (c) orientation after P_2 and P_4 finish eating

fork, associated with each edge. Process P_i is considered to have the fork associated with the edge (i, j), if it has precedence over P_j in any conflict resolution.

The algorithm for dining philosophers obeys the following two rules:

- *Eating rule*: A process can eat only if it has all the forks for the edges incident to it, that is, a process can eat only when it is a source.

- *Edge reversal*: On finishing the eating session, a process reverses orientations of all the outgoing edges to incoming edges.

Now let us look at the rules for transmitting forks. We do not require that once a philosopher has finished eating it sends all the forks to its neighbors. This is because its neighbors may be thinking and therefore not interested in eating. Thus we require that if a philosopher is hungry (interested in eating) and does not have the fork, then it should explicitly request the fork. To request the fork, we use a request token associated with each fork. Although a fork is not transmitted after eating, we still need to capture the fact that the other philosopher has priority over this fork to satisfy the edge reversal rule. Thus we need to distinguish the case when a philosopher has a fork but has not used it from the case when the philosopher has the fork and has used it for eating. This is done conveniently by associating a boolean variable *dirty* with each fork. Once a philosopher has eaten from a fork, it becomes dirty. Before a fork is sent to the neighbor, it is cleaned.

Our solution is based on keeping an acyclic conflict resolution graph as mentioned earlier. Philosopher u has priority over philosopher v if the edge between u and v points to v. The direction of the edge is from u to v if (1) u holds the fork and it is clean, (2) v holds the fork and it is dirty, or (3) the fork is in transit from v to u.

The forks are initially placed so that the conflict resolution graph is initially acyclic. The algorithm ensures that the graph stays acyclic. Observe that when a fork is cleaned before it is sent, the conflict graph does not change. The change in the conflict graph occurs only when a philosopher eats, thereby reversing all edges incident to it. The algorithm for the dining philosophers problem is given in Figure 8.8. In this algorithm, we have assumed that the conflict graph is a complete graph for simplicity.

We use the following boolean variables for each process P_i:

- $fork[j]$: Process P_i holds the fork that is shared with P_j.

- $request[j]$: Process P_i holds the request token for the fork that is shared with P_j.

- $dirty[j]$: The fork that is shared with P_j is dirty.

It is easy to see that the conflict resolution graph is always acyclic. It is acyclic initially by our initialization. The only action that changes direction of any edge in the graph is eating (which dirties the fork). A philosopher can eat only when she has all the forks corresponding to the edges that she shares with other philosophers. By the act of eating, all those forks are dirtied and therefore all those edges point toward the philosopher after eating. This transformation cannot create a cycle.

Observe that when a fork is transmitted, it is cleaned before transmission and thus does not result in any change in the conflict resolution graph.

The conflict graph for the mutual exclusion on N processes is a complete graph on N nodes. For any philosopher to eat, she will need to request only those forks that she is missing. This can be at most $N - 1$. This results in $2(N - 1)$ messages in the worst case. Note that if a process never requests critical section after some time, it will eventually relinquish all its forks and will not be disturbed after that. Thus, the number of messages in the average case is proportional only to the number of processes who are active in accessing the resource.

8.7   Token-Based Algorithms

Token-based algorithms use the auxiliary resource *token* to resolve conflicts in a resource coordination problem. The issue in these algorithms is how the requests for the token are made, maintained, and served. A centralized algorithm is an instance of a token-based algorithm in which the coordinator is responsible for keeping the token. All the requests for the token go to the coordinator.

In a token ring approach, all processes are organized in a ring. The token circulates around the ring. Any process that wants to enter the critical section

```
public class DinMutex extends Process implements Lock {
    private static final int thinking = 0, hungry = 1, eating = 2;
    boolean fork[] = null,  dirty[] = null, request[] = null;
    int myState = thinking;
    public DinMutex(Linker initComm) {
        super(initComm);
        fork = new boolean[N];  dirty = new boolean[N];
        request = new boolean[N];
        for (int i = 0; i < N; i++) {
            if ((myId > i) && (isNeighbor(i))) {
                fork[i] = false;  request[i] = true;
            } else { fork[i] = true; request[i] = false; }
            dirty[i] = true;
        }
    }
    public synchronized void requestCS() {
        myState = hungry;
        if (haveForks()) myState = eating;
        else
            for (int i = 0; i < N; i++)
                if (request[i] && !fork[i]) {
                    sendMsg(i, "Request");  request[i] = false;
                }
        while (myState != eating) myWait();
    }
    public synchronized void releaseCS() {
        myState = thinking;
        for (int i = 0; i < N; i++) {
            dirty[i] = true;
            if (request[i]) { sendMsg(i, "Fork");  fork[i] = false; }
        }
    }
    boolean haveForks() {
        for (int i = 0; i < N; i++)
            if (!fork[i]) return false;
        return true;
    }
    public synchronized void handleMsg(Msg m, int src, String tag) {
        if (tag.equals("Request")) {
            request[src] = true;
            if ((myState != eating) && fork[src] && dirty[src]) {
                sendMsg(src, "Fork");  fork[src] = false;
                if (myState == hungry){
                    sendMsg(src, "Request");  request[src] = false;
                }
            }
        } else if (tag.equals("Fork")) {
            fork[src] = true; dirty[src] = false;
            if (haveForks()) {
                myState = eating; notify();
            }
        }
    }
}
```

Figure 8.8: An algorithm for dining philosopher problem

waits for the token to arrive at that process. It then grabs the token and enters the critical section. This algorithm is shown in Figure 8.9. The algorithm is initiated by the coordinator who sends the token to the next process in the ring. The local state of a process is simply the boolean variable `haveToken` which records whether the process has the token. By ensuring that a process enters the critical section only when it has the token, the algorithm guarantees the safety property trivially.

In this algorithm, the token is sent to the next process in the ring after a fixed period of time. The reader is invited to design an algorithm in which the token moves only on receiving a request.

8.8   Quorum-Based Algorithms

Token-based algorithms are vulnerable to failures of processes holding the token. We now present quorum-based algorithms, which do not suffer from such single point of failures. The main idea behind a quorum-based algorithm is that instead of asking permission to enter the critical section from either just one process as in token-based algorithms, or from all processes, as in timestamp-based algorithms in Chapter 2, the permission is sought from a subset of processes called the *request set*. If any two request sets have nonempty intersection, then we are guaranteed that at most one process can have permission to enter the critical section. A simple example of this strategy is that of requiring permission from a majority of processes. In this case, a request set is any subset of processes with at least $\lceil \frac{N+1}{2} \rceil$ processes.

Voting systems and crumbling walls are some examples of quorum systems. In voting systems, each process is assigned a number of votes. Let the total number of votes in the system be V. A quorum is defined to be any subset of processes with a combined number of votes exceeding $V/2$. If each process is assigned a single vote, then such a quorum system is also called a *majority voting system*.

When applications require *read* or *write* accesses to the critical section, then the voting systems can be generalized to two kinds of quorums—*read* quorums and *write* quorums. These quorums are defined by two parameters R and W such that $R + W > V$ and $W > V/2$. For a subset of processes if the combined number of votes exceeds R, then it is a *read* quorum and if it exceeds W, then it is a *write* quorum.

To obtain quorums for *crumbling walls*, processes are logically arranged in rows of possibly different widths. A quorum in a crumbling wall is the union of one full row and a representative from every row below the full rows. For example, consider a system with 9 processes such that P_1 to P_3 are in row 1, P_4 to P_6 are in row 2 and P_7 to P_9 are in row 3. In this system, $\{P_4, P_5, P_6, P_9\}$ is a quorum because it contains the entire second row and a representative, P_9, from the third row. Let

```
import java.util.Timer;
public class CircToken extends Process implements Lock {
    boolean haveToken;
    boolean wantCS = false;
    public CircToken(Linker initComm, int coordinator) {
        super(initComm);
        haveToken = (myId == coordinator);
    }
    public synchronized void initiate() {
        if (haveToken) sendToken();
    }
    public synchronized void requestCS() {
        wantCS = true;
        while (!haveToken) myWait();
    }
    public synchronized void releaseCS() {
        wantCS = false;
        sendToken();
    }
    void sendToken() {
        if (haveToken && !wantCS) {
            int next = (myId + 1) % N;
            Util.println("Process " + myId + "has sent the token");
            sendMsg(next, "token");
            haveToken = false;
        }
    }
    public synchronized void handleMsg(Msg m, int src, String tag) {
        if (tag.equals("token")) {
            haveToken = true;
            if (wantCS)
                notify();
            else {
                Util.mySleep(1000);
                sendToken();
            }
        }
    }
}
```

Figure 8.9: A token ring algorithm for the mutual exclusion problem

$CW(n_1, n_2, \ldots, n_d)$ be a wall with d rows of width n_1, n_2, $\ldots$, n_d, respectively. We assume that processes in the wall are numbered sequentially from left to right and top to bottom. Our earlier example of the crumbling wall can be concisely written as $CW(3,3,3)$. $CW(1)$ denotes a wall with a single row of width 1. This corresponds to a centralized algorithm. The crumbling wall $CW(1, N-1)$ is called the *wheel coterie* because it has $N-1$ "spoke" quorums of the form $\{1, i\}$ for $i = 2, \ldots, N$ and one "rim" quorum $\{2, \ldots, N\}$. In a triangular quorum system, processes are arranged in a triangle such that the ith row has i processes. If there are d rows, then each quorum has exactly d processes. In a grid quorum system, $N(= d^2)$ processes are arranged in a grid such that there are d rows each with d processes. A quorum consists of the union of one full row and a representative from every row below the full rows.

It is important to recognize that the simple strategy of getting permission to enter the critical section from one of the quorums can result in a deadlock. In the majority voting system, if two requests gather $N/2$ votes each (for an even value of N), then neither of the requests will be granted. Quorum-based systems require additional messages to ensure that the system is deadlock-free. The details of ensuring deadlock freedom are left to the reader (see Problem 8.9).

8.9 Problems

8.1. How will you modify the centralized mutual exclusion algorithm to ensure fairness. (*Hint*: Use vector clocks modified appropriately.)

8.2. The mutual exclusion algorithm by Lamport requires that any request message be acknowledged. Under what conditions does a process not need to send an *acknowledgment* message for a *request* message?

8.3. Some applications require two types of access to the critical section—*read* access and *write* access. For these applications, it is reasonable for two *read* accesses to happen concurrently. However, a *write* access cannot happen concurrently with either a *read* access or a *write* access. Modify algorithms presented in this chapter for such applications.

8.4. Build a multiuser *Chat* application in Java that ensures that a user can type its message only in its critical section. Ensure that your system handles a dynamic number of users, that is, allows users to join and leave a chat session.

8.5. Show that any finite directed acyclic graph has at least one source.

8.6. When can you combine the request token message with a fork message? With this optimization, show that a philosopher with d neighbors needs to send or receive at most $2d$ messages before making transition from hungry state to eating state.

8.7. Show that the solution to the dining problem does not deny the possibility of simultaneous eating from different forks by different philosophers (when there is no conflict in requirements of forks).

8.8. (due to Raymond [Ray89]) In the decentralized algorithm, a process is required to send the message to everybody to request the token. Design an algorithm in which all processes are organized in the form of a logical binary tree. The edges in the tree are directed as follows. Each node except the one with the token has exactly one outgoing edge such that if that edge is followed, it will lead to the node with the token. Give the actions required for requesting and releasing the critical section. What is the message complexity of your algorithm?

8.9. (due to Maekawa [Mae85]) Let all processes be organized in a rectangular grid. We allow a process to enter the critical section only if it has permission from all the processes in its row and its column. A process grants permission to another process only if it has not given permission to some other process. What properties does this algorithm satisfy? What is the message complexity of the algorithm? How will you ensure deadlock freedom?

8.10. Compare all the algorithms for mutual exclusion discussed in this chapter using the following metrics: the response time and the number of messages.

8.11. Discuss how you will extend each of the mutual exclusion algorithms to tolerate failure of a process. Assume perfect failure detection of a process.

8.12. Extend all algorithms discussed in this chapter to solve k-mutual exclusion problem, in which at most k processes can be in the critical section concurrently.

8.13. (due to Agrawal and El-Abbadi [AEA91]) In the tree-based quorum system, processes are organized in a rooted binary tree. A quorum in the system is defined recursively to be either the union of the root and a quorum in one of the two subtrees, or the union of quorums of subtrees. Analyze this coterie for availability and load.

8.10   Bibliographic Remarks

Lamport's algorithm for mutual exclusion [Lam78] was initially presented as an application of logical clocks. The number of messages per invocation of the critical section in Lamport's algorithm can be reduced as shown by Ricart and Agrawala [RA81]. The token-based algorithm can be decentralized as shown by Suzuki and Kasami [SK85]. The tree-based algorithm in the problem set is due to Raymond [Ray89]. The use of majority voting systems for distributed control is due to Thomas [Tho79], and the use of weighted voting systems with R and W parameters is due to Gifford [Gif79]. Maekawa [Mae85] introduced grid-based quorums and quorums based on finite projective planes. The tree-based quorum in the problem set is due to Agrawal and El-Abbadi [AEA91]. The triangular quorum systems are due to Lovasz [Lov73]. The notion of crumbling walls is due to Peleg and Wool [PW95].

Chapter 9

Global Snapshot

9.1 Introduction

One of the difficulties in a distributed system is that no process has access to the global state of the system, that is, it is impossible for a process to know the current global state of the system (unless the computation is frozen). For many applications, it is sufficient to capture a global state that happened in the *past* instead of the *current* global state. For example, in case of a failure the system can restart from such a global state. As another example, suppose that we were interested in monitoring the system for the property that the token in the system has been lost. This property is *stable*, that is, once it is true it stays true forever; therefore, we can check this property on an old global state. If the token is found to be missing in the old global state, then we can conclude that the token is also missing in the current global state. An algorithm that captures a global state is called a *global snapshot algorithm*.

A global snapshot algorithm is a useful tool in building distributed systems. Computing a global snapshot is beautifully exemplified by Chandy and Lamport as the problem of taking a picture of a big scene such as a sky filled with birds. The scene is so big that it cannot be captured by a single photograph, and therefore multiple photographs must be taken and composed together to form the global picture. The multiple photographs cannot be taken at the same time instant because there is no shared physical clock in a distributed system. Furthermore, the act of taking a picture cannot change the behavior of the underlying process. Thus birds may fly from one part of the sky to the other while the local pictures are being taken. Despite these problems, we require that the composite picture be meaningful. For example, it should give us an accurate count of the number of birds. We next define what is meant by "meaningful" global state.

Consider the following definition of a global state: A *global state* is a set of local states that occur simultaneously. This definition is based on physical time. We use the phrase "time-based model" to refer to such a definition. A different definition of a global state based on the "happened-before model" is possible. In the happened-before model, a global state is a set of local states that are all concurrent with each other. By *concurrent*, we mean that no two states have a happened-before relationship with each other. A global state in the time-based model is also a global state in the happened-before model; if two states occur simultaneously, then they cannot have any happened-before relationship. However, the converse is not true; two concurrent states may or may not occur simultaneously in a given execution.

We choose to use the definition for the global state from the happened-before model for two reasons.

1. It is impossible to determine whether a given global state occurs in the time-based model without access to perfectly synchronized local clocks. For example, the statement "there exists a global state in which more than two processes have access to the critical section" cannot be verified in the time-based model. In the happened-before model, however, it is possible to determine whether a given global state occurs.

2. Program properties that are of interest are often more simply stated in the happened-before model than in the time-based model, which makes them easier to understand and manipulate. This simplicity and elegance is gained because the happened-before model inherently accounts for different execution schedules. For example, an execution that does not violate mutual exclusion in the time-based model may do so with a different execution schedule. This problem is avoided in the happened-before model.

It is instructive to observe that a consistent global state is not simply a product of local states. To appreciate this, consider a distributed database for a banking application. Assume for simplicity that there are only two sites that keep the accounts for a customer. Also assume that the customer has $500 at the first site and $300 at the second site. In the absence of any communication between these sites, the total money of the customer can be easily computed to be $800. However, if there is a transfer of $200 from site A to site B, and a simple procedure is used to add up the accounts, we may falsely report that the customer has a total of $1000 in his or her accounts (to the chagrin of the bank). This happens when the value at the first site is used before the transfer and the value at the second site after the transfer. It is easily seen that these two states are not concurrent. Note that $1000 cannot be justified even by the messages in transit (or, that "the check is in the mail").

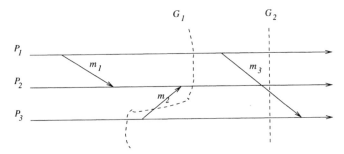

Figure 9.1: Consistent and inconsistent cuts

Figure 9.1 depicts a distributed computation. The dashed lines labeled G_1 and G_2 represent global states that consist of local states at P_1, P_2, and P_3, where G_1 and G_2 intersect the processes. Because a global state can be visualized in such a figure as a *cut* across the computation, the term, "cut" is used interchangeably with "global state." The cut G_1 in this computation is not consistent because it records the message m_2 as having been received but not sent. This is clearly impossible. The cut G_2 is consistent. The message m_3 in this cut has been sent but not yet received. Thus it is a part of the channel from process P_1 to P_3.

Formally, in an event-based model of a computation $(E, \rightarrow)$, with total order $\prec$ on events in a single process, we define a *cut* as any subset $F \subseteq E$ such that

$$f \in F \wedge e \prec f \Rightarrow e \in F.$$

We define a *consistent cut*, or a global snapshot, as any subset $F \subseteq E$ such that

$$f \in F \wedge e \rightarrow f \Rightarrow e \in F.$$

9.2   Chandy and Lamport's Global Snapshot Algorithm

In this section, we describe an algorithm to take a global snapshot (or a consistent cut) of a distributed system. Our example of the distributed database in the previous section illustrates the importance of recording only the consistent cuts. The computation of the snapshot is initiated by one or more processes. We assume that all channels are unidirectional and satisfy the FIFO property. Assuming that channels are unidirectional is not restrictive because a bidirectional channel can simply be modeled by using two unidirectional channels. The assumption that channels are FIFO is essential to the correctness of the algorithm as explained later.

The interface that we study in this chapter is called `Camera`. It allows any application that uses a camera to invoke the method `globalState`, which records a consistent global state of the system.

```
public interface Camera extends MsgHandler {
    void globalState ();
}
```

The class `Camera` can be used by any application that implements the interface `CamUser`. Thus, the application is required to implement the method `localState`, which records the local state of the application whenever invoked.

```
public interface CamUser extends MsgHandler {
    void localState ();
}
```

The algorithm is shown in Figure 9.3. We associate with each process a variable called *color* that is either white or red. Intuitively, the computed global snapshot corresponds to the state of the system just before the processes turn red. All processes are initially white. After recording the local state, a process turns red. Thus the state of a local process is simply the state just before it turned red.

There are two difficulties in the design of rules for changing the color for the global snapshot algorithm: (1) we need to ensure that the recorded local states are mutually concurrent, and (2) we also need a mechanism to capture the state of the channels. To address these difficulties, the algorithm relies on a special message called a *marker*. Once a process turns red, it is required to send a marker along all its outgoing channels before it sends out any message. A process is required to turn red on receiving a marker if it has not already done so. Since channels are FIFO, the above mentioned rule guarantees that no white process ever receives a message sent by a red process. This in turn guarantees that local states are mutually concurrent.

Now let us turn our attention to the problem of computing states of the channels. Figure 9.2 shows that messages in the presence of colors can be of four types:

1. *ww messages*: These are the messages sent by a white process to a white process. These messages correspond to the messages sent and received before the global snapshot.

2. *rr messages*: These are the messages sent by a red process to a red process. These messages correspond to the messages sent and received after the global snapshot.

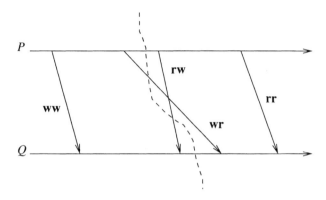

Figure 9.2: Classification of messages

3. *rw messages*: These are the messages sent by a red process received by a white process. In the figure, they cross the global snapshot in the backward direction. The presence of any such message makes the global snapshot inconsistent. The reader should verify that such messages are not possible if a *marker* is used.

4. *wr messages*: These are the messages sent by a white process received by a red process. These messages cross the global snapshot in the forward direction and form the state of the channel in the global snapshot because they are in transit when the snapshot is taken.

To record the state of the channel, P_j starts recording all messages it receives from P_i after turning red. Since P_i sends a marker to P_j on turning red, the arrival of the marker at P_j from P_i indicates that there will not be any further white messages from P_i sent to P_j. It can, therefore, stop recording messages once it has received the marker.

The program shown in Figure 9.3 uses `chan[k]` to record the state of the kth incoming channel and `closed[k]` to stop recording messages along that channel. In the program, we say that P_j is a *neighbor* of P_i if there is a channel from P_i to P_j. In our implementation, we have assumed that channels are bidirectional.

Lines 10–17 initialize the variables of the algorithm. All channels are initialized to empty. For each neighboring process P_k, `closed[k]` is initialized to false. The method `globalState` turns the process red, records the local state, and sends the *marker* message on all outgoing channels. Lines 25–34 give the rule for receiving a marker message. If the process is white, it turns red by invoking `globalState`. Line 27 sets `closed[src]` to true because there cannot be any message of type *wr* in that channel after the marker is received. The method `isDone` determines whether the process has recorded its local state and all incoming channels. Lines 29–33 print all the messages recorded as part of the channels. Lines 36–38 handle application messages. The condition on line 36 is true if the application message is of type *wr*.

In the algorithm, any change in the value of `color` must be reported to all neighbors. On receiving any such notification, a process is required to update its own color. This may result in additional messages because of the method `globalState`. The net result is that if one process turns red, all processes that can be reached directly or indirectly from that process also turn red.

The Chandy-Lamport algorithm requires that a marker be sent along all channels. Thus it has an overhead of e messages, where e is the number of unidirectional channels in the system. We have not discussed the overhead required to combine local snapshots into a global snapshot. A simple method would be for all processes to send their local snapshots to a predetermined process, say, P_0.

9.3 Global Snapshots for non-FIFO Channels

We now describe an algorithm due to Mattern that works even if channels are not FIFO. We cannot rely on the marker any more to distinguish between white and red messages. Therefore, we include the color in all the outgoing messages for any process besides sending the marker. Further, even after P_i gets a red message from P_j or the marker, it cannot be sure that it will not receive a white message on that channel. A white message may arrive later than a red message due to the overtaking of messages. To solve this problem we include in the marker the total number of white messages sent by that process along that channel. The receiver keeps track of the total number of white messages received and knows that all white messages have been received when this count equals the count included in the marker. We leave the details of the algorithm to the reader as an exercise.

9.4 Channel Recording by the Sender

Chandy and Lamport's algorithm requires the receiver to record the state of the channel. Since messages in real channels may get lost, it may be advantageous for senders to record the state of the channel. We will assume that control messages can be sent over unidirectional channels even in the reverse direction.

The mechanism to ensure that we do not record inconsistent global state is based on the coloring mechanism discussed earlier. A process sends white messages before it has recorded its local state and red messages after it has recorded the local state. By ensuring that a white process turns red before accepting a red message,

```
1  import java.util.*;
2  public class RecvCamera extends Process implements Camera {
3      static final int white = 0, red = 1;
4      int myColor = white;
5      boolean closed [];
6      CamUser app;
7      LinkedList chan[] = null;
8      public RecvCamera(Linker initComm, CamUser app) {
9          super(initComm);
10         closed = new boolean[N];
11         chan = new LinkedList[N];
12         for (int i = 0; i < N; i++)
13             if (isNeighbor(i)) {
14                 closed[i] = false;
15                 chan[i] = new LinkedList();
16             } else closed[i] = true;
17         this.app = app;
18     }
19     public synchronized void globalState() {
20         myColor = red;
21         app.localState(); // record local State;
22         sendToNeighbors("marker", myId); // send Markers
23     }
24     public synchronized void handleMsg(Msg m, int src, String tag) {
25         if (tag.equals("marker")) {
26             if (myColor == white) globalState();
27             closed[src] = true;
28             if (isDone()){
29                 System.out.println("Channel State: Transit Messages ");
30                 for (int i = 0; i < N; i++)
31                     if (isNeighbor(i))
32                         while (!chan[i].isEmpty())
33                             System.out.println(
34                                 ((Msg) chan[i].removeFirst()).toString());
35             }
36         } else { // application message
37             if ((myColor == red) && (!closed[src]))
38                 chan[src].add(m);
39             app.handleMsg(m, src, tag); // give it to app
40         }
41     }
42     boolean isDone() {
43         if (myColor == white) return false;
44         for (int i = 0; i < N; i++)
45             if (!closed[i]) return false;
46         return true;
47     }
48 }
```

Figure 9.3: Chandy and Lamport's snapshot algorithm

we are guaranteed that there are no *rw* messages and therefore we will record only a consistent global snapshot.

Now let us turn our attention to recording the state of channels. We assume that the sender records all the messages that it sends out on any outgoing channel before it turned red. Whenever a process turns red, it sends a marker message on all its incoming channels (in the reverse direction) indicating the messages it has received on that channel so far. The sender can now compute the state of the channel by removing from its buffer all messages that have been received according to the marker.

In this scheme, the sender may end up storing a large number of messages before the marker arrives. Assuming that all control messages (marker and acknowledgment messages) follow FIFO ordering, we can reduce the storage burden at the sender by requiring the receiver to send acknowledgments. When the sender receives an acknowledgment and has not received the marker, it can delete the message from the storage. To identify each message uniquely, we use sequence numbers with messages as encapsulated by the class **SeqMessage** given below.

```
public class SeqMessage {
    Msg m;
    int seqNo;
    public SeqMessage(Msg m, int seqNo) {
        this.m = m;
        this.seqNo = seqNo;
    }
    public int getSeqNo() {
        return seqNo;
    }
    public Msg getMessage() {
        return m;
    }
}
```

Thus, the algorithm can be summarized by the following rules.

1. Every process is white before recording its state and red after recording its state. A white process sends white messages and a red process sends a red message.

2. A white process turns red before accepting a red message or a marker.

3. On turning red, a process sends markers on all incoming channels in the reverse direction.

4. A white process acknowledges a white message.

5. A white process records any message sent. On receiving an acknowledgment, the corresponding message is removed from the record.

Since this algorithm requires every application message to include the color and the sequence number, we extend the Linker class as shown in Figure 9.4. The method sendMsg works as follows. If the message is either a marker or an acknowledgment message, then no special action is required, and super.sendMsg is invoked. If it is a white application message, then it is recorded as part of the channel history. The method sendMsg also appends the tag "white" or "red" with the message and includes a sequence number.

The algorithm for recording a global snapshot with channel states recorded by the sender is shown in Figure 9.5. For simplicity we have assumed a completely connected topology.

The method globalState is identical to Chandy and Lamport's algorithm except that the markers are sent on the incoming channels in the reverse direction. When a *marker* message is received, a white process invokes the method globalState at line 26. Also, that incoming channel is closed at line 27. When an acknowledgement message is received then the corresponding message is removed from the channel history at line 31. This is accomplished by the method removeM. When an application message is received, a white process sends an acknowledgment for a white message at line 37. If the message is red, then the process also turns red by invoking globalState at line 39.

Note that this algorithm also does not require channels for application messages to be FIFO. If channels are known to be FIFO then the receiver only needs to record the sequence number of the last message it received before turning red. The algorithm does require the ability to send control messages in the reverse direction for any application channel. Furthermore, it requires control messages to follow FIFO order. (Why?) If the underlying network does not support FIFO, then sequence numbers can be used to ensure FIFO ordering of messages.

9.5   Application: Checkpointing a Distributed Application

As a simple example, let us try our snapshot algorithm on the circulating token algorithm discussed in the Chapter 2. Figure 9.6 gives a program that constructs a circulating token and a camera. The computation of the global snapshot is initiated by the method globalState.

```java
import java.util.*; import java.net.*; import java.io.*;
public class CameraLinker extends Linker {
    static final int white = 0, red = 1;
    int seqNo[] = null;
    SenderCamera cam;
    public CameraLinker(String basename, int myId, int numProc)
                                                    throws Exception {
        super(basename, myId, numProc);
        seqNo = new int[numProc];
        for (int i = 0; i < numProc; i++)
            seqNo[i] = 0;
    }
    public void initCam(SenderCamera cam){
        this.cam = cam;
    }
    public void sendMsg(int destId, String tag, String msg) {
        if ((tag.equals("marker")) || (tag.equals("ack")))
            super.sendMsg(destId, tag, msg);
        else { // send seq numbers with app msgs
            seqNo[destId]++;
            Msg m = new Msg(myId, destId, tag, msg);
            if (cam.myColor == white) {
                cam.recordMsg(destId, new SeqMessage(m, seqNo[destId]));
                super.sendMsg(destId, "white",
                    String.valueOf(seqNo[destId]) + " " + m.toString()+" ");
            } else
                super.sendMsg(destId, "red",
                    String.valueOf(seqNo[destId]) + " " + m.toString()+" ");
        }
    }
}
```

Figure 9.4: Linker extended for use with SenderCamera

```
1  import java.util.*;
2  public class SenderCamera extends Process implements Camera {
3      static final int white = 0, red = 1;
4      public int myColor = white;
5      CamUser app;
6      boolean closed [];
7      MsgList outChan[] = null;
8      public SenderCamera(CameraLinker initComm, CamUser app) {
9          super(initComm);
10         this.app = app;
11         closed = new boolean[N]; outChan = new MsgList[N];
12         for (int i = 0; i < N; i++)
13             if (isNeighbor(i)) {
14                 closed[i] = false;
15                 outChan[i] = new MsgList();
16             } else closed[i] = true;
17         initComm.initCam(this);
18     }
19     public synchronized void globalState() {
20         myColor = red;
21         app.localState(); // record local State;
22         sendToNeighbors("marker", myId); // send Markers
23     }
24     public synchronized void handleMsg(Msg m, int src, String tag){
25         if (tag.equals("marker")) {
26             if (myColor == white) globalState();
27             closed[src] = true;
28             if (isDone()) System.out.println("Done recording");
29         } else if (tag.equals("ack")) {
30             int seqNo = m.getMessageInt();
31             outChan[src].removeM(seqNo);
32         } else { // application message
33             StringTokenizer st=new StringTokenizer(m.getMessage()+"#");
34             int seqNo = Integer.parseInt(st.nextToken());
35             Msg appMsg = Msg.parseMsg(st);
36             if ((myColor == white) && (tag.equals("white")))
37                 sendMsg(src, "ack", seqNo);
38             if ((myColor == white) && (tag.equals("red")))
39                 globalState();
40             app.handleMsg(appMsg, src, appMsg.getTag());
41         }
42     }
43     boolean isDone() {
44         if (myColor == white) return false;
45         for (int i = 0; i < N; i++)
46             if (!closed[i]) return false;
47         return true;
48     }
49     public synchronized void recordMsg(int destId, SeqMessage sm){
50         outChan[destId].add(sm);
51     }
52 }
```

Figure 9.5: A global snapshot algorithm based on sender recording

```
import java.util.Random;
public class CameraTester {
    public static void main(String [] args) throws Exception {
        String baseName = args[0];
        int myId = Integer.parseInt(args[1]);
        int numProc = Integer.parseInt(args[2]);
        Camera camera = null;
        CamCircToken sp = null;
        if (args[3].equals("RecvCamera")) {
            Linker comm = new Linker(baseName, myId, numProc);
            sp = new CamCircToken(comm, 0);
            camera = new RecvCamera(comm, sp);
        }
        if (args[3].equals("SenderCamera")) {
            CameraLinker comm = new CameraLinker(args[0], myId, numProc);
            sp = new CamCircToken(comm, 0);
            camera = new SenderCamera(comm, sp);
        }
        sp.initiate();
        for (int i = 0; i < numProc; i++)
            if (i != myId) (new ListenerThread(i, camera)).start();
        if (myId == 0) camera.globalState();
    }
}
```

Figure 9.6: Invocation of the global snapshot algorithm

The global snapshot algorithm can be used for providing fault tolerance in distributed systems. On failure, the system can be restarted from the last snapshot. Global snapshots can also be used for distributed debugging. Inspection of intermediate snapshots may sometimes reveal the source of an error.

9.6   Problems

9.1. Show that if G and H are consistent cuts of a distributed computation $(E, \rightarrow)$, then so are $G \cup H$ and $G \cap H$.

9.2. The global snapshot algorithms discussed in this chapter do not freeze the underlying computation. In some applications it may be okay for the underlying application to be frozen while the snapshot algorithm is in progress. How can the snapshot algorithm be simplified if this is the case? Give an algorithm for global snapshot computation and its Java implementation.

9.3. Extend the Java implementation of Chandy and Lamport's algorithm to allow repeated computation of global snapshots.

9.4. The original algorithm proposed by Chandy and Lamport does not require FIFO but a condition weaker than that. Specify the condition formally.

9.5. How can you use Lamport's logical clock to compute a consistent global snapshot?

9.6. Give Java implementation of global snapshot algorithm when channels are not FIFO.

9.7. Extend Chandy and Lamport's algorithm to compute a *transitless global state*. A consistent global state is transitless if there are no messages in any channel in that global state. Note that a process may have to record its local state multiple times until the recorded local state can be part of a transitless global state. Give Java implementation of your algorithm.

9.8. Give an example of a distributed computation in the interleaving model (with the events of the superimposed global snapshot algorithm) in which the recorded global snapshot does not occur in the computation.

9.9. How will you use snapshot algorithms to detect that the application has reached a deadlock state?

9.7 Bibliographic Remarks

Chandy and Lamport [CL85] were the first to give an algorithm for computation of a meaningful global snapshot (a colorful description of this algorithm is given by Dijkstra [Dij85]). Spezialetti and Kearns have given efficient algorithms to disseminate a global snapshot to processes initiating the snapshot computation [SK86]. Bouge [Bou87] has given an efficient algorithm for repeated computation of snapshots for synchronous computations. In the absence of the FIFO assumption, as shown by Taylor [Tay89], any algorithm for a snapshot is either inhibitory (that is, it may delay actions of the underlying application) or requires piggybacking of control information on basic messages. Lai and Yang [LY87] and Mattern [Mat93] have given snapshot algorithms that require only the piggybacking of control information. Helary [Hel89] has proposed an inhibitory snapshot algorithm.

Chapter 10

Global Properties

10.1 Introduction

In this chapter, we introduce another useful tool for monitoring distributed computations. A distributed computation is generally monitored to detect if the system has reached a global state satisfying a certain property. For example, a token ring system may be monitored for the loss of the token. A distributed database system may be monitored for deadlocks. The global snapshot algorithm discussed in Chapter 9 can be used to detect a stable predicate in a distributed computation. To define stable predicates, we use the notion of the reachability of one global state from another. For two consistent global states G and H, we say that $G \leq H$ if H is reachable from G. A predicate B is *stable* iff

$$\forall G, H : G \leq H : B(G) \Rightarrow B(H)$$

In other words, a property B is stable if once it becomes true, it stays true. Some examples of stable properties are deadlock, termination, and loss of a token. Once a system has deadlocked or terminated, it remains in that state. A simple algorithm to detect a stable property is as follows. Compute a consistent global state. If the property B is true in that global state, then we are done. Otherwise, we repeat the process after some period of time. It is easily seen that if the stable property ever becomes true, the algorithm will detect it. Conversely, if the algorithm detects that some stable property B is true, then the property must have become true in the past (and is therefore also true currently).

Formally, if the global snapshot computation was started in the global state G_i, the algorithm finished by the global state G_f, and the recorded state is G_*, then

163

the following is true:

1. $B(G_*) \Rightarrow B(G_f)$

2. $\neg B(G_*) \Rightarrow \neg B(G_i)$

Note that the converses of statements 1 and 2 may not hold.

At this point it is important to observe some limitations of the snapshot algorithm for detection of global properties:

- The algorithm is not useful for unstable predicates. An unstable predicate may turn true only between two snapshots.

- In many applications (such as debugging), it is desirable to compute the least global state that satisfies some given predicate. The snapshot algorithm cannot be used for this purpose.

- The algorithm may result in an excessive overhead depending on the frequency of snapshots. A process in Chandy and Lamport's algorithm is forced to take a local snapshot on receiving a marker even if it knows that the global snapshot that includes its local snapshot cannot satisfy the predicate being detected. For example, suppose that the property being detected is termination. Clearly, if a process is not terminated, then the entire system could not have terminated. In this case, computation of the global snapshot is a wasted effort.

10.2 Unstable Predicate Detection

In this section, we discuss an algorithm to detect unstable predicates. We will assume that the given global predicate, say, B, is constructed from local predicates using boolean connectives. We first show that B can be detected using an algorithm that can detect q, where q is a pure conjunction of local predicates. The predicate B can be rewritten in its disjunctive normal form. Thus

$$B = q_1 \vee \ldots \vee q_k \qquad k \geq 1$$

where each q_i is a pure conjunction of local predicates. Next, observe that a global cut satisfies B if and only if it satisfies at least one of the q_i's. Thus the problem of detecting B is reduced to solving k problems of detecting q, where q is a pure conjunction of local predicates.

As an example, consider a distributed program in which x, y, and z are in three different processes. Then,

$$even(x) \wedge ((y < 0) \vee (z > 6))$$

can be rewritten as

$$(even(x) \wedge (y < 0)) \vee (even(x) \wedge (z > 6))$$

where each disjunct is a conjunctive predicate.

Note that even if the global predicate is not a boolean expression of local predicates, but is satisfied by a finite number of possible global states, it can also be rewritten as a disjunction of conjunctive predicates. For example, consider the predicate $(x = y)$, where x and y are in different processes. $(x = y)$ is not a *local* predicate because it depends on both processes. However, if we know that x and y can take values $\{0, 1\}$ only, we can rewrite the preceding expression as follows:

$$((x = 0) \wedge (y = 0)) \vee ((x = 1) \wedge (y = 1)).$$

Each of the disjuncts in this expression is a conjunctive predicate.

In this chapter we study methods to detect global predicates that are conjunctions of local predicates. We will implement the interface **Sensor**, which abstracts the functionality of a global predicate evaluation algorithm. This interface is shown below:

```
public interface Sensor extends MsgHandler {
    void localPredicateTrue(VectorClock vc);
}
```

Any application that uses Sensor is required to call `localPredicateTrue` whenever its local predicate becomes true and provide its `VectorClock`. It also needs to implement the following interface:

```
public interface SensorUser extends MsgHandler {
    void globalPredicateTrue(int G[]);
    void globalPredicateFalse(int pid);
}
```

The class that implements **Sensor** calls these methods when the value of the global predicate becomes known. If the global predicate is true in a consistent global state G, then the vector clock for the global state is passed as a parameter to the method. If the global predicate is false, then the process id of the process that terminated is passed as a parameter.

We have emphasized conjunctive predicates and not disjunctive predicates. The reason is that disjunctive predicates are quite simple to detect. To detect a disjunctive predicate $l_1 \vee l_2 \vee \ldots \vee l_N$, where l_i denotes a local predicate in the process P_i, it is sufficient for the process P_i to monitor l_i. If any of the processes finds its local predicate true, then the disjunctive predicate is true.

Formally, we define a weak conjunctive predicate (WCP) to be true for a given computation if and only if there exists a consistent global cut in that run in which all conjuncts are true. Intuitively, detecting a weak conjunctive predicate is generally useful when one is interested in detecting a combination of states that is unsafe. For example, violation of mutual exclusion for a two-process system can be written as "P_1 is in the critical section and P_2 is in the critical section." It is necessary and sufficient to find a set of incomparable states, one on each process in which local predicates are true, to detect a weak conjunctive predicate. We now present an algorithm to do so. This algorithm finds the *least* consistent cut for which a WCP is true.

In this algorithm, one process serves as a checker. All other processes involved in detecting the WCP are referred to as *application processes*. Each application process checks for local predicates. It also maintains the vector clock algorithm. Whenever the local predicate of a process becomes true for the *first* time since the most recently sent message (or the beginning of the trace), it generates a debug message containing its local timestamp vector and sends it to the checker process.

Note that a process is not required to send its vector clock every time the local predicate is detected. If two local states, say, s and t, on the same process are separated only by internal events, then they are indistinguishable to other processes so far as consistency is concerned, that is, if u is a local state on some other process, then $s||u$ if and only if $t||u$. Thus it is sufficient to consider at most one local state between two external events and the vector clock need not be sent if there has been no message activity since the last time the vector clock was sent.

The checker process is responsible for searching for a consistent cut that satisfies the WCP by considering a sequence of candidate cuts. If the candidate cut either is not a consistent cut or does not satisfy some term of the WCP, the checker can efficiently eliminate one of the states along the cut. The eliminated state can never be part of a consistent cut that satisfies the WCP. The checker can then advance the cut by considering the successor to one of the eliminated states on the cut. If the checker finds a cut for which no state can be eliminated, then that cut satisfies the WCP and the detection algorithm halts. The algorithm for the checker process is shown in Figure 10.1.

The checker receives local snapshots from the other processes in the system. These messages are used by the checker to create and maintain data structures that describe the global state of the system for the current cut. The data structures are divided into two categories: queues of incoming messages and those data structures that describe the state of the processes.

The queue of incoming messages is used to hold incoming local snapshots from

```
import java.util.*;
public class CentSensor extends Process implements Runnable, Sensor {
    final static int red = 0, green = 1;
    LinkedList q[]; // q[i] stores vector timestamps from process i
    int cut[][], color[], gstate[];
    boolean finished[]; // process i finished
    SensorUser app; final int checker = Symbols.coordinator;
    public CentSensor(VCLinker initComm, SensorUser app) {
        super(initComm);
        cut = new int[N][N]; q = new LinkedList[N];
        color = new int[N]; gstate = new int[N]; finished = new boolean[N];
        for (int i = 0; i < N; i++) {
            q[i] = new LinkedList(); color[i] = red; finished[i] = false;
        }
        this.app = app;
        if (myId == checker) new Thread(this).start();
    }
    public synchronized void localPredicateTrue(VectorClock vc){
        if (myId == checker)
            handleMsg(new Msg(0,0,"trueVC", vc.toString()),0,"trueVC");
        else
            ((VCLinker)comm).simpleSendMsg(checker,"trueVC",vc.toString());
    }
    public synchronized void run() {
        int i = Util.searchArray(color, red);
        while (i != -1) {
            while (q[i].isEmpty() && !finished[i]) myWait();
            if (finished[i]) {
                app.globalPredicateFalse(i);
                return;
            }
            cut[i] = (int[]) q[i].removeFirst();
            paintState(i);
            i = Util.searchArray(color, red);
        }
        for (int j = 0; j < N; j++) gstate[j] = cut[j][j];
        app.globalPredicateTrue(gstate);
    }
    public synchronized void handleMsg(Msg m, int src, String tag){
        if (tag.equals("trueVC")) {
            int[] receiveTag = new int[N];
            Util.readArray(m.getMessage(), receiveTag);
            q[src].add(receiveTag); notify();
        } else if (tag.equals("finished")) {
            finished[src] = true; notify();
        }
    }
    void paintState(int i) {
        color[i] = green;
        for (int j = 0; j < N; j++)
            if (color[j] == green)
                if (Util.lessThan(cut[i], cut[j])) color[i] = red;
                else if (Util.lessThan(cut[j], cut[i])) color[j] = red;
    }
}
```

Figure 10.1: WCP (weak conjunctive predicate) detection algorithm—checker process.

application processes. We require that messages from an individual process be received in FIFO order. We abstract the message-passing system as a set of N FIFO queues, one for each process. We use the notation $q[1 \dots N]$ to label these queues in the algorithm.

The checker also maintains information describing one state from each process P_i. cut[i] represents the state from P_i using the vector clock. Thus, cut[i][j] denotes the jth component of the vector clock of cut[i]. The color[i] of a state cut[i] is either red or green and indicates whether the state has been eliminated in the current cut. A state is green only if it is concurrent with all other green states. A state is red only if it cannot be part of a consistent cut that satisfies the WCP.

The aim of advancing the cut is to find a new candidate cut. However, we can advance the cut only if we have eliminated at least one state along the current cut and if a message can be received from the corresponding process. The data structures for the processes are updated to reflect the new cut. This is done by the procedure paintState. The parameter i is the index of the process from which a local snapshot was most recently received. The color of cut[i] is temporarily set to green. It may be necessary to change some green states to red to preserve the property that all green states are mutually concurrent. Hence, we must compare the vector clock of cut[i] to each of the other green states. Whenever the states are comparable, the smaller of the two is painted red.

Let N denote the number of processes involved in the WCP and m denote the maximum number of messages sent or received by any process.

The main time complexity is involved in detecting the local predicates and time required to maintain vector clocks. In the worst case, one debug message is generated for each program message sent or received, so the worst-case message complexity is $O(m)$. In addition, program messages have to include vector clocks.

The main space requirement of the checker process is the buffer for the local snapshots. Each local snapshot consists of a vector clock that requires $O(N)$ space. Since there are at most $O(mN)$ local snapshots, $O(N^2 m)$ total space is required to hold the component of local snapshots devoted to vector clocks. Therefore, the total amount of space required by the checker process is $O(N^2 m)$.

We now discuss the time complexity of the checker process. Note that it takes only two comparisons to check whether two vectors are concurrent. Hence, each invocation of *paintState* requires at most N comparisons. This function is called at most once for each state, and there are at most mN states. Therefore, at most $N^2 m$ comparisons are required by the algorithm.

10.3 Application: Distributed Debugging

Assume that a programmer is interested in developing an application in which there is a *leader* or a *coordinator* at all times. Since the leader has to perform more work than other nodes, the programmer came up with the idea of circulating a token in the network and requiring that whichever node has the token acts as the leader. We will assume that this is accomplished using the class CircToken discussed in Chapter 8. Now, the programmer wants to ensure that his program is correct. He constructs the bad condition as "there is no coordinator in the system." This condition can be equivalently written as "P_1 does not have the token, and P_2 does not have the token," and so on for all processes. To see if this condition becomes true, the programmer must modify his program to send a vector clock to the sensor whenever the local condition "does not have the token" becomes true. Figure 10.2 shows the circulating token application modified to work with the class Sensor. Figure 10.3 shows the main application that runs the application with the sensor. This program has an additional command-line argument that specifies which sensor algorithm needs to be invoked as sensor—the centralized algorithm discussed in this section, or the distributed algorithm discussed in the next section.

When the programmer runs the program, he may discover that the global condition actually becomes true, that is, there is a global state in which there is no coordinator in the system. This simple test exposed the fallacy in the programmer's thinking. The token may be in transit and at that time there is no coordinator in the system.

We leave it for the reader to modify the circulating token application in which a process continues to act as the leader until it receives an acknowledgment for the token. This solution assumes that the application work correctly even if there are two processes acting as the leader temporarily.

10.4 A Token-Based Algorithm for Detecting Predicates

Up to this point we have described detection of WCP on the basis of a checker process. The checker process in the vector-clock-based centralized algorithm requires $O(N^2m)$ time and space, where m is the number of messages sent or received by any process and N is the number of processes over which the predicate is defined. We now introduce token-based algorithms that distribute the computation and space requirements of the detection procedure. The distributed algorithm has $O(N^2m)$ time, space, and message complexity, distributed such that each process performs $O(Nm)$ work.

We introduce a new set of N *monitor processes*. One monitor process is mated

```
public class SensorCircToken extends CircToken
implements MsgHandler, SensorUser {
    VCLinker comm;
    Sensor checker;
    int coordinator;
    int algoCode;
    public SensorCircToken(VCLinker comm, int coordinator, int algoCode){
        super(comm, coordinator);
        this.comm = comm;
        this.coordinator = coordinator;
        this.algoCode = algoCode;
    }
    public void initiate () {
        if ( algoCode == 0)
            checker = new CentSensor(comm, this);
        else
            checker = new DistSensor(comm, this);
        if (!haveToken) checker.localPredicateTrue(comm.vc);
        super.initiate ();
    }
    public synchronized void sendToken() {
        super.sendToken ();
        if (!haveToken) checker.localPredicateTrue(comm.vc);
    }
    public synchronized void handleMsg(Msg m, int src, String tag){
        checker.handleMsg(m, src, tag);
        super.handleMsg(m, src, tag);
    }
    public void globalPredicateTrue(int v[]){
        System.out.println ("*************************************");
        System.out.println ("Predicate true at:" + Util.writeArray(v));
    }
    public void globalPredicateFalse(int pid){
        System.out.println ("*************************************");
        System.out.println ("Predicate false. Proc " + pid + " finished");
    }
}
```

Figure 10.2: Circulating token with vector clock

```
public class SensorTester {
    public static void main(String[] args) throws Exception {
        String baseName = args[0];
        int myId = Integer.parseInt(args[1]);
        int numProc = Integer.parseInt(args[2]);
        VCLinker comm = new VCLinker(baseName, myId, numProc);
        int algoCode = Integer.parseInt(args[3]);
        SensorCircToken sp = new SensorCircToken(
                    comm, Symbols.coordinator, algoCode);
        sp.initiate();
        for (int i = 0; i < numProc; i++)
            if (i != myId) (new ListenerThread(i, sp)).start();
    }
}
```

Figure 10.3: An application that runs circulating token with a sensor

to each application process. The application processes interact according to the distributed application. In addition, the application processes send local snapshots to monitor processes. The monitor processes interact with each other but do not send any information to the application processes.

The distributed WCP detection algorithm shown in Figure 10.4 uses a unique token. The token contains two vectors. The first vector is labeled G. This vector defines the current candidate cut. If $G[i]$ has the value k, then state k from process P_i is part of the current candidate cut. Note that all states on the candidate cut satisfy local predicates. However, the states may not be mutually concurrent, that is, the candidate cut may not be a consistent cut. The token is initialized with $\forall i : G[i] = 0$.

The second vector is labeled $color$, where $color[i]$ indicates the color for the candidate state from application process P_i. The color of a state can be either red or $green$. If $color[i]$ equals red, then the state $(i, G[i])$ and all its predecessors have been eliminated and can never satisfy the WCP. If $color[i] = green$, then there is no state in G such that $(i, G[i])$ happened before that state. The token is initialized with $\forall i : color[i] = red$.

The token is sent to monitor process M_i only when $color[i] = red$. When it receives the token, M_i waits to receive a new candidate state from P_i and then checks for violations of consistency conditions with this new candidate. This activity is repeated until the candidate state does not causally precede any other state on the candidate cut, that is, the candidate can be labeled green. Next, M_i examines the token to see if any other states violate concurrency. If it finds any j such that $(j, G[j])$ happened before $(i, G[i])$, then it makes $color[j]$ red. Finally, if all states

```
var
    // vector clock from the candidate state
    candidate: array[1..n] of integer initially 0;

Upon receiving the token (G, color)
    while (color[i] = red) do
        receive candidate from application process Pi;
        if (candidate[i] > G[i]) then
            G[i] := candidate[i];
            color[i] := green;
        endif;
    endwhile;
    for j := 1 to  n, (j ≠ i) do
        if (candidate[j] ≥ G[j]) then
            G[j] := candidate[j];
            color[j] := red;
        endif
    endfor
    if (∃j : color[j] = red) then send token to Mj;
    else detect := true;
```

Figure 10.4: Monitor process algorithm at P_i

in G are green, that is, G is consistent, then M_i has detected the WCP. Otherwise, M_i sends the token to a process whose color is red.

The implementation for the algorithm is given in Figure 10.5. It uses three types of messages. The *trueVC* message is sent by the application process to the monitor process whenever the local predicate becomes true in a message interval. This message includes the value of the vector clock when the local predicate became true. This vector is stored in the queue q. The *Token* message denotes the token used in the description of the algorithm. Whenever a monitor process receives the token, it invokes the method `handleToken` described later. For simplicity of implementation, we send the G vector and the `color` vector separately. The *finished* message from the application process indicates that it has ended and that there will not be any more messages from it.

Let us now look at the `handleToken` method. The goal of the process is to make the entry `color[i]` green. If there is no pending vector in the queue q, then the monitor process simply waits for either a *trueVC* or a *finished* message to arrive. If there is no pending vector and the finished message has been received, then we know that the global predicate can never be true and thus it is declared to be false for this computation. If a vector, `candidate`, is found such that `candidate[i] > G[i]`, then the global cut is advanced to include `candidate[i]`. This advancement may result in `color[j]` becoming red if `candidate[j] ≥ G[j]`. The method `getRed` determines the first process that has red color. If the array `color` is completely green, `getRed` returns -1, and the global predicate is detected to be true. Otherwise, the token is sent to the process returned by `getRed`.

Let us analyze the time complexity of the algorithm. It is easy to see that whenever a process receives the token, it deletes at least one local state, that is, it receives at least one message from the application process. Every time a state is eliminated, $O(N)$ work is performed by the process with the token. There are at most mN states; therefore, the total computation time for all processes is $O(N^2m)$. The work for any process in the distributed algorithm is at most $O(Nm)$. The analysis of message and space complexity is left as an exercise (see Problem 10.4).

10.5 Problems

10.1. Show that it is sufficient to send the vector clock once after each message is sent irrespective of the number of messages received.

10.2. Assume that the given global predicate is a simple conjunction of local predicates. Further assume that the global predicate is stable. In this scenario, both Chandy and Lamport's algorithm and the weak conjunctive algorithm

```
import java.util.*;
public class DistSensor extends Process implements Runnable,Sensor {
    final static int red = 0, green = 1;
    int candidate [], color [],G[];
    boolean finished = false, haveToken = false;
    LinkedList q = new LinkedList ();
    SensorUser app;
    public DistSensor(VCLinker initComm, SensorUser app) {
        super(initComm); this.app = app;
        candidate = new int [N]; color = new int [N]; G = new int [N];
        for (int j=0; j < N; j++) { color [j] = red; G[j] = 0;}
        if (myId == Symbols.coordinator) haveToken=true;
        new Thread(this).start ();
    }
    public synchronized void run (){
        while (!finished) {
            while (!haveToken) myWait ();
            handleToken ();
        }
    }
    public synchronized void handleToken () {
        while (color [myId] == red) {
            while (q.isEmpty() && !finished) myWait ();
            if (q.isEmpty() && finished) {
                app.globalPredicateFalse (myId); return;
            }
            candidate = (int []) q.removeFirst ();
            if (candidate [myId] > G[myId]) {
                G[myId] = candidate [myId]; color [myId] = green;
            }
        }
        for (int j = 0; j < N; j++)
            if ((j != myId) && (candidate [j] >= G[j])) {
                G[j] = candidate [j]; color [j] = red;
            }
        int j = Util.searchArray (color, red);
        if (j != -1) sendToken (j);
        else { app.globalPredicateTrue (G); finished = true; }
    }
    public synchronized void handleMsg (Msg m, int src, String tag) {
        if (tag.equals ("TokenG")) Util.readArray (m.getMessage (), G);
        else if (tag.equals ("Tokencolor")) {
            Util.readArray (m.getMessage (), color);
            haveToken = true;
        } else if (tag.equals ("finished")) finished = true;
        notifyAll ();
    }
    void sendToken (int j) {
        ((VCLinker) comm).simpleSendMsg (j, "TokenG", Util.writeArray (G));
        ((VCLinker) comm).simpleSendMsg (j,"Tokencolor", Util.writeArray (color));
        haveToken = false;
    }
    public synchronized void localPredicateTrue (VectorClock vc) {
        q.add(vc.v); notifyAll ();
    }
}
```

Figure 10.5: Token-based WCP detection algorithm.

can be used to detect the global predicate. What are the advantages and disadvantages of using each of them?

10.3. Show that if the given weak conjunctive predicate has a conjunct from each of the processes, then direct dependency clocks can be used instead of the vector clocks in the implementation of sensors. Give an example showing that if there is a process that does not have any conjunct in the global predicate, then direct dependency clocks cannot be used.

10.4. Show that the message complexity of the vector-clock-based distributed algorithm is $O(mN)$, the bit complexity (number of bits communicated) is $O(N^2 m)$, and the space complexity is $O(mN)$ entries per process.

10.5. The main drawback of the single-token WCP detection algorithm is that it has no concurrency—a monitor process is active only if it has the token. Design an algorithm that uses multiple tokens in the system. [*Hint:* Partition the set of monitor processes into g groups and use one token-algorithm for each group. Once there are no longer any red states from processes within the group, the token is returned to a predetermined process (say, P_0). When P_0 has received all the tokens, it merges the information in the g tokens to identify a new global cut. Some processes may not satisfy the consistency condition for this new cut. If so, a token is sent into each group containing such a process.]

10.6. Design a hierarchical algorithm to detect WCP based on ideas in the previous exercise.

10.7. Show the following properties of the vector-clock-based algorithm for WCP detection: for any i,
   1. $G[i] \neq 0 \land color[i] = red \Rightarrow \exists j : j \neq i : (i, G[i]) \rightarrow (j, G[j])$;
   2. $color[i] = green \Rightarrow \forall k : (i, G[i]) \not\rightarrow (k, G[k])$;
   3. $(color[i] = green) \land (color[j] = green) \Rightarrow (i, G[i]) \| (j, G[j])$.
   4. If $(color[i] = red)$, then there is no global cut satisfying the WCP which includes $(i, G[i])$.

10.8. Show the following claim for the vector-clock-based distributed WCP detection algorithm: The flag *detect* is true with G if and only if G is the smallest global state that satisfies the WCP.

*10.9. (due to Hurfin et al.[HMRS95]) Assume that every process communicates with every other process directly or indirectly infinitely often. Design a distributed algorithm in which information is piggybacked on existing program messages to detect a conjunctive predicate under this assumption, that is, the algorithm does not use any additional messages for detection purposes.

10.6   Bibliographic Remarks

Detection of conjunctive properties was first discussed by Garg and Waldecker[GW92]. Distributed online algorithms for detecting conjunctive predicates were first presented by Garg and Chase [GC95]. Hurfin et al.[HMRS95] were the first to give a distributed algorithm that does not use any additional messages for predicate detection. Their algorithm piggybacks additional information on program messages to detect conjunctive predicates. Distributed algorithms for offline evaluation of global predicates are also discussed in Venkatesan and Dathan [VD92]. Stoller and Schneider [SS95] have shown how Cooper and Marzullo's algorithm can be integrated with that of Garg and Waldecker to detect conjunction of global predicates. Lower bounds on these algorithms were discussed by Garg [Gar92].

Chapter 11

Detecting Termination and Deadlocks

11.1 Introduction

Termination and deadlocks are crucial predicates in a distributed system. Generally, computations are expected to terminate and be free from deadlocks. It is an important problem in distributed computing to develop efficient algorithms for termination and deadlock detection. Note that both termination and deadlock are stable properties and therefore can be detected using any global snapshot algorithm. However, these predicates can be detected even more efficiently than general stable predicates. The reason for this efficiency is that these predicates are not only stable but also *locally stable*—the state of each process involved in the predicate does not change when the predicate becomes true. We will later define and exploit the locally stable property of the predicates to design efficient distributed algorithms.

To motivate termination detection, we consider a class of distributed computations called *diffusing* computations. We give a diffusing computation for the problem of determining the shortest path from a fixed process. The diffusing computation algorithm works except that one does not know when the computation has terminated.

11.2 Diffusing Computation

Consider a computation on a distributed system that is started by a special process called *environment*. This process starts up the computation by sending messages to some of the processes. Each process in the system is either *passive* or *active*. It is assumed that a passive process can become active only on receiving a message (an active process can become passive at any time). Furthermore, a message can be sent by a process only if it is in the active state. Such a computation is called a *diffusing computation*. Algorithms for many problems such as computing the breadth-first search-spanning tree in an asynchronous network or determining the shortest paths from a processor in a network can be structured as diffusing computations.

We use a distributed shortest-path algorithm to illustrate the concepts of a diffusing computation. Assume that we are interested in finding the shortest path from a fixed process called a *coordinator* (say, P_0) to all other processes. Each process initially knows only the average delay of all its *incoming* links in the array edgeWeight. A diffusing computation to compute the shortest path is quite simple. Every process P_i maintains the following variables:

1. cost: represents the cost of the shortest path from the coordinator to P_i as known to P_i currently

2. parent: represents the predecessor of P_i in the shortest path from the coordinator to P_i as known to P_i currently

The coordinator acts as the environment and starts up the diffusing computation by sending the cost of the shortest path to be 0 using a message type *path*. Any process P_i that receives a message from P_j of type *path* with cost c determines whether its current cost is greater than the cost of reaching P_j plus the cost of reaching from P_j to P_i. If that is indeed the case, then P_i has discovered a path of shorter cost and it updates the cost and parent variables. Further, any such update results in messages to its neighbors about its new cost. The algorithm is shown in Figure 11.1. Each process calls the method initiate to start the program. This call results in the coordinator sending out messages with cost 0. The method handleMsg simply handles messages of type *path*.

The algorithm works fine with one catch. No process ever knows when it is done, that is, the cost variable will not decrease further. In this chapter, we study how we can extend the computation to detect termination. Figure 11.2 shows the interface implemented by the termination detection algorithm. Any application which uses a TermDetector must invoke initiate at the beginning of the program, sendAction on sending a message, and turnPassive on turning passive.

From properties of a diffusing computation, it follows that if all processes are passive in the system and there are no messages in transit, then the computation has terminated. Our problem is to design a protocol by which the environment process can determine whether the computation has terminated. Our solution is based on an algorithm by Dijkstra and Scholten.

```
public class ShortestPath extends Process {
    int parent = -1;
    int cost = -1;
    int edgeWeight [] = null;
    public ShortestPath (Linker initComm, int initCost []) {
        super (initComm);
        edgeWeight = initCost;
    }
    public synchronized void initiate () {
        if (myId == Symbols.coordinator) {
            parent = myId;
            cost = 0;
            sendToNeighbors ("path", cost);
        }
    }
    public synchronized void handleMsg (Msg m, int src, String tag){
        if (tag.equals ("path")) {
            int dist = m.getMessageInt ();
            if ((parent == -1) || (dist + edgeWeight[src] < cost)) {
                parent = src;
                cost = dist + edgeWeight[src];
                System.out.println ("New cost is " + cost);
                sendToNeighbors ("path", cost);
            }
        }
    }
}
```

Figure 11.1: A diffusing computation for the shortest path

```
public interface TermDetector {
    public void initiate ();
    public void sendAction ();
    public void turnPassive ();
    public void handleMsg (Msg m, int srcsId, String tag);
}
```

Figure 11.2: Interface for a termination detection algorithm

11.3 Dijkstra and Scholten's Algorithm

We say that a process is in a *green* state if it is passive and all of its outgoing channels are empty; otherwise, it is in a *red* state. How can a process determine whether its outgoing channel is empty? This can be done if the receiver of the channel signals the sender of the channel the number of messages received along that channel. If the sender keeps a variable $D[i]$ (for deficit) for each outgoing channel i, which records the number of messages sent minus the number of messages that have been acknowledged via signals, it can determine that the channel i is empty by checking whether $D[i] = 0$. Observe that $D[i] \geq 0$ is always true. Therefore, if O is the set of all outgoing channels, it follows that

$$\forall i \in O : D[i] = 0$$

is equivalent to

$$\sum_{i \in O} D[i] = 0.$$

Thus it is sufficient for a process to maintain just one variable D that represents the total deficit for the process.

It is clear that if all processes are in the green state, then the computation has terminated. To check this condition, we will maintain a set T with the following invariant (I0):

(I0) All red processes are part of the set T.

Observe that green processes may also be part of T—the invariant is that there is no red process outside T. When the set T becomes empty, termination is true.

When the diffusing computation starts, the environment is the only red process initially (with nonempty outgoing channels); the invariant is made true by keeping environment in the set T. To maintain the invariant that all red processes are in T, we use the following rule. If P_j turns P_k red (by sending a message), and P_k is not in T, then we add P_k to T.

We now induce a directed graph (T, E) on the set T by defining the set of edges E as follows. We add an edge from P_j to P_k, if P_j was responsible for addition of P_k to the set T. We say that P_j is the parent of P_k. From now on we use the terms *node* and *process* interchangeably. Because every node (other than the environment) has exactly one parent and an edge is drawn from P_j to P_k only when P_k is not part of T, the edges E form a spanning tree on T rooted at the environment. Our algorithm will maintain this as invariant:

(I1) The edges E form a spanning tree of nodes in T rooted at the environment.

Up to now, our algorithm only increases the size of T. Because detection of termination requires the set to be empty, we clearly need a mechanism to remove nodes from T. Our rule for removal is simple—a node is removed from T only if it is a green-leaf node. When a node is removed from T, the incoming edge to that node is also removed from E. Thus the invariants (I0) and (I1) are maintained by this rule. To implement this rule, a node needs to keep track of the number of its children in T. This can be implemented by keeping a variable at each node *numchild* initialized to 0 that denotes the number of children it has in T. Whenever a new edge is formed, the child reports this to the parent by a special acknowledgment that also indicates that a new edge has been formed. When a leaf leaves T, it reports this to the parent, who decrements the count. If the node has no parent (it must be the environment) and it leaves the set T, then termination is detected. By assuming that a green-leaf node eventually reports to its parent, we conclude that once the computation terminates, it is eventually detected. Conversely, if termination is detected, then the computation has indeed terminated on account of invariant (I0).

Observe that the property that a node is green is not stable and hence a node, say, P_k, that is green may become active once again on receiving a message. However, because a message can be sent only by an active process, we know that some active process (which is already a part of the spanning tree) will be now responsible for the node P_k. Thus the tree T changes with time but maintains the invariant that all active nodes are part of the tree.

11.3.1 An Optimization

The algorithm given above can be optimized for the number of messages by combining messages from the reporting process and the messages for detecting whether a node is green. To detect whether an outgoing channel is empty, we assumed a mechanism by which the receiver tells the sender the number of messages it has received. One implementation could be based on control messages called *signal*. For every message received, a node is eventually required to send a signal message to the sender. To avoid the use of report messages, we require that a node not send the signal message for the message that made it active until it is ready to report to leave T. When it is ready to report, the signal message for the message that made it active is sent. With this constraint we get an additional property that a node will not turn green unless all its children in the tree have reported. Thus we have also eliminated the need for maintaining *numchild*: only a leaf node in the tree can be green. A node is ready to report when it has turned green, that is, it is passive and $D = 0$. The algorithm obtained after the optimization is shown in Figure 11.3.

The algorithm uses `state` to record the state of the process, `D` to record the deficit, and `parent` to record the parent of the process. There is no action required on `initiate`. The method `handleMsg` reduces deficit on receiving a *signal* message at line 15. If `D` becomes 0 for the environment process, then termination is detected at line 18. On receiving an application message, a node without parent sets the source of the message as the parent. In this case, no *signal* is sent back. This signal is sent at line 20 or line 38 when this node is passive and its `D` is 0. If the receiving node had a parent, then it simply sends a *signal* message back at line 29. The method `sendAction` increments the deficit and the method `turnPassive` changes `state` to passive and sends a *signal* to the parent if `D` is 0.

Now we can solve the original problem of computing the shortest path as shown in Figure 11.4.

11.4 Termination Detection without Acknowledgment Messages

Dijkstra and Scholten's algorithm required overhead of one acknowledgment message per application message. We now present an algorithm due to Safra as described by Dijkstra which does not use acknowledgment messages. This algorithm is based on a token going around the ring. The token collects the information from all processes and determines whether the computation has terminated. The algorithm shown in Figure 11.5 requires each process to maintain the following variables:

1. `state`: The state of a process is either *active* or *passive* as defined earlier.

2. `color`: The color of a process is either *white* or *black*. If the process is white, then it has not received any message since the last visit of the token. This variable is initialized to *white*.

3. `c`: This is an integer variable maintained by each process. It records the value of the number of messages sent by the process minus the number of messages received by that process. This variable is initialized to 0.

Process P_0 begins the detection probe by sending token to the next process when it is passive. The token consists of two fields: `color` and `count`. The `color` simply records if the token has seen any *black* process. The `count` records sum of all c variables seen in this round.

When a process receives the token, it keeps the token until it becomes passive. It then forwards the token to the next process, maintaining the invariants on the color of the token and the count of the token. Thus, if a black process forwards the token, the token turns black; otherwise the token keeps its color. The `count`

```
1 public class DSTerm extends Process implements TermDetector {
2     final static int passive = 0, active = 1;
3     int state = passive;
4     int D = 0;
5     int parent = -1;
6     boolean envtFlag;
7     public DSTerm(Linker initComm) {
8         super(initComm);
9         envtFlag = (myId == Symbols.coordinator);
10    }
11    public synchronized void initiate() {
12    }
13    public synchronized void handleMsg(Msg m, int src, String tag) {
14        if (tag.equals("signal")) {
15            D = D - 1;
16            if (D == 0) {
17                if (envtFlag)
18                    System.out.println("Termination Detected");
19                else if (state == passive) {
20                    sendMsg(parent, "signal");
21                    parent = -1;
22                }
23            }
24        } else { // application message
25            state = active;
26            if ((parent == -1) && !envtFlag) {
27                parent = src;
28            } else
29                sendMsg(src, "signal");
30        }
31    }
32    public synchronized void sendAction() {
33        D = D + 1;
34    }
35    public synchronized void turnPassive() {
36        state = passive;
37        if ((D == 0) && (parent != -1)) {
38            sendMsg(parent, "signal");
39            parent = -1;
40        }
41    }
42 }
```

Figure 11.3: Termination detection algorithm

```
public class TermShortestPath extends ShortestPath {
    TermDetector td = null;
    public TermShortestPath(Linker initComm, int initCost [],
                            TermDetector td) {
        super(initComm, initCost);
        this.td = td;
    }
    public synchronized void initiate () {
        super.initiate ();
        td.initiate ();
    }
    public synchronized void sendMsg(int dest, String tag, int msg) {
        super.sendMsg(dest, tag, msg);
        td.sendAction ();
    }
    public synchronized void handleMsg(Msg m, int src, String tag) {
        td.handleMsg(m, src, tag);
        super.handleMsg(m, src, tag);
        td.turnPassive ();
    }
}
```

Figure 11.4: A diffusing computation for the shortest path with termination

variable in the token is increased by c. The process resets its own color to *white* after sending the token.

Process P_0 is responsible for detecting termination. On receiving the token, P_0 detects termination, if its own color is *white*, it is *passive*, the token is *white* and the sum of token *count* and c is 0. If termination is not detected, then P_0 can start a new round of token passing. The correctness of this algorithm will be apparent after the discussion of locally stable predicates.

11.5   Locally Stable Predicates

We now show a technique that can be used for efficient detection of not only termination but many other locally stable predicates as well. A stable predicate B is *locally stable* if no process involved in the predicate can change its state relative to B once B holds. In other words, the values of all the variables involved in the predicate do not change once the predicate becomes true. The predicate B, "the distributed computation has terminated," is locally stable. It is clear that if B is true, the states of processes will not change. Similarly, once there is a deadlock in the system the processes involved in the deadlock do not change their state.

Now consider the predicate B, "there is at most one token in the system." This predicate is stable in a system which cannot create tokens. It is not locally stable because the state of a process can change by sending or receiving a token even when the predicate is true.

Since a locally stable predicate is also stable, one can use any global snapshot algorithm to detect it. However, computing a single global snapshot requires $O(e)$ messages, where e is the number of unidirectional channels. We will show that for locally stable predicates, one need not compute a *consistent* global state.

We first generalize the notion of a consistent cut to a consistent interval. An *interval* is a pair of cuts (possibly inconsistent) X and Y such that $X \subseteq Y$. We denote an interval by $[X, Y]$.

An interval of cuts $[X, Y]$ is *consistent* if there exists a consistent cut G such that $X \subseteq G \subseteq Y$. Note that $[G, G]$ is a consistent interval iff G is consistent. We now show that an interval $[X, Y]$ is consistent iff

$$\forall e, f : (f \in X) \wedge (e \to f) \Rightarrow e \in Y \tag{11.1}$$

First assume that $[X, Y]$ is a consistent interval. This implies that there exists a consistent cut G such that $X \subseteq G \subseteq Y$. We need to show that Equation (11.1) is true. Pick any e, f such that $f \in X$ and $e \to f$. Since $f \in X$ and $X \subseteq G$, we get that $f \in G$. From the fact that G is consistent, we get that $e \in G$. But $e \in G$ implies that $e \in Y$ because $G \subseteq Y$. Therefore Equation (11.1) is true.

```java
import java.util.*;
public class TermToken extends Process implements TermDetector {
    final static int passive = 0, active = 1, white = 0, black = 1;
    int state = passive, color = white;
    int c = 0;
    int next;
    boolean haveToken = false;
    int tokenCount = 0, tokenColor = white;
    public TermToken(Linker initComm) {
        super(initComm);
        next = (myId + 1) % N;
    }
    public synchronized void initiate() {
        if (myId == Symbols.coordinator) {
            if (state == passive) sendToken();
            else haveToken = true;
        }
    }
    public synchronized void handleMsg(Msg m, int src, String tag) {
        if (tag.equals("termToken")) {
            haveToken = true;
            StringTokenizer st = new StringTokenizer(m.getMessage());
            tokenColor = Integer.parseInt(st.nextToken());
            tokenCount = Integer.parseInt(st.nextToken());
            if (myId == Symbols.coordinator) {
                if ((c + tokenCount == 0) && (color == white) &&
                        (state == passive) && (tokenColor == white)) {
                    System.out.println("Termination Detected");
                    haveToken = false;
                }
            }
            if ((state == passive) && haveToken) sendToken();
        } else { // application message
            state = active;
            color = black;
            c = c - 1;
        }
    }
    public synchronized void sendAction() {
        c = c + 1;
    }
    public synchronized void turnPassive() {
        state = passive;
        if (haveToken) sendToken();
    }
    void sendToken() {
        if (myId == Symbols.coordinator)
            sendMsg(next, "termToken", white, 0);
        else if ((color == black) || (tokenColor == black))
            sendMsg(next, "termToken", black, c + tokenCount);
        else
            sendMsg(next, "termToken", white, c + tokenCount);
        haveToken = false;
        color = white;
    }
}
```

Figure 11.5: Termination detection by token traversal.

Conversely, assume that Equation (11.1) is true. We define the cut G as follows:

$$G = \{e \in E \mid \exists f \in X : (e \to f) \lor (e = f)\}$$

Clearly, $X \subseteq G$ from the definition of G and $G \subseteq Y$ because of Equation (11.1). We only need to show that G is consistent. Pick any c, d such that $c \to d$ and $d \in G$. From the definition of G, there exists $f \in X$ such that $d = f$ or $d \to f$. In either case, $c \to d$ implies that $c \to f$ and therefore $c \in G$. Hence, G is consistent.

Our algorithm will exploit the observation presented above as follows. It repeatedly computes consistent intervals $[X, Y]$ and checks if B is true in Y and the values of variables have not changed in the interval. If both these conditions are true, then we know that there exists a consistent cut G in the interval with the same values of (relevant) variables as Y and therefore has B true. Conversely, if a predicate is locally stable and it turns true at a global state G, then all consistent intervals $[X, Y]$ such that $G \subseteq X$ will satisfy both the conditions checked by the algorithm.

Note that computing a consistent interval is easier than computing a consistent cut. To compute a consistent interval, we need to compute any two cuts X and Y, such that $X \subseteq Y$ and Equation (11.1) holds. To ensure that Equation (11.1) holds, we will use the notion of *barrier synchronization*. Let X and Y be any cuts such that $X \subseteq Y$ (i.e., $[X, Y]$ is an interval) and Y has at least one event on every process. We say that an interval $[X, Y]$ is barrier-synchronized if

$$\forall g \in X \land h \in E - Y : g \to h$$

Intuitively, this means that every event in X happened before every event that is not in Y. If $[X, Y]$ are barrier synchronized, then they form a consistent interval. Assume, if possible, that $[X, Y]$ is not a consistent interval. Then there exist e, f such that $f \in X$, $e \to f$, but $e \notin Y$. But $e \notin Y$ implies that $f \to e$ which contradicts $e \to f$.

Barrier synchronization can be achieved in a distributed system in many ways. For example

1. P_0 sends a token to P_1 which sends it to the higher-numbered process until it reaches P_{N-1}. Once it reaches P_{N-1}, the token travels in the opposite direction. Alternatively, the token could simply go around the ring twice. These methods require every process to handle only $O(1)$ messages with total $O(N)$ messages for all processes but have a high latency.

2. All processes send a message to P_0. After receiving a message from all other processes, P_0 sends a message to everybody. This method requires total $O(N)$ messages and has a low latency but requires the coordinator to handle $O(N)$ messages.

3. All processes send messages to everybody else. This method is symmetric and has low latency but requires $O(N^2)$ messages.

Clearly, in each of these methods a happened-before path is formed from every event before the barrier synchronization to every process after the synchronization.

Now detecting a locally stable predicate B is simple. The algorithm repeatedly collects two barrier synchronized cuts $[X, Y]$. If the predicate B is true in cut Y and the values of the variables in the predicate B have not changed during the interval, then B is announced to be true in spite of the fact that B is evaluated only on possibly inconsistent cuts X and Y.

11.6   Application: Deadlock Detection

We illustrate the technique for detecting locally stable predicates for *deadlocks*. A deadlock in a distributed system can be characterized using the wait-for graph (WFG): a graph with nodes as processes and an edge from P_i to P_j if P_i is waiting for P_j for a resource to finish its job or *transaction*. Thus, an edge from P_i to P_j means that there exist one or more resources held by P_j without which P_i cannot proceed. We have assumed that a process needs all the resources for which it is waiting to finish its job. Clearly, if there is a cycle in the WFG, then processes involved in the cycle will wait forever. This is called a *deadlock*.

A simple approach to detecting deadlocks based on the idea of locally stable predicates is as follows. We use a coordinator to collect information from processes in the system. Each process P_i maintains its local WFG, that is, all the edges in the WFG that are outgoing from P_i. It also maintains a bit *changed$_i$*, which records if its WFG has changed since its last report to the coordinator. The coordinator periodically sends a request message to all processes requesting their local WFGs. On receiving this request, a process sends its local WFG if the *changed$_i$* bit is true and "notChanged" message if *changed$_i$* is false. On receiving all local WFGs, the coordinator can combine them to form the global WFG. If this graph has a cycle, the coordinator sends a message to all processes to send their reports again. If *changed$_i$* is false for all processes involved in the cycle, then the coordinator reports deadlock.

In this algorithm, even though WFGs are constructed possibly on inconsistent global states, we know, thanks to barrier synchronization, that there exists a consistent global state with the same WFG. Therefore, any deadlock reported actually happened in a consistent global state.

We leave the Java implementation of this algorithm as an exercise.

11.7 Problems

11.1. What is the message complexity of Dijkstra and Scholten's algorithm?

11.2. Give an algorithm based on diffusing computation to determine the breadth-first search tree from a given processor.

11.3. Extend Dijkstra and Scholten's algorithm for the case when there can be multiple initiators of the diffusing computation.

11.4. Prove the correctness of the token-based algorithm for termination detection.

11.5. Give a Java implementation of the two-phase deadlock detection algorithm.

11.8 Bibliographic Remarks

The spanning-tree-based algorithm discussed in this chapter is a slight variant of the algorithm proposed by Dijkstra and Scholten [DS80]. The token-based termination algorithm is due to Safra as described by Dijkstra [Dij87]. The notion of locally stable predicates is due to Marzullo and Sabel [MS94]. The notion of consistent interval and the algorithm of detecting locally stable predicates by using two cuts is due to Atreya, Mittal and Garg [AMG03]. The two-phase deadlock detection algorithm is due to Ho and Ramamoorthy [HR82].

Chapter 12

Message Ordering

12.1 Introduction

Distributed programs are difficult to design and test because of their nondeterministic nature, that is, a distributed program may exhibit multiple behaviors on the same external input. This nondeterminism is caused by reordering of messages in different executions. It is sometimes desirable to control this nondeterminism by restricting the possible message ordering in a system.

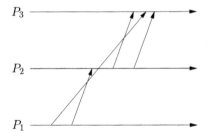

Figure 12.1: A FIFO computation that is not causally ordered

A *fully asynchronous* computation does not have any restriction on the message ordering. It permits maximum concurrency, but algorithms based on fully asynchronous communication can be difficult to design because they are required to work for all ordering of the messages. Therefore, many systems restrict message delivery to a FIFO order. This results in simplicity in design of distributed algorithms based on the FIFO assumption. For example, we used the FIFO assumption in Lamport's algorithm for mutual exclusion and Chandy and Lamport's algorithm for a global snapshot.

A FIFO-ordered computation is implemented generally by using sequence numbers for messages. However, observe that by using FIFO ordering, a program loses some of its concurrency. When a message is received out of order, its processing must be delayed.

A stronger requirement than FIFO is that of *causal ordering*. Intuitively, causal ordering requires that a single message not be overtaken by a sequence of messages. For example, the computation in Figure 12.1 satisfies FIFO ordering of messages but does not satisfy causal ordering. A sequence of messages from P_1 to P_2 and from P_2 to P_3 overtakes a message from P_1 to P_3 in this example. Causal ordering of messages is useful in many contexts. In Chapter 8, we considered the problem of mutual exclusion. Assume that we use a centralized coordinator for granting requests to the access of the critical section. The fairness property requires that the requests be honored in the order they are made (and not in the order they are received). It is easy to see that if the underlying system guaranteed a causal ordering of messages, then the order in which requests are received cannot violate the happened-before order in which they are made. For another example of the usefulness of causal ordering, see Problem 12.1.

The relationship among various message orderings can be formally specified on the basis of the happened-before relation. For convenience, we denote the receive event corresponding to the send event s_i by r_i and vice versa. The message is represented as (s_i, r_i). We also use $s_i \rightsquigarrow r_i$ to denote that r_i is the receive event corresponding to the send event s_i. Finally, we use $e \prec f$ to denote that e occurred before f in the same process.

Now, FIFO and causally ordered computations can be defined as follows:.

FIFO: Any two messages from a process P_i to P_j are received in the same order as they were sent. Formally, let s_1 and s_2 be any two send events and r_1 and r_2 be the corresponding receive events. Then

$$s_1 \prec s_2 \quad \Rightarrow \quad \neg(r_2 \prec r_1) \qquad\qquad \text{(FIFO)}$$

Causally Ordered: Let any two send events s_1 and s_2 in a distributed computation be related such that the first send happened before the second send. Then, the second message cannot be received before the first message by any process. Formally, this can be expressed as

$$s_1 \rightarrow s_2 \quad \Rightarrow \quad \neg(r_2 \prec r_1) \qquad\qquad \text{(CO)}$$

12.2   Causal Ordering

P_i::
>   **var**
>> M:array$[1..N,\ 1..N]$ of integer initially $\forall j,k : M[j,k] = 0$;
>
>   To send a message to P_j:
>> $M[i,j] := M[i,j] + 1$;
>>   piggyback M as part of the message;
>
>   To receive a message with matrix W from P_j
>>   **enabled if** $(W[j,i] = M[j,i]+1) \wedge (\forall k \neq j : M[k,i] \geq W[k,i])$
>> $M := max(M,W)$;

Figure 12.2: An algorithm for causal ordering of messages at P_i

We now describe an algorithm to ensure causal ordering of messages. We assume that a process never sends any message to itself. Each process maintains a matrix M of integers. The entry $M[j,k]$ at P_i records the number of messages sent by process P_j to process P_k as known by process P_i. The algorithm for process P_i is given in Figure 12.2. Whenever a message is sent from P_i to P_j, first the entry $M[i,j]$ is incremented to reflect the fact that one more message is known to be sent from P_i to P_j. The matrix M is piggybacked with the message. Whenever messages are received by the communication system at P_i, they are first checked for eligibility before delivery to P_i. If a message is not eligible, it is simply buffered until it becomes eligible. A message m from P_j is eligible to be received when

1. The entry $W[j,i]$ is one more than the entry $M[j,i]$ that records the number of messages received by P_i from P_j.

2. The number of messages sent from any other process $P_k (k \neq j)$ to P_i, as indicated by the matrix W in the message, is less than or equal to the number recorded in the matrix M. Formally, this condition is

$$\forall k \neq j : M[k,i] \geq W[k,i]$$

If for some k, $W[k,i] > M[k,i]$, then there is a message that was sent in the causal history of the message and has not arrived yet. Therefore, P_i must wait for that message to be delivered before it can accept the message m.

Whenever a message is accepted for delivery, the information at matrix M is updated with the matrix W received in the message.

The structure of a causal message is shown in Figure 12.3, and the Java implementation of the causal ordering algorithm is shown in Figure 12.4. The causal ordering algorithm extends the class `Linker` to include the matrix in outgoing messages. The method `sendMsg` increments the entry $M[myId][destId]$ to account for this message and attaches the matrix M with it. The method `multicast` is used for sending a message to multiple sites. In this method, we first increment $M[myId][destId]$ for all $destId$ in the list of destinations. It is this matrix that is sent with every message.

The method `okayToReceive` determines whether a message can be delivered to the process. The method `receiveMsg` uses two `LinkedList` for storing messages. The `deliverQ` stores all messages that are deliverable to the application layer. The `pendingQ` stores all messages that are received but are not deliverable. When the application layer asks for a message, the `pendingQ` is traversed first to check whether some messages are deliverable. Deliverable messages are moved from the `pendingQ` to the `deliveryQ` by the method `checkPendingQ`. If `deliveryQ` is empty, then we wait for a message to arrive by calling the blocking method `super.receiveMsg`. On receiving this message, it is put in the `pendingQ` and the method `checkPendingQ` is invoked again. If `deliveryQ` is nonempty, the first message from that queue is delivered and the matrix M updated to record the delivery of this message.

```
public class CausalMessage {
    Msg m;
    int N;
    int W[][];
    public CausalMessage (Msg m, int N, int matrix [][]) {
        this.m = m;
        this.N = N;
        W = matrix;
    }
    public int [][] getMatrix () {
        return W;
    }
    public Msg getMessage () {
        return m;
    }
}
```

Figure 12.3: Structure of a causal message

```
import java.util.*; import java.net.*; import java.io.*;
public class CausalLinker extends Linker {
    int M[][];
    LinkedList deliveryQ = new LinkedList(); // deliverable messages
    LinkedList pendingQ = new LinkedList(); // messages with matrix
    public CausalLinker(String basename, int id, int numProc)
                                                throws Exception {
        super(basename, id, numProc);
        M = new int[N][N]; Matrix.setZero(M);
    }
    public synchronized void sendMsg(int destId, String tag, String msg){
        M[myId][destId]++;
        super.sendMsg(destId, "matrix", Matrix.write(M));
        super.sendMsg(destId, tag, msg);
    }
    public synchronized void multicast(IntLinkedList destIds,
                                        String tag, String msg) {
        for (int i=0; i<destIds.size(); i++)
            M[myId][destIds.getEntry(i)]++;
        for (int i=0; i<destIds.size(); i++) {
            int destId = destIds.getEntry(i);
            super.sendMsg(destId, "matrix", Matrix.write(M));
            super.sendMsg(destId, tag, msg);
        }
    }
    boolean okayToRecv(int W[][], int srcId) {
        if (W[srcId][myId] > M[srcId][myId]+1) return false;
        for (int k = 0; k < N; k++)
            if ((k!=srcId) && (W[k][myId] > M[k][myId])) return false;
        return true;
    }
    synchronized void checkPendingQ() {
        ListIterator iter = pendingQ.listIterator(0);
        while (iter.hasNext()) {
            CausalMessage cm = (CausalMessage) iter.next();
            if (okayToRecv(cm.getMatrix(), cm.getMessage().getSrcId())){
                iter.remove(); deliveryQ.add(cm);
            }
        }
    }
    // polls the channel given by fromId to add to the pendingQ
    public Msg receiveMsg(int fromId) throws IOException {
        checkPendingQ();
        while (deliveryQ.isEmpty()) {
            Msg matrix = super.receiveMsg(fromId); // matrix
            int [][] W = new int[N][N];
            Matrix.read(matrix.getMessage(), W);
            Msg m1 = super.receiveMsg(fromId); //app message
            pendingQ.add(new CausalMessage(m1, N, W));
            checkPendingQ();
        }
        CausalMessage cm = (CausalMessage) deliveryQ.removeFirst();
        Matrix.setMax(M, cm.getMatrix());
        return cm.getMessage();
    }
}
```

Figure 12.4: CausalLinker for causal ordering of messages

12.2.1   Application: Causal Chat

To illustrate an application of causal ordering, we consider a chat application in which a user can send messages to multiple other users. This simple program, shown in Figure 12.5, takes as input from the user a message and the list of destination process identifiers. This message is then multicast to all the process identifiers in the list.

The application takes as an argument the message ordering to be used. The user can verify that if the plain `Linker` class were used in this application, then the following scenario would be possible. If P_0 sends a query to both P_1 and P_2, and P_1 sends a reply to the query to both P_0 and P_2, then P_2 may receive the reply before the query. On the other hand, if the class `CausalLinker` is used, then such a scenario is not possible.

12.3   Synchronous Ordering

Synchronous ordering is a stronger requirement than causal ordering. A computation satisfies synchronous ordering of messages if it is equivalent to a computation in which all messages are logically instantaneous. Figure 12.6 gives an example of a synchronously ordered computation and Figure 12.7, an example of a computation that does not satisfy synchronous ordering.

Algorithms for synchronous systems are easier to design than those for causally ordered systems. The model of synchronous message passing lets us reason about a distributed program under the assumption that messages are instantaneous or "points" rather then "intervals" (i.e., we can always draw the time diagrams for the distributed programs with the message arrows being vertical). If we assume messages as points instead of intervals, we can order the messages as a partial order and therefore, we can have vector clocks with respect to messages. One application for synchronous ordering of messages is that it enables us to reason about distributed objects as if they were centralized. Assume that a process invokes an operation on a remote object by sending a message. If synchronous ordering of messages is assumed, then all operations on the objects can be ordered according to when the messages are sent because messages can be considered instantaneous.

A computation is synchronous if its time diagram can be drawn such that all message arrows are vertical, that is, all external events can be assigned a timestamp such that time increases within a single process, and for any message its send and receive are assigned the same timestamp. Formally, let $\mathcal{E}$ be the set of all external events. Then, a computation is synchronous iff there exists a mapping T from $\mathcal{E}$ to

```
import java.io.*; import java.util.*;
public class Chat extends Process {
    public Chat(Linker initComm) {
        super(initComm);
    }
    public synchronized void handleMsg(Msg m, int src, String tag){
        if (tag.equals("chat")) {
            System.out.println("Message from " + src +":");
            System.out.println(m.getMessage());
        }
    }
    public String getUserInput(BufferedReader din) throws Exception {
        System.out.println("Type your message in a single line:");
        String chatMsg = din.readLine();
        return chatMsg;
    }
    public IntLinkedList getDest(BufferedReader din) throws Exception {
        System.out.println("Type in destination pids with -1 at end:");
        System.out.println("Only one pid for synch order:");
        IntLinkedList destIds = new IntLinkedList(); //dest for msg
        StringTokenizer st = new StringTokenizer(din.readLine());
        while (st.hasMoreTokens()) {
            int pid = Integer.parseInt(st.nextToken());
            if (pid == -1) break;
            else destIds.add(pid);
        }
        return destIds;
    }
    public static void main(String[] args) throws Exception {
        String baseName = args[0];
        int myId = Integer.parseInt(args[1]);
        int numProc = Integer.parseInt(args[2]);
        Linker comm = null;
        if (args[3].equals("simple"))
            comm = new Linker(baseName, myId, numProc);
        else if (args[3].equals("causal"))
            comm = new CausalLinker(baseName, myId, numProc);
        else if (args[3].equals("synch"))
            comm = new SynchLinker(baseName, myId, numProc);
        Chat c = new Chat(comm);
        for (int i = 0; i < numProc; i++)
            if (i != myId) (new ListenerThread(i, c)).start();
        BufferedReader din = new BufferedReader(
        new InputStreamReader(System.in));
        while (true) {
            String chatMsg = c.getUserInput(din);
            if (chatMsg.equals("quit")) break;
            IntLinkedList destIds = c.getDest(din);
            if (args[3].equals("synch"))
                comm.sendMsg(destIds.getEntry(0), "chat", chatMsg);
            else
                comm.multicast(destIds, "chat", chatMsg);
        }
    }
}
```

Figure 12.5: A chat program

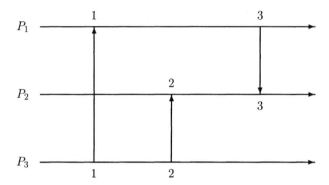

Figure 12.6: A computation that is synchronously ordered

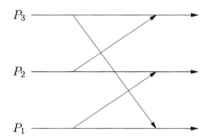

Figure 12.7: A computation that is not synchronously ordered

the set of natural numbers such that for all $s, r, e, f \in \mathcal{E}$

$$s \rightsquigarrow r \Rightarrow T(s) = T(r)$$

and

$$e \prec f \Rightarrow T(e) < T(f)$$

We call this condition SYNC. It is easy to see that, for any two external events e and f

$$(e \rightarrow f) \wedge \neg(e \rightsquigarrow f) \quad \Rightarrow \quad T(e) < T(f). \qquad (12.1)$$

We show that the hierarchy associated with the various message orderings is

Synchronous $\subseteq$ causally ordered $\subseteq$ FIFO $\subseteq$ asynchronous.

FIFO $\subseteq$ asynchronous is obvious. A causally ordered computation satisfies FIFO because

$$s_1 \prec s_2 \quad \Rightarrow \quad s_1 \rightarrow s_2.$$

We only need to show that if a computation is synchronous then it is also causally ordered. Because the communication is synchronous, there exists a function T satisfying SYNC.

For any set of send events s_1, s_2 and receive events r_1, r_2 such that $s_1 \rightsquigarrow r_1$, $s_2 \rightsquigarrow r_2$ and $s_1 \rightarrow s_2$:

$$T(s_1) = T(r_1), \quad T(s_2) = T(r_2), \quad \text{and} \quad T(s_1) < T(s_2).$$

It follows that $T(r_1) < T(r_2)$. Therefore, (12.1) implies

$$\neg(r_2 \rightarrow r_1).$$

The algorithm for synchronous ordering uses control messages. Note that control messages do not have to be synchronously ordered. Thus $\mathcal{E}$ includes the send and receive events only of application messages. It does not include send and receive of control messages sent by the algorithm to ensure synchronous ordering.

The algorithm shown in Figure 12.8 is for the process P_i. All processes have the same algorithm. Observe that the protocol to implement synchronous message ordering cannot be completely symmetric. If two processes desire to send messages to each other, then there is no symmetric synchronous computation that allows this—one of them must succeed before the other. To introduce asymmetry, we use process numbers to totally order all processes. We classify messages into *big* messages and *small* messages. A message sent from a (bigger) process to a smaller process is a *big* message and a message from a (smaller) process to a bigger process is called a *small* message. We assume that processes do not send messages to themselves.

In our algorithm, a process can be in two states—*active* or *passive*. Every process is initially active. We first consider the algorithm for a big message. A process is allowed to send a message to a smaller process only when it is active. After sending the message, it turns passive until it receives an *ack* message from the receiver of the message. While passive, it cannot send any other message, nor can it accept any other message. Note that the protocol for a message from a bigger process requires only one control message (*ack*).

To send a message to a bigger process, say, P_j, process P_i first needs permission from P_j. P_i can request the permission at any time. P_j can grant permission only when it is active. Furthermore, after granting the permission, P_j turns passive until it receives the message for which it has granted the permission. Thus the protocol for a message from a smaller process requires two control messages (*request* and *permission*). The implementation of synchronous ordering in Java is shown in Figure 12.9.

To prove correctness of the algorithm, we show that one can assign timestamps to all messages such that the timestamps of messages are in increasing order for any process. Each process maintains a local variable c that serves as the timestamping function for messages. The rules used by the algorithm are:

1. *Timestamp proposal*: When a process sends a *big* message, it increments c and sends c as the proposed timestamp with the message. For a *small* message, the timestamp is proposed in the *permission* message sent from the bigger process. Again, to make the proposal c is incremented and sent as a proposal. Thus the proposal of the timestamp is made by the bigger process for both types of messages. Note that as soon as a proposal is made, the process turns passive and cannot make any further proposals. A process can propose a timestamp only if it is active.

2. *Timestamp finalization*: When a process receives a proposal for a timestamp t, it can finalize the timestamp only if it is active. The timestamp assigned to this message is $max(c + 1, t)$. This timestamp is sent with the *ack* message or the *app* message, depending on whether the message is big or small. The new value of c is set to the finalized timestamp. When the proposer receives the final timestamp of the message, it assigns that timestamp to the message and sets its own clock to the maximum of the timestamp received and its own timestamp.

It is easy to verify that

P_i ::

    var

        $state$: $\{active, passive\}$ initially $active$;

    To send m to P_j, $(j < i)$
        enabled if $(state = active)$:
        send m to P_j
        $state := passive$;

    Upon receive m from P_j, $(j > i)$
        enabled if $(state = active)$:
        send ack to P_j;

    Upon receive ack:
        $state := active$;

    To send a message $(message\_id, m)$ to P_j, $(j > i)$
        send *request(message_id)* to P_j;

    Upon receive *request(message_id)* from P_j, $(j < i)$
        enabled if $(state = active)$:
        send *permission(message_id)* to P_j
        $state := passive$;

    Upon receive *permission(message_id)* from P_j, $(j > i)$
        enabled if $(state = active)$:
        send m to P_j;

    Upon receive m from P_j, $(j < i)$
        $state := active$;

Figure 12.8: The algorithm at P_i for synchronous ordering of messages

```
import java.io.*;
public class SynchLinker extends Linker {
    final static int passive = 0, active = 1;
    int state = active;
    private boolean granted;
    public SynchLinker(String basename, int id, int numProc)
    throws Exception {
        super(basename, id, numProc);
    }
    public synchronized void sendMsg(int destId, String tag, String msg) {
        if (destId < myId) { // big message
            waitForActive();
            super.sendMsg(destId, "app", " ");
            super.sendMsg(destId, tag, msg);
            state = passive;
        } else { // small message
            granted = false;
            super.sendMsg(destId, "request", " ");
            while (!granted) Util.myWait(this); // wait for permission
            super.sendMsg(destId, "app", " ");
            super.sendMsg(destId, tag, msg);
        }
    }
    synchronized void turnActive(){
        state = active; notifyAll();
    }
    synchronized void waitForActive(){
        while (state != active) Util.myWait(this);
    }
    synchronized void grant(){
        granted = true; notifyAll();
    }
    public Msg receiveMsg(int fromId) throws IOException {
        boolean done = false;
        Msg m = null;
        while (!done) { // app msg received
            m = super.receiveMsg(fromId);
            String tag = m.getTag();
            if (tag.equals("app")) {
                if (m.getSrcId() > myId) { // big message
                    waitForActive();
                    m = super.receiveMsg(fromId);
                    super.sendMsg(fromId, "ack", " ");
                } else { // small message
                    m = super.receiveMsg(fromId);
                    turnActive();
                }
                done = true;
            } else if (tag.equals("ack")) turnActive();
            else if (tag.equals("request")) {
                waitForActive();
                super.sendMsg(fromId, "permission", " ");
            } else if (tag.equals("permission")) grant();
        }
        return m;
    }
}
```

Figure 12.9: The algorithm for synchronous ordering of messages

1. No process decreases its clock, and each process increases its clock by at least one for successive messages.

2. The send and receive points of a message have the same timestamp.

12.4 Total Order for Multicast Messages

For synchronous ordering, we had assumed that messages were point-to-point. In applications where a message may be sent to multiple processes, it is often desirable that all messages be delivered in the same order at all processes. For example, consider a server that is replicated at multiple sites for fault tolerance. If a client makes a request to the server, then all copies of the server should handle requests in the same order. The total ordering of messages can be formally specified as follows:

For all messages x and y and all processes P and Q, if x is received at P before y, then y is not received before x at Q. (**Total Order**)

We require that y not be received before x, rather than that x be received before y, to address the case where x is not sent to Q. Observe that we do not require that a message be broadcast to all processes.

In this section we discuss algorithms for the total ordering of messages. Observe that the property of total order of messages does not imply causal or even FIFO property of messages. Consider the case when P sends messages m_1 followed by m_2. If all processes receive m_2 before m_1, then the total order is satisfied even though FIFO is not. If messages satisfy causal order in addition to the total order, then we will call this ordering of messages *causal total order*.

The algorithms for ensuring total order are very similar to mutual exclusion algorithms. After all, mutual exclusion algorithms ensure that all accesses to the critical section form a total order. If we ensure that messages are received in the "critical section" order, then we are done. We now discuss centralized and distributed algorithms for causal total ordering of messages.

12.4.1 Centralized Algorithm

We first modify the centralized algorithm for mutual exclusion to guarantee causal total ordering of messages. We assume that channels between the coordinator process and other processes satisfy the FIFO property. A process that wants to multicast a message simply sends it to the coordinator. This step corresponds to requesting the lock in the mutual exclusion algorithm. Furthermore, in that algorithm, the coordinator maintains a request queue, and whenever a request by a process becomes eligible, it sends the lock to that process. In the algorithm for total ordering of messages, the coordinator will simply multicast the message corresponding to the request instead of sending the lock. Since all multicast messages originate from the coordinator, and the channels are FIFO, the total-order property holds.

In this centralized algorithm, the coordinator has to perform more work than the other nodes. One way to perform load balancing over time is by suitably rotating the responsibility of the coordinator among processes. This can be achieved through the use of a token. The token assigns sequence numbers to broadcasts, and messages are delivered only in this sequence order.

12.4.2 Lamport's Algorithm for Total Order

We modify Lamport's algorithm for mutual exclusion to derive an algorithm for total ordering of messages. As in that algorithm, we assume FIFO ordering of messages. We also assume that a message is broadcast to all processes. To simulate multicast, a process can simply ignore a message that is not meant for it. Each process maintains a logical clock (used for timestamps) and a queue (used for storing undelivered messages). The algorithm is given by the following rules:

- To send a broadcast message, a process sends a timestamped message to all processes including itself. This step corresponds to requesting the critical section in the mutual exclusion algorithm.

- On receiving a broadcast message, the message and its timestamp are stored in the queue, and a timestamped acknowledgment is returned.

- A process can deliver the message with the smallest timestamp, t, in the request queue if it has received a message with timestamp greater than t from every other process. This step corresponds to executing the critical section for the mutual exclusion algorithm.

In this algorithm, the total order of messages delivered is given by the logical clock of send events of the broadcast messages.

12.4.3 Skeen's Algorithm

Lamport's algorithm is wasteful when most messages are multicast and not broadcast. Skeen's algorithm requires messages proportional to the number of recipients of a message and not the total number of processes in the system.

The distributed algorithm of Skeen also assumes that processes have access to Lamport's logical clock. The algorithm is given by the following rules:

- To send a multicast message, a process sends a timestamped message to all the destination processes.

- On receiving a message, a process marks it as *undeliverable* and sends the value of the logical clock as the proposed timestamp to the initiator.

- When the initiator has received all the proposed timestamps, it takes the maximum of all proposals and assigns that timestamp as the final timestamp to that message. This value is sent to all the destinations.

- On receiving the final timestamp of a message, it is marked as deliverable.

- A deliverable message is delivered to the site if it has the smallest timestamp in the message queue.

In this algorithm, the total order of message delivery is given by the final timestamps of the messages.

12.4.4   Application: Replicated State Machines

Assume that we are interested in providing a fault-tolerant service in a distributed system. The service is expected to process *requests* and provide *outputs*. We would also like the service to tolerate up to t faults where each fault corresponds to a crash of a processor. We can build such a service using $t + 1$ processors in a distributed system as follows. We structure our service as a *deterministic* state machine. This means that if each nonfaulty processor starts in the same initial state and executes the requests in the same order, then each will produce the same output. Thus, by combining outputs of the collection, we can get a t fault-tolerant service. The key requirement for implementation is that all state machines process all requests in the same order. The total ordering of messages satisfies this property.

12.5   Problems

12.1. Assume that you have replicated data for fault tolerance. Any file (or a record) may be replicated at more than one site. To avoid updating two copies of the data, assume that a token-based scheme is used. Any site possessing the token can update the file and broadcast the update to all sites that have that file. Show that if the communication is guaranteed to be causally ordered, then the scheme described above will ensure that all updates at all sites happen in the same order.

12.2. Let M be the set of messages in a distributed computation. Given a message x, we use $x.s$ to denote the send event and $x.r$ to denote the receive event. We say that a computation is *causally* ordered if

$$\forall x, y \in M : (x.s \rightarrow y.s) \Rightarrow \neg(y.r \rightarrow x.r).$$

We say that a computation is *mysteriously* ordered if

$$\forall x, y \in M : (x.s \to y.r) \Rightarrow \neg(y.s \to x.r).$$

(a) Prove or disprove that every causally ordered computation is also mysteriously ordered.
(b) Prove or disprove that every mysteriously ordered computation is also causally ordered.

12.3. Show the relationship between conditions (C1), (C2), and (C3) on message delivery of a system.

$$s_1 \to s_2 \Rightarrow \neg(r_2 \to r_1) \qquad\qquad (C1)$$

$$s_1 \prec s_2 \Rightarrow \neg(r_2 \to r_1) \qquad\qquad (C2)$$

$$s_1 \to s_2 \Rightarrow \neg(r_2 \prec r_1) \qquad\qquad (C3)$$

where s_1 and s_2 are sends of any two messages and r_1 and r_2 are the corresponding receives. Note that a computation satisfies a delivery condition if and only if the condition is true for all pairs of messages.

12.4. Assume that all messages are broadcast messages. How can you simplify the algorithm for guaranteeing causal ordering of messages under this condition?

12.5. Consider a system of $N+1$ processes $\{P_0, P_1, \ldots, P_N\}$ in which processes P_1 through P_N can only send messages to P_0 or receive messages from P_0. Show that if all channels in the system are FIFO, then any computation on this system is causally ordered.

12.6. In this chapter, we have used the happened-before model for modeling the dependency of one message to the other. Thus all messages within a process are totally ordered. For some applications, messages sent from a process may be independent. Give an algorithm to ensure causal ordering of messages when the send events from a single process do not form a total order.

12.7. Suppose that a system is composed of nonoverlapping groups such that any communication outside the group is always through the group leader, that is, only a group leader is permitted to send or receive messages outside the group. How will you exploit this structure to reduce the overhead in causal ordering of messages?

12.8. Design an algorithm for synchronous ordering for point-to-point messages that does not use a static priority scheme. (*Hint*: Impose an acyclic directed graph on processes. The edge from P_i to P_j means that P_i is bigger than P_j for the purpose of sending messages. Give a rule by which the direction of edges is reversed, such that acyclicity of the graph is maintained.)

12.9. Prove the correctness of Lamport's algorithm for providing causal total ordering of messages.

12.10. Prove the correctness of Skeen's algorithm for providing total ordering of messages.

12.11. Build a multiuser *Chat* application in Java that guarantees that all users see all messages in the same order.

12.6   Bibliographic Remarks

Causal ordering was first proposed by Birman and Joseph [BJ87]. The algorithm for causal ordering described in this chapter is essentially the same as that described by Raynal, Schiper, and Toueg [RST91]. The algorithm for implementing synchronous ordering is taken from a paper by Murty and Garg [MG95]. For a discussion on total ordering of messages, see the article by Birman and Joseph [BJ87]. The distributed algorithm for causal total ordering of messages is implicit in the replicated state machine construction described by Lamport [Lam78]. Skeen's algorithm is taken from the reference [Ske82].

Chapter 13

Leader Election

13.1 Introduction

Many distributed systems superimpose a logical ring topology on the underlying network to execute control functions. An important control function is that of electing a leader process. The leader can serve as a coordinator for centralized algorithms for problems such as mutual exclusion. Electing a leader in a ring can also be viewed as the problem of breaking symmetry in a system. For example, once a deadlock is detected in the form of a cycle, we may wish to remove one of the nodes in the cycle to remove the deadlock. This can be achieved by electing the leader.

We abstract the leader election problem using the interface `Election` shown below.

```
public interface Election extends MsgHandler {
    void startElection ();
    int getLeader (); //blocks till the leader is known
}
```

Any implementation of `Election` should provide the method `startElection`, which is invoked by one or more processes in the system. The method `getLeader` returns the identity of the leader. If the identity of the leader is not known, then this method blocks until the leader is elected.

The leader election problem is similar to the mutual exclusion problem discussed in Chapter 8. In both problems, we are interested in choosing one of the processes as a privileged process. Coordinator-based or token-based solutions for mutual exclusion are not applicable for the leader election problem, because deciding which process can serve as the coordinator or has the token is precisely the leader election problem. If processes have unique identifiers and the underlying communication network is completely connected, then we can apply Lamport's mutual exclusion algorithm to determine the leader—the first process to enter the critical section is deemed as the leader. However, this algorithm requires every process to communicate with every other process in the worst case. We will explore more efficient algorithms for the ring topology.

13.2   Ring-Based Algorithms

A ring is considered anonymous if processes in the ring do not have unique identifiers. Furthermore, every process has an identical state machine with the same initial state.

It is not difficult to see that there is no deterministic algorithm for leader election in an anonymous ring. The reason is that we have complete symmetry initially—no process is distinguishable from other processes. Because there is a unique leader, we know that the system can never terminate in a symmetric state. Thus the algorithm has not terminated in the initial state. We now show an execution that moves the system from one symmetric state to the other. Assume that any process in the ring takes a step. By symmetry, this step is possible at all processes. Thus in the adversarial execution all processes take the same step. Since the algorithm is deterministic, the system must again reach a symmetric state. Therefore, the system could not have terminated (i.e., the leader could not have been elected yet). We can repeat this procedure forever.

Observe that our argument uses the fact that the algorithm is deterministic. A randomized algorithm can solve the leader election problem in expected finite time (see Problem 13.1).

13.2.1   Chang–Roberts Algorithm

Now assume that each process has a unique identifier. In such a system, a leader can be elected in a ring by a very simple algorithm due to Chang and Roberts. The algorithm ensures that the process with the maximum identifier gets elected as the leader. In the algorithm shown in Figure 13.1, every process sends messages only to its left neighbor and receives messages from its right neighbor. A process can send an *election* message along with its identifier to its left, if it has not seen any message with a higher identifier than its own identifier. It also forwards any message that has an identifier greater than its own; otherwise, it swallows that message. If a process receives its own message, then it declares itself as the leader by sending a *leader* message. When a process receives its own *leader* message, it knows that everybody knows the leader.

In the algorithm, one or more processes may spontaneously wake up and initiate the election using the method `startElection`. When a process wakes up on receiving a message from a process with a smaller identifier, it circulates its own *election* message.

Note that the algorithm does not require any process to know the total number of processes in the system.

```java
public class RingLeader extends Process implements Election {
    int number;
    int leaderId = -1;
    int next;
    boolean awake = false;
    public RingLeader(Linker initComm, int number) {
        super(initComm);
        this.number = number;
        next = (myId + 1) % N;
    }
    public synchronized int getLeader(){
        while (leaderId == -1) myWait();
        return leaderId;
    }
    public synchronized void handleMsg(Msg m, int src, String tag) {
        int j = m.getMessageInt(); // get the number
        if (tag.equals("election")) {
            if (j > number)
                sendMsg(next, "election", j); // forward the message
            else if (j == number) // I won!
                sendMsg(next, "leader", myId);
            else if ((j < number) && !awake) startElection();
        } else if (tag.equals("leader")) {
            leaderId = j;
            notify();
            if (j != myId) sendMsg(next, "leader", j);
        }
    }
    public synchronized void startElection() {
        awake = true;
        sendMsg(next, "election", number);
    }
}
```

Figure 13.1: The leader election algorithm

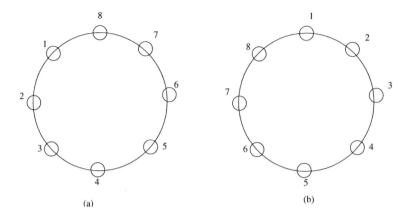

Figure 13.2: Configurations for the worst case (a) and the best case (b)

The worst case of this algorithm is when N processes with identifiers $1 \ldots N$ are arranged clockwise in decreasing order (see Figure 13.2(a)). The message initiated by process j will travel j processes before it is swallowed by a larger process. Thus the total number of *election* messages in the worst case is

$$\sum_{j=1}^{j=N} j = O(N^2).$$

In addition, there are N *leader* messages. The best case is when the same identifiers are arranged clockwise in the increasing order. In that case, only $O(N)$ election messages are required. On an average, the algorithm requires $O(N \log N)$ messages (see Problem 13.2).

13.2.2   Hirschberg–Sinclair Algorithm

In this section we assume that the ring is bidirectional so that messages can be sent to the left or the right neighbor. The main idea of the algorithm is to carry out elections on increasingly larger sets. The algorithm works in asynchronous rounds such that a process P_i tries to elect itself in round r. Only processes that win their election in round r can proceed to round $r + 1$. The invariant satisfied by the algorithm is that process P_i is a leader in round r iff P_i has the largest identifier of all nodes that are at distance 2^r or less from P_i. It follows that any two leaders after round r must be at least 2^r distance apart. In other words, after round r, there are at most $N/(2^{r-1} + 1)$ leaders. With each round, the number of leaders decreases, and in $O(\log N)$ rounds there is exactly one leader. It can be shown by using induction that there are at most $O(N)$ messages per round, which gives us a bound of $O(N \log N)$. The details of the algorithm and its proof of correctness are left as exercises.

13.3   Election on General Graphs

First assume that the graph is completely connected, that is, every process can talk to every other process directly. In this case, we can modify Lamport's mutual exclusion algorithm for leader election. One or more processes start the election. Any process that enters the critical section first is considered the leader.

Note that a process need not acknowledge another process's request if it knows that there is a request with a lower timestamp. Moreover, there is no need for release messages for the leader election problem. As soon as a process enters the critical section, it can inform all other processes that it has won the election. If c processes start the election concurrently, then this algorithm takes at most $2cN$ messages for "request" and "acknowledgment," and N messages for the final broadcast of who the leader is.

Now consider the case when the graph is not completely connected. We assume that every process initially knows only the identities of its neighbors. In this case, we can simulate the broadcast from a node v by constructing a spanning tree rooted at v.

13.3.1   Spanning Tree Construction

We assume that there is a distinguished process *root*. Later we will remove this assumption. The algorithm shown in Figure 13.3 is initiated by the root process by sending an *invite* message to all its neighbors. Whenever a process P_i receives an *invite* message (from P_j) for the first time, it sends that message to all its neighbors except P_j. To P_j it sends an *accept* message, indicating that P_j is the parent of P_i. If P_i receives an *invite* message from some other process thereafter, it simply replies with a *reject* message. Every node keeps a count of the number of nodes from which it has received messages in the variable *numreports*. When this value reaches the total number of neighbors, P_i knows that it has heard from all processes that it had sent the *invite* message (all neighbors except the *parent*). At this point, P_i can be sure that it knows all its children and can halt.

This algorithm is also called the *flooding algorithm* because it can be used to broadcast a message m, when there is no predefined spanning tree. The algorithm for flooding a message is simple. Whenever a process P_i receives a message m (from P_j) for the first time, it sends that message to all its neighbors except P_j.

```
public class SpanTree extends Process {
    public int parent = -1; // no parent yet
    public IntLinkedList children = new IntLinkedList ();
    int numReports = 0;
    boolean done = false;
    public SpanTree(Linker initComm, boolean isRoot) {
        super(initComm);
        if (isRoot) {
            parent = myId;
            if (initComm.neighbors.size () == 0)
                done = true;
            else
                sendToNeighbors ( "invite", myId);
        }
    }
    public synchronized void waitForDone () { // block till children known
        while (!done) myWait ();
    }
    public synchronized void handleMsg(Msg m, int src, String tag) {
        if (tag.equals ("invite")) {
            if (parent == -1) {
                numReports++;
                parent = src;
                sendMsg(src, "accept");
                for (int i = 0; i < N; i++)
                    if ((i != myId) && (i != src) && isNeighbor (i))
                        sendMsg(i, "invite");
            } else
                sendMsg(src, "reject");
        } else if ((tag.equals ("accept")) || (tag.equals ("reject"))) {
            if (tag.equals ("accept")) children.add(src);
            numReports++;
            if (numReports == comm.neighbors.size ()) {
                done = true;
                notify ();
            }
        }
    }
}
```

Figure 13.3: A spanning tree construction algorithm

What if there is no distinguished process? We assume that each process has a unique *id*, but initially every process knows only its own *id*. In this case, each node can start the spanning tree construction assuming that it is the distinguished process. Thus many instances of spanning tree construction may be active concurrently. To distinguish these instances, all messages in the spanning tree started by P_i contain the *id* for P_i. By ensuring that only the instance started by the process with the largest *id* succeeds, we can build a spanning tree even when there is no distinguished process. The details of the algorithm are left as an exercise.

13.4 Application: Computing Global Functions

One of the fundamental difficulties of distributed computing is that no process has access to the global state. This difficulty can be alleviated by developing mechanisms to compute functions of the global state. We call such functions *global functions*. More concretely, assume that we have x_i located at process P_i. Our aim is to compute a function $f(x_1, x_2, \ldots, x_N)$ that depends on states of all processes.

First, we present an algorithm for convergecast and broadcast on a network, assuming that there is a predefined spanning tree. The convergecast requires information from all nodes of the tree to be collected at the root of the tree. Once all the information is present at the root node, it can compute the global function and then broadcast the value to all nodes in the tree. Both the convergecast and the broadcast require a spanning tree on the network.

The algorithms for convergecast and broadcast are very simple if we assume a rooted spanning tree. For convergecast, the algorithm is shown in Figure 13.4. Each node in the spanning tree is responsible to report to its *parent* the information of its subtree. The variable *parent*, for a node x, is the identity of the neighbor of x, which is the parent in the rooted spanning tree. For the root, this value is *null*. The variable *numchildren* keeps track of the total number of its children, and *numreports* keeps track of the number of its children who have reported. When the root node hears from all its children, it has all the information needed to compute the global function.

The broadcast algorithm shown in Figure 13.5 is dual of the convergecast algorithm. The algorithm is initiated by the root process by sending the broadcast message to all its children. In this algorithm, messages traverse down the tree.

We now combine the convergecast and the broadcast algorithms to provide a service that can compute a global function. For simplicity, we assume that the global function is commutative and associative, such as *min, max, sum,* and *product*. This allows internal nodes to send intermediate results to the parent node during the convergecast process. The `GlobalService` interface is shown below.

```
var
    parent: process id;// initialized based on the spanning tree
    numchildren: integer; // initialized based on the spanning tree
    numreports: integer initially 0;

on receiving a report from P_j
    numreports := numreports + 1;
    if (numreports = numchildren) then
        if (parent = null) then // root node
            compute global function;
        else send report to parent;
    endif;
```

Figure 13.4: A convergecast algorithm

```
P_root ::
    send m to all children;

P_i :: i ≠ root
    on receiving a message m from parent
        send m to all children;
```

Figure 13.5: A broadcast algorithm

```
public interface GlobalService extends MsgHandler {
    public void initialize (int x, FuncUser prog );
    public int computeGlobal ();
}
```

Any program that wants to compute a global function can invoke `computeGlobal` with its value and the global function to be computed as arguments. The `FuncUser` is required to have a binary function called `func` as shown below.

```
public interface FuncUser {
  public int func(int x, int y);
}
```

Now we can give an implementation for `GlobalService` based on the ideas of convergecast and broadcast. The Java implementation is shown in Figure 13.6.

The program uses two types of messages, *subTreeVal* and *globalFunc*, for convergecast and broadcast respectively. The list `pending` keeps track of all the children that have not reported using the *subTreeVal* message. Whenever a *subTreeVal* message is received, it is combined with `myValue` using `prog.func()`. Whenever the `pending` list becomes empty, that node has the value of the global function for its subtree. If the node is a root, it can initiate the broadcast; otherwise it sends its `myValue` to its parent and waits for the *globalFunc* message to arrive. The final answer is given by the value that comes with this message.

The class `GlobalFunc` can be used to compute a global function as illustrated by the class `GlobalFuncTest` in Figure 13.7.

13.5 Problems

13.1. An algorithm on a ring is considered *nonuniform* if every process knows the total number of processes in the ring. Show that there exists a randomized nonuniform algorithm to elect a leader on an anonymous ring that terminates with probability 1. [*Hint*: Consider an algorithm with rounds in which initially all processes are eligible. In each round, an eligible process draws at random from $0 \ldots m$ (where $m > 0$). The subset of processes that draw the maximum element from the set selected is eligible for the next round. If there is exactly one eligible process, then the algorithm terminates. Analyze the expected number of rounds as a function of N and m.]

13.2. Show that the Chang–Roberts algorithm requires $O(N \log N)$ messages on average.

13.3. Modify the Chang–Roberts algorithm such that a process keeps track of *maxid*, the largest identifier it has seen so far. It swallows any message with any identifier that is smaller than *maxid*. What are the worst and the expected number of messages for this variant of the algorithm?

13.4. Give an $O(N \log N)$ algorithm for leader election on a bidirectional ring.

```java
import java.util.*;
public class GlobalFunc extends Process implements GlobalService {
    FuncUser prog;
    SpanTree tree = null;
    IntLinkedList pending = new IntLinkedList();
    int myValue;
    int answer;
    boolean answerRecvd;
    boolean pendingSet = false;
    public GlobalFunc(Linker initComm, boolean isRoot) {
        super(initComm);
        tree = new SpanTree(comm, isRoot);
    }
    public void initialize(int myValue, FuncUser prog) {
        this.myValue = myValue;
        this.prog = prog;
        tree.waitForDone();
        Util.println(myId + ":" + tree.children.toString());
    }
    public synchronized int computeGlobal() {
        pending.addAll(tree.children);
        pendingSet = true;
        notifyAll();
        while (!pending.isEmpty()) myWait();
        if (tree.parent == myId) { // root node
            answer = myValue;
        } else { //non-root node
            sendMsg(tree.parent, "subTreeVal", myValue);
            answerRecvd = false;
            while (!answerRecvd) myWait();
        }
        sendChildren(answer);
        return answer;
    }
    void sendChildren(int value) {
        ListIterator t = tree.children.listIterator(0);
        while (t.hasNext()) {
            Integer child = (Integer) t.next();
            sendMsg(child.intValue(), "globalFunc", value);
        }
    }
    public synchronized void handleMsg(Msg m, int src, String tag) {
        tree.handleMsg(m, src, tag);
        if (tag.equals("subTreeVal")) {
            while (!pendingSet) myWait();
            pending.remove(new Integer(src));
            myValue = prog.func(myValue, m.getMessageInt());
            if (pending.isEmpty()) notifyAll();
        } else if (tag.equals("globalFunc")) {
            answer = m.getMessageInt();
            answerRecvd = true;
            notifyAll();
        }
    }
}
```

Figure 13.6: Algorithm for computing a global function

```java
public class GlobalFuncTester implements FuncUser {
    public int func(int x, int y) {
        return x + y;
    }
    public static void main(String[] args) throws Exception {
        int myId = Integer.parseInt(args[1]);
        int numProc = Integer.parseInt(args[2]);
        Linker comm = new Linker(args[0], myId, numProc);
        GlobalFunc g = new GlobalFunc(comm, (myId == 0));
        for (int i = 0; i < numProc; i++)
            if (i != myId)
                (new ListenerThread(i, g)).start();
        int myValue = Integer.parseInt(args[3]);
        GlobalFuncTester h = new GlobalFuncTester();
        g.initialize(myValue, h);
        int globalSum = g.computeGlobal();
        System.out.println("The global sum is " + globalSum);
    }
}
```

Figure 13.7: Computing the global sum

13.6 Bibliographic Remarks

The impossibility result on anonymous rings is due to Angluin [Ang80]. The $O(N^2)$ algorithm is due to Chang and Roberts [CR79]. The $O(N \log N)$ algorithm discussed in the chapter is due to Hirschberg and Sinclair [HS80]. Dolev, Klawe and Rodeh [DKR82] and Peterson [Pet82] have presented an $O(N \log N)$ algorithm for unidirectional rings. For lower bounds of $\Omega(N \log N)$, see papers by Burns [Bur80] and Pachl, Korach, and Rotem [PKR82].

Chapter 14

Synchronizers

14.1 Introduction

The design of distributed algorithms is easier if we assume that the underlying network is synchronous rather than asynchronous. A prime example is that of computing a breadth-first search (BFS) tree in a network. In this chapter, we assume that the network has N nodes, E edges, and its diameter is D. Assume that we are given a distinguished node v and our job is to build a breadth-first search tree rooted at v. A synchronous algorithm for this task is quite simple. We build the tree level by level. The node v is initially at level 0. A node at level i is required to send messages to its neighbors at pulse i. A process that receives one or more of these messages, and does not have a level number assigned yet, chooses the source of one of these messages as its parent and assigns itself level number $i + 1$. It is clear that if the graph is connected, then every node will have its level number assigned in at most D pulses assuming that any message sent at pulse i is received at pulse $i + 1$.

What if the underlying network is not synchronous? The corresponding problem on an asynchronous network is more difficult. This motivates methods by which a synchronous network can be simulated by an asynchronous network. We show that, in the absence of failures, this is indeed possible using a mechanism called a *synchronizer*. To simulate the synchronous algorithm on an asynchronous network, all we need is to use one of the synchronizers discussed in this chapter.

A synchronous network can be abstracted with the notion of a *pulse*, which is a counter at each process with the property that any message sent in pulse i is received at pulse $i + 1$. A synchronizer is simply a mechanism that indicates to a process when it can generate a pulse. In this chapter we will study synchronizers and their complexity.

To define properties of synchronizers formally, we associate a pulse number with each state s on a process. It is initialized to 0 for all processes. A process can go from pulse i to $i + 1$ only if it knows that it has received and acted on all the messages sent during pulse $i - 1$.

Given the notion of a pulse, the execution of a synchronous algorithm can be modeled as a sequence of pulses. In each pulse, a process first receives messages from neighbors that were sent in previous round. It then performs internal computation based on the received messages. It also sends messages to its neighbors as required by the application. It can execute the next pulse only when indicated by the synchronizer. Thus a synchronizer can be abstracted by the following interface:

```
public interface Synchronizer extends MsgHandler {
        public void initialize (MsgHandler initProg );
        public void sendMessage(int destId , String tag , int msg);
        public void nextPulse (); // block for the next pulse
}
```

There are two aspects of the complexity of a synchronizer—the message complexity and the time complexity. The *message complexity* indicates the additional number of messages required by the synchronizer to simulate a synchronous algorithm on top of an asynchronous network. The *time complexity* is the number of time units required to simulate one pulse, where a *time unit* is defined as the time required for an asynchronous message.

Some synchronizers have a nontrivial initialization cost. Let M_{init} be the number of messages and T_{init} be the time required for initialization of the synchronizer. Let M_{pulse} and T_{pulse} respectively be the number of messages and the time required to simulate one pulse of a synchronous algorithm. If a synchronous algorithm requires T_{synch} rounds and M_{synch} messages, then the complexity of the asynchronous protocol based on the synchronizer is given by

$$M_{asynch} = M_{init} + M_{synch} + M_{pulse} * T_{synch}$$

$$T_{asynch} = T_{init} + T_{pulse} * T_{synch}$$

We model the topology of the underlying network as an undirected, connected graph. We assume that processes never fail. It is not possible to simulate a synchronous algorithm on an asynchronous network when processes can fail. In Chapter

15, we show algorithms that can achieve consensus despite process failures in synchronous systems and that consensus is impossible in asynchronous systems when even a single process may fail. This implies that process failures cannot be tolerated in simulating synchrony. We also assume that all channels are reliable. Again, Chapter 15 shows that the consensus problem is impossible to solve when channels are unreliable.

14.2   A Simple Synchronizer

A simple synchronizer can be built using a rule stipulating that every process send exactly one message to all neighbors in each pulse. With this rule, a process can simply wait for exactly one message from each of its neighbors. To implement this rule, even if the synchronous algorithm did not require P_i to send any message to its neighbor P_j in a particular round, it must still send a "null" message to P_j. Furthermore, if the synchronous algorithm required P_i to send multiple messages, then these messages must be packed as a single message and sent to P_j.

The simple synchronizer generates the next pulse for process p at pulse i when it has received exactly one message sent during pulse i from each of its neighbors. The algorithm is shown in Figure 14.1 and its Java implementation, in Figure 14.2.

```
Pj::
var
     pulse: integer initially 0;

round i :
     pulse := pulse + 1;
     wait for exactly one message with (pulse = i) from each neighbors;
     simulate the round i of the synchronous algorithm;
     send messages to all neighbors with pulse;
```

Figure 14.1: Algorithm for the simple synchronizer at P_j

The algorithm in Figure 14.2 ensures that a process in pulse i receives only the messages sent in pulse $i - 1$.

The implementation in Java assumes FIFO and uses the following variables:

- pendingS: list of neighbors who have not been sent any message in this pulse

```java
import java.util.LinkedList;
public class SimpleSynch extends Process implements Synchronizer {
    int pulse = 0;
    MsgHandler prog;
    boolean rcvEnabled [];
    IntLinkedList pendingS = new IntLinkedList ();
    IntLinkedList pendingR = new IntLinkedList ();
    public SimpleSynch (Linker initComm) {
        super (initComm);
        rcvEnabled = new boolean [N];
        for (int i = 0; i < N; i++)
            rcvEnabled [i] = false;
    }
    public synchronized void initialize (MsgHandler initProg) {
        prog = initProg;
        pendingS.addAll (comm.neighbors);
        notifyAll ();
    }
    public synchronized void handleMsg (Msg m, int src, String tag) {
        while (! rcvEnabled [src]) myWait ();
        pendingR.removeObject (src);
        if (pendingR.isEmpty ()) notifyAll ();
        if (! tag.equals ("synchNull"))
            prog.handleMsg (m, src, tag);
        rcvEnabled [src] = false;
    }
    public synchronized void sendMessage (int destId, String tag, int msg) {
        if (pendingS.contains (destId)) {
            pendingS.removeObject (destId);
            sendMsg (destId, tag, msg);
        } else
            System.err.println ("Error: sending two messages/pulse");
    }
    public synchronized void nextPulse () {
        while (! pendingS.isEmpty ()) { // finish last pulse by sending null
            int dest = pendingS.removeHead ();
            sendMsg (dest, "synchNull", 0);
        }
        pulse ++;
        Util.println ("**** new pulse ****:" + pulse);
        pendingS.addAll (comm.neighbors);
        pendingR.addAll (comm.neighbors);
        for (int i = 0; i < N; i++)
            rcvEnabled [i] = true;
        notifyAll ();
        while (! pendingR.isEmpty ()) myWait ();
    }
}
```

Figure 14.2: Implementation of the simple synchronizer

- `pendingR`: list of neighbors from which no message has been received in this pulse

- `rcvEnabled[j]`: whether the process can receive a message from P_j in this round.

The method `initialize` sets `pendingS` and `pendingR` for all neighbors and the variable `pulse` to 0. We have assumed that the communication topology is given by an undirected graph and that `comm.neighbors` has the list of all neighbors.

The method `handleMsg` is implemented as follows. When a message is received at the application, it is determined whether any message has already been received from the source in the current pulse. If there is such a message, then this message belongs to the next pulse and the process waits for `rcvEnabled[src]` to become true. Otherwise, this message is meant for this pulse and `source` is removed from the list `pendingR`. At this point, the tag of the message is checked to see if it is a null message (of type *synchNull*) used only for the synchronizer. If it is not, the message is passed on to the application. If a message has been received in this pulse from each of the neighbors, that is, `pendingR` is empty, then the application can continue to the next pulse and the thread that may be blocked in `nextPulse` is signaled. To send a message, we simply remove the destination from the list `pendingS`.

Whenever the application layer calls `nextPulse`, the synchronizer first ensures that every neighbor is sent exactly one message in the last pulse. After incrementing the pulse number, it waits to receive exactly one message from every neighbor. This is achieved bu waiting for the list `pendingR` to be empty. When this condition becomes true, it is ready for the next pulse.

Note that there is no special requirement for initialization of this synchronizer. When any process starts pulse 1, within D time units all other processes will also start pulse 1. Therefore, the complexity of initializing the simple synchronizer is

$$M_{init} = 0; \quad T_{init} = D.$$

Because each pulse requires a message along every link in both directions, we get the complexity of simulating a pulse as

$$M_{pulse} = 2E; \quad T_{pulse} = 1.$$

14.2.1 Application: BFS Tree Construction

Let us use the simple synchronizer for computing the BFS tree in a network. Figure 14.3 gives an algorithm that will compute the BFS tree on a synchronous network, but not necessarily the BFS tree on an *asynchronous* network. The algorithm has two methods: `initiate` and `handleMsg`. The method `initiate` is invoked by the root from which we would like to compute the tree. In this method, the root sends an *invite* message to all its neighbors. Any node that receives an *invite* message for the first time becomes part of the tree with its parent as the node that sent the invitation. This node in turn sends invitations to all its neighbors. In an asynchronous network, this algorithm may not produce a BFS tree. Figure 14.4 gives an algorithm that runs with the simple synchronizer to ensure that the tree computed is the BFS tree even on asynchronous networks.

```
public class Tree extends Process {
    int parent = −1;
    int level;
    public Tree(Linker initComm, boolean isRoot) {
        super(initComm);
        if (isRoot) initiate();
    }
    public void initiate() {
        parent = myId;
        level = 0;
        for (int i = 0; i < N; i++)
            if (isNeighbor(i))
                sendMsg(i, "invite", level + 1);
    }
    public synchronized void handleMsg(Msg m, int src, String tag) {
        if (tag.equals("invite")) {
            if (parent == −1) {
                parent = src;
                level = m.getMessageInt();
                for (int i = 0; i < N; i++)
                    if (isNeighbor(i) && (i != src))
                        sendMsg(i, "invite", level + 1);
            }
        }
    }
}
```

Figure 14.3: An algorithm that generates a tree on an asynchronous network

14.3 Synchronizer α

The synchronizer α is very similar to the simple synchronizer. We cover this synchronizer because it is a special case of a more general synchronizer γ that will be covered later. All the synchronizers discussed from now on are based around the

```java
public class SynchBfsTree extends Process {
    int parent = -1;
    int level;
    Synchronizer s;
    boolean isRoot;
    public SynchBfsTree(Linker initComm,
                        Synchronizer initS, boolean isRoot) {
        super(initComm);
        s = initS;
        this.isRoot = isRoot;
    }
    public void initiate() {
        if (isRoot) {
            parent = myId;
            level = 0;
        }
        s.initialize(this);
        for (int pulse = 0; pulse < N; pulse++) {
            if ((pulse == 0) && isRoot) {
                for (int i = 0; i < N; i++)
                    if (isNeighbor(i))
                        s.sendMessage(i, "invite", level + 1);
            }
            s.nextPulse();
        }
    }
    public void handleMsg(Msg m, int src, String tag) {
        if (tag.equals("invite")) {
            if (parent == -1) {
                parent = src;
                level = m.getMessageInt();
                Util.println(myId + " is at level " + level);
                for (int i = 0; i < N; i++)
                    if (isNeighbor(i) && (i != src))
                        s.sendMessage(i, "invite", level + 1);
            }
        }
    }
}
```

Figure 14.4: BFS tree algorithm using a synchronizer

concept of *safety* of a process. Process P is safe for pulse i if it knows that all messages sent from P in pulse i have been received.

The α synchronizer generates the next pulse at process P if all its neighbors are safe. This is because if all neighbors of P are safe, then all messages sent to process P have been received.

To implement the α synchronizer, it is sufficient for every process to inform all its neighbors whenever it is safe for a pulse. How can a process determine whether it is safe? This is a simple matter if all messages are required to be acknowledged.

The algorithm for α synchronizer is given in Figure 14.5. We have assumed FIFO ordering of messages. The algorithm maintains a variable `acksNeeded` that records the number of unacknowledged messages for the current pulse. It also maintains `unsafe`, the list of neighbors that are unsafe for this node for the current pulse. At the beginning of each pulse, `acksNeeded` is initialized to 0 and `unsafe` to the list of all neighbors.

The synchronizer handles two types of messages: *synchAck* and *safe*. The *synchAck* message acknowledges an application message and `acksNeeded` is decremented whenever the *synchAck* message is received. The *safe* message is handled by removing the source of the message from the `unsafe` list. When an application message is received, it is checked whether a *safe* message has been received from that neighbor. Since a process sends *safe* messages only at the end of the pulse, if a safe message has already been received, then this message is meant for the next pulse and is recorded in `nextPulseMsgs` as in `SimpleSynch`. Otherwise, an acknowledgment is sent and the message is delivered to the application layer.

The method `nextPulse` is implemented as follows. First, the node waits for all pending acknowledgments. Once all acknowledgments are received, it knows that it is safe and sends the *safe* message to all neighbors. It then waits for all its neighbors to be safe. When that condition becomes true, the node is ready for the next pulse. At the beginning of the pulse all the messages in `nextPulseMsgs` are delivered.

The complexity of synchronizer α is given below:

$$T_{init} = D; \qquad M_{init} = D$$

$$T_{pulse} = O(1); \qquad M_{pulse} = O(E)$$

14.4 Synchronizer β

Although the synchronizers discussed so far appear to be efficient, they have high message complexity when the topology of the underlying network is dense. For large networks, where every node may be connected to a large number of nodes, it may be impractical to send a message to all neighbors in every pulse. The message

```java
import java.util.LinkedList;
public class AlphaSynch extends Process implements Synchronizer {
    int pulse = -1;
    int acksNeeded = 0;
    IntLinkedList unsafe = new IntLinkedList ();
    LinkedList nextPulseMsgs = new LinkedList (); //msgs for next pulse
    boolean meSafe;
    MsgHandler prog;
    public AlphaSynch(Linker initComm) {
        super(initComm);
    }
    public synchronized void initialize (MsgHandler initProg) {
        prog = initProg;
        startPulse ();
        notifyAll ();
    }
    void startPulse (){
        unsafe.addAll(comm.neighbors);
        meSafe = false;
        pulse ++;
        Util.println ("**** new pulse ****:" + pulse);
    }
    public synchronized void handleMsg(Msg m, int src, String tag) {
        while ( pulse < 0) myWait();
        if ( tag.equals ("synchAck")) {
            acksNeeded--;
            if ( acksNeeded == 0) notifyAll ();
        } else if ( tag.equals ("safe")) {
            while (! unsafe.contains (src)) myWait();
            unsafe.removeObject (src);
            if ( unsafe.isEmpty ()) notifyAll ();
        } else { // application message
            sendMsg(src, "synchAck", 0);
            while (! unsafe.contains (src)) myWait();
            if ( meSafe) nextPulseMsgs.add(m);
            else prog.handleMsg(m, src, tag);
        }
    }
    public synchronized void sendMessage(int destId, String tag, int msg) {
        acksNeeded++;
        sendMsg(destId, tag, msg);
    }
    public synchronized void nextPulse () {
        while ( acksNeeded != 0) myWait();
        meSafe = true;
        sendToNeighbors ("safe", 0);
        while (! unsafe.isEmpty ()) myWait();
        startPulse ();
        while (! nextPulseMsgs.isEmpty ()) { //act on msgs received earlier
            Msg m = (Msg) nextPulseMsgs.removeFirst ();
            prog.handleMsg(m, m.getSrcId (), m.getTag ());
        }
        notifyAll ();
    }
}
```

Figure 14.5: Alpha synchronizer

complexity can be reduced at the expense of time complexity as illustrated by the β synchronizer.

The β synchronizer assumes the existence of a rooted spanning tree in the network. A node in the tree sends a message *subtree safe* when all nodes in its subtree are safe. When the root of the tree is safe and all its children are safe, then we can conclude that all nodes in the tree are safe. Now a simple broadcast of this fact via a *pulse* message can start the next pulse at all nodes. The broadcast can be done using the rooted spanning tree.

The initialization phase of this synchronizer requires a spanning tree to be built. This can be done using $O(N \log N + E)$ messages and $O(N)$ time. For each pulse, we require messages only along the spanning tree. Thus the message complexity for each pulse is $O(N)$. Each pulse also takes time proportional to the height of the spanning tree, which in the worst case is $O(N)$. In summary, the complexity of the β synchronizer is

$$T_{init} = O(N); \qquad M_{init} = O(N \log N + E)$$

$$T_{pulse} = O(N); \qquad M_{pulse} = O(N).$$

14.5 Synchronizer γ

We have seen that the α synchronizer takes $O(1)$ time but has high message complexity $O(E)$, and the β synchronizer has low message complexity $O(N)$ but requires $O(N)$ time per pulse. We now describe the γ synchronizer which is a generalization of both α and β synchronizers. It takes a parameter k such that when k is $N - 1$, it reduces to the α synchronizer and when k is 2, it reduces to the β synchronizer.

The γ synchronizer is based on *clustering*. In the initialization phase, the network is divided into clusters. Within each cluster the algorithm is similar to the β synchronizer and between clusters it is similar to the α synchronizer. Thus each cluster has a cluster spanning tree. The root of the cluster spanning tree is called the *cluster leader*. We say that two clusters are *neighboring* if there is an edge connecting them. For any two neighboring clusters, we designate one of the edges as the *preferred* edge.

The algorithm works as follows. There are two phases in each pulse. In both phases, the messages first travel upward in the cluster tree and then travel downward. The goal of the first phase is to determine when the cluster is safe and inform all cluster nodes when it is so. In this phase, *subtree safe* messages first propagate up the cluster tree. When the root of the cluster gets messages from all its children and it is safe itself, it propagates the *cluster safe* message down the cluster tree. This phase corresponds to the β synchronizer running on the cluster. We also require that the nodes that are incident on preferred edges also send out *our cluster safe* (*ocs*) messages over preferred edges.

The goal of the second phase is to determine whether all neighboring clusters are safe. In this sense, it is like an α synchronizer. It uses two additional message types: *neighboring cluster safe* (*ncs*) and *pulse*. When a leaf in the cluster tree receives the *our cluster safe* message from all preferred edges incident on it, it sends *ncs* to its parent. Now consider an internal node in the cluster tree that has received *ncs* messages from all its children and has received *ocs* on all preferred edges incident on it. If it is not the cluster leader, then it propagates the *ncs* message upward; otherwise, it broadcasts the *pulse* message in its group.

For any clustering scheme c, let E_c denote the number of tree edges and preferred edges and H_c denote the maximum height of a tree in c. The complexity of the γ synchronizer is given by

$$M_{pulse} = O(E_c)$$

$$T_{pulse} = O(H_c)$$

We now show that any graph can be decomposed into clusters so that there is an appropriate tradeoff between the cluster height and the number of tree and preferred edges. In particular, we claim that for each k in the range $2 \leq k < N$, there exists a clustering c such that $E_c \leq kN$ and $H_c \leq \log N / \log k$.

We give an explicit construction of the clustering. In this scheme, we add clusters one at a time. Assume that we have already constructed r clusters and there are still some nodes left that are not part of any cluster. We add the next cluster as follows.

Each cluster C consists of multiple layers. For the first layer, any node that is not part of any cluster so far is chosen. Assume that i layers ($i \geq 1$) of the cluster C have already been formed. Let S be the set of neighbors of the node in layer i that are not part of any cluster yet. If the size of S is at least $(k-1)$ times the size of C, then S is added as the next layer of the cluster C; otherwise, C's construction is finished.

Let us compute H_c and E_c for this clustering scheme. Since each cluster with level i has at least k^{i-1} nodes, it follows that H_c is at most $\log N / \log k$. E_c has two components—tree edges and preferred edges. The tree edges are clearly at most N. To count the preferred edges, we charge a preferred edge between two clusters to the first cluster that is created in our construction process. Note that for a cluster C, its construction is finished only when there are at most $(k-1)|C|$ neighboring nodes. Thus, for the cluster C, there can be at most $(k-1)|C|$ preferred edges charged to it. Adding up the contribution from all clusters, we get that the total number of preferred edges is at most $(k-1)N$.

14.6 Problems

14.1. Give the Java code for the β synchronizer.

14.2. Give the Java code for the γ synchronizer.

14.3. What is the message complexity of the asynchronous algorithm for constructing a breadth-first search tree when it is obtained by combining the synchronous algorithm with (a) the α synchronizer, (b) the β synchronizer, and (c) the $\gamma(k)$ synchronizer?

14.4. Show how synchronizers can be used in a distributed algorithm to solve a set of simultaneous equations by an iterative method.

*14.5. (due to Awerbuch[Awe85]) Give a distributed algorithm to carry out the clustering used by the γ synchronizer.

*14.6. (due to Luby[Lub85]) Let $G = (V, E)$ be an undirected graph corresponding to the topology of a network. A set $V' \subseteq V$ is said to be *independent* if there is no edge between any two vertices in V'. An independent set is *maximal* if there is no independent set that strictly contains V'. Give a distributed synchronous randomized algorithm that terminates in $O(\log |V|)$ rounds. Also, give an algorithm that works on asynchronous networks.

14.7 Bibliographic Remarks

The concept of synchronizers, and the synchronizers α, β, and γ were introduced by Awerbuch [Awe85]. The reader is referred to the books by Raynal and Helary [RH90] and Tel [Tel94] for more details on synchronizers.

Chapter 15

Agreement

15.1 Introduction

Consensus is a fundamental problem in distributed computing. Consider a distributed database in which a transaction spans multiple sites. In this application it is important that either all sites agree to commit or all sites agree to abort the transaction. In absence of failures, this is a simple task. We can use either a centralized scheme or a quorum-based scheme. What if processes can fail? It may appear that if links are reliable, the system should be able to tolerate at least failure of a single process. In this chapter, we show the surprising result that even in the presence of one unannounced process death, the consensus problem is impossible to solve. This result (FLP) is named after Fischer, Lynch and Paterson who first discovered it.

The FLP result for consensus shows a fundamental limitation of asynchronous computing. The problem itself is very basic—processes need to agree on a single bit. Most problems we have discussed such as leader election, mutual exclusion, and computation of global functions are harder than the consensus problem because any solution to these problems can be used to solve the consensus problem. The impossibility of consensus implies that all these problems are also impossible to solve in the presence of process failures.

The FLP result is remarkable in another sense. It assumes only a mild form of failures in the environment. First, it assumes only process failures and not link failures. Any message sent takes a finite but unbounded amount of time. Furthermore, it assumes that a process fails only by crashing and thus ceasing all its activities. Thus it does not consider failures in which the process omits certain steps of the protocol or colludes with other processes to foil the protocol. Since the impossibility result holds under weak models of failure, it is also true for stronger failure models.

15.2   Consensus in Asynchronous Systems (Impossibility)

The consensus problem is as follows. We assume that there are $N, (N \geq 2)$ processes in the system and that the value of N is known to all processes. Each process starts with an initial value of $\{0,1\}$. This is modeled as a one bit input register x. A nonfaulty process decides by entering a decision state. We require that *some* process eventually make a decision. Making a decision is modeled by output registers. Each process also has an output register y that indicates the value decided or committed on by the process. The value of 0 in y indicates that the process has decided on the value 0. The same holds for the value 1. The value $\perp$ indicates that the process has not agreed on any value. Initially, we require all processes to have $\perp$ in their register y. We require that once a process has decided, it does not change its value, that is, output registers are write-once. We also assume that each process has unbounded storage.

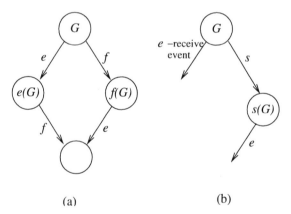

(a)   (b)

Figure 15.1: (a) Commutativity of disjoint events; (b) asynchrony of messages

Before we list formal requirements of the consensus problem, we discuss our assumptions on the environment.

- *Initial independence*: We allow processes to choose their input in an independent manner. Thus, all input vectors are possible.

- *Commute property of disjoint events:* Let G be any global state such that two events e and f are enabled in it. If e and f are on different processes, then they commute. This is shown in Figure 15.1(a). We use the notation $e(G)$ for the global state reached after executing event e at G. Similarly, we use $s(G)$ to denote the global state reached after executing a sequence of events s at the global state G. The global state reached after executing ef at G is identical to the one reached after executing fe at G.

- *Asynchrony of events*: The asynchronous message system is modeled as a buffer with two operations. The operation $send(p, m)$ by process p places (p, m) in the buffer. The operation $receive()$ from p by any process q deletes (p, m) and returns m or returns *null*. The system may return *null* to model the fact that the asynchronous messages may take an unbounded amount of time. The condition we impose on the message system is that if the $receive()$ event is performed an unbounded number of times, then every message is eventually delivered. The asynchrony assumption states that any *receive* event may be arbitrarily delayed. In Figure 15.1(b), the event e is an enabled event after executing a sequence of events s at state G because $e \notin s$. Note that this assumption does not state that $se(G) = es(G)$. The event e commutes with s only when the process on which e is executed is completely disjoint from processes that have events in s.

Our model of a faulty process is as follows. We only consider infinite runs. A faulty process is one that takes only a finite number of steps in that run. A run is *admissible* if at most one process is faulty. Since the message system is reliable, all messages sent to nonfaulty processes are eventually delivered. A run is *deciding* if some process reaches a decision state in that run.

The requirements of the protocol can be summarized as:

- *Agreement*: Two nonfaulty processes cannot commit on different values.

- *Nontriviality*: Both values 0 and 1 should be possible outcomes. This requirement eliminates protocols that return a fixed value 0 or 1 independent of the initial input.

- *Termination*: A nonfaulty process decides in finite time.

We now show the FLP result—there is no protocol that satisfies agreement, nontriviality, and termination in an asynchronous system in presence of one fault. The main idea behind the proof consists of showing that there exists an admissible run that remains forever indecisive. Specifically, we show that (1) there is an initial

global state in which the system is indecisive, and (2) there exists a method to keep
the system indecisive.

To formalize the notion of *indecision*, we use the notion of valences of a global
state. Let $G.V$ be the set of decision values of global state reachable from G. Since
the protocol is correct, $G.V$ is nonempty. We say that G is bivalent if $|G.V| = 2$
and univalent if $|G.V| = 1$. In the latter case, we call G 0-valent if $G.V = \{0\}$ and
1-valent if $G.V = \{1\}$. The bivalent state captures the notion of indecision.

We first show that every consensus protocol has a bivalent initial global state.
Assume, if possible, that the protocol does not have any bivalent initial global state.
By the nontriviality requirement, the protocol must have both 0-valent and 1-valent
global states. Let us call two global states *adjacent* if they differ in the local state of
exactly one process. Since any two initial global states can be connected by a chain
of initial global states each adjacent to the next, there exist adjacent 0-valent and
1-valent global states. Assume that they differ in the state of p. We now apply to
both of these global states a sequence in which p takes no steps. Since they differ
only in the state of p, the system must reach the same decision value, which is a
contradiction.

Our next step is to show that we can keep the system in an indecisive state. Let
G be a bivalent global state of a protocol. Let event e on process p be applicable
to G, and $\mathcal{G}$ be the set of global states reachable from G without applying e. Let
$\mathcal{H} = e(\mathcal{G})$. We claim that $\mathcal{H}$ contains a bivalent global state. Assume, if possible,
that $\mathcal{H}$ contains no bivalent global states. We show a contradiction.

We first claim that $\mathcal{H}$ contains both 0-valent and 1-valent states. Let E_i ($i \in$
$\{0..1\}$) be an i-valent global state reachable from G. If $E_i \in \mathcal{G}$, then define $F_i =$
$e(E_i)$. Otherwise, e was applied in reaching E_i. In this case, there exists $F_i \in \mathcal{H}$
from which E_i is reachable. Thus $\mathcal{H}$ contains both 0-valent and 1-valent states.

We call two global states neighbors if one results from the other in a single step.

We now claim that there exist neighbors G_0, G_1 such that $H_0 = e(G_0)$ is 0-valent,
and $H_1 = e(G_1)$ is 1-valent. Let t be the smallest sequence of events applied to G
without applying e such that $et(G)$ has different valency from $e(G)$. To see that
such a sequence exists, assume that $e(G)$ is 0-valent. From our earlier claim about
$\mathcal{H}$, there exists a global state in $\mathcal{H}$ which is 1-valent. Let t be a minimal sequence
that leads to a 1-valent state. The case when $e(G)$ is 1-valent is similar. The last
two global states reached in this sequence give us the required neighbors.

Without loss of generality let $G_1 = f(G_0)$, where f is an event on process q. We
now do a case analysis:

Case 1: p is different from q [see Figure 15.2(a)]
This implies that f is applicable to H_0, resulting in H_1. This is a contradiction
because H_0 is 0-valent, and H_1 is 1-valent.

Case 2: $p = q$ [see Figure 15.2(b)]

Consider any finite deciding run from G_0 in which p takes no steps. Let s be the corresponding sequence. Let $K = s(G_0)$. From the commute property, s is also applicable to H_i and leads to i-valent global states $E_i = s(H_i)$. Again, by the commute property, $e(K) = E_0$ and $e(f(K)) = E_1$. Hence K is bivalent, which is a contradiction.

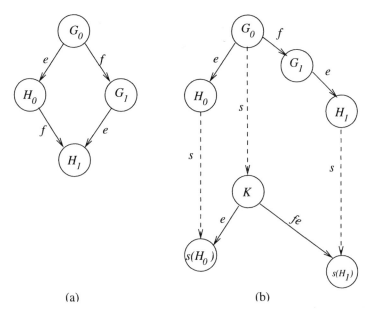

(a)   (b)

Figure 15.2: (a) Case 1: $proc(e) \neq proc(f)$; (b) case 2: $proc(e) = proc(f)$

The intuition behind the case analysis above is as follows. Any protocol that goes from a bivalent global state to a univalent state must have a critical step in which the decision is taken. This critical step cannot be based on the order of events done by different processes because execution of events at different processes commutes. This observation corresponds to case 1. This implies that the critical step must be taken by one process. But this method also does not work because other processes cannot distinguish between the situation when this process is slow and the situation when the process has crashed. This observation corresponds to case 2.

We are now ready for the main result that no consensus protocol satisfies agreement, nontriviality, and termination despite one fault. To show this result, we construct an admissible nondeciding run as follows. The run is started from any bivalent initial global state G_0 and consists of a sequence of stages. We ensure that every stage begins from a bivalent global state G. We maintain a queue of processes and maintain the message buffer as a FIFO queue. In each stage the process p at the head of the queue receives the earliest message m (if any). Let e be the event corresponding to p receiving the message m. From our earlier claims, we know that there is a bivalent global state H reachable from G by a sequence in which e is the last event applied. We then move the process to the back of the queue and repeat this set of steps forever. This method guarantees that every process executes infinitely often and every message sent is eventually received. Thus, the protocol stays in bivalent global states forever.

15.3 Application: Terminating Reliable Broadcast

Impossibility of consensus in the presence of a failure implies that many other interesting problems are impossible to solve in asynchronous systems as well. Consider, for example, the problem of the terminating reliable broadcast specified as follows. Assume that there are N processes in the system $P_0, \ldots, P_{N-1}$ and that P_0 wishes to broadcast a single message to all processes (including itself). The terminating reliable broadcast requires that a correct process always deliver a message even if the sender is faulty and crashes during the protocol. The message in that case may be "sender faulty." The requirements of the problem are

- *Termination*: Every correct process eventually delivers some message.

- *Validity*: If the sender is correct and broadcasts a message m, then all correct processes eventually deliver m.

- *Agreement*: If a correct process delivers a message m, then all correct processes deliver m.

- *Integrity*: Every correct process delivers at most one message, and if it delivers m different from "sender faulty," then the sender must have broadcast m.

We now show that the terminating reliable broadcast (TRB) is impossible to solve in an asynchronous system. We show this by providing an algorithm for consensus given an algorithm for TRB. The algorithm for consensus is simple. Process P_0 is required to broadcast its input bit using the TRB protocol. If a correct process receives a message different from "sender faulty" it decides on the bit received; otherwise, it decides on 0. It is easy to verify that this algorithm satisfies the termination, agreement, and nontriviality requirements of the consensus problem.

15.4   Consensus in Synchronous Systems

We have seen that consensus is impossible to solve in asynchronous systems even in the presence of a single crash. We show that the main difficulty in solving consensus lies in the asynchrony assumption. Thus there exist protocols to solve consensus when the system is synchronous. A system is synchronous if there is an upper bound on the message delay and on the duration of actions performed by processes. We show that under suitable conditions not only crash failures but also malevolent faults in which faulty processes can send arbitrary messages can be tolerated by consensus algorithms.

In general, we can classify the faults in a distributed system as follows:

- *Crash*: In the crash model, a fault corresponds to a processor halting. When the processor halts, it does not perform any other action and stays halted forever. The processor does not perform any wrong operation such as sending a corrupted message. As we have seen earlier, crashes may not be detectable by other processors in asynchronous systems, but they are detectable in synchronous systems.

- *Crash+link*: In this model, either a processor can crash or a link may go down. If a link goes down, then it stays down. When we consider link failures, it is sometimes important to distinguish between two cases—one in which the network is *partitioned* and the second in which the underlying communication graph stays connected. When the network gets partitioned, some pairs of nodes can never communicate with each other.

- *Omission*: In this model, a processor fails either by sending only a proper subset of messages that it is required to send by the algorithm or by receiving only a proper subset of messages that have been sent to it. The fault of the first kind is called a *send omission*, and that of the second kind is called a *receive omission*.

- *Byzantine failure*: In this model, a processor fails by exhibiting arbitrary behavior. This is an extreme form of a failure. A system that can tolerate a Byzantine fault can tolerate any other fault.

In this chapter, we will consider only the crash and Byzantine failures. We assume that links are reliable for crash failures. A processor that is not faulty is called a *correct* processor.

15.4.1   Consensus under Crash Failures

In this section, we will be concerned mainly with *algorithms* for synchronous systems. It is generally advantageous to prove impossibility results with as weak a specification of the problem as possible because the same proof will hold for a stronger specification. However, when designing algorithms it is better for the algorithm to satisfy a strong specification because the same algorithm will work for all weaker specifications.

We first generalize the set of values on which consensus is required. Instead of a single bit, the set of values can be any totally ordered set. We will assume that each process P_i has as its input a value v_i from this set. The goal of the protocol is to set the value y at each process such that the following constraints are met. The value y can be set at most once and is called the value *decided* by the process. Thus the requirements of the protocol are:

- *Agreement*: Two nonfaulty processes cannot decide on different values.

- *Validity*: If all processes propose the same value, then the decided value should be that proposed value. It is easy to verify that this condition implies the nontriviality condition discussed in Section 15.2.

- *Termination*: A nonfaulty process decides in finite time.

An algorithm for achieving consensus in the presence of crash failures is quite simple. In the algorithm we use the parameter f to denote the maximum number of processors that can fail. The algorithm shown in Figure 15.3 works based on rounds. Each process maintains V, which contains the set of values that it knows have been proposed by processors in the system. Initially, a process P_i knows only the value it proposed. The algorithm takes $f + 1$ rounds for completion; thus the algorithm assumes that the value of f is known. In each round, a process sends to all other processes, values from V that it has not sent before. So, initially the process sends its own value and in later rounds it sends only those values that it learns for the first time in the previous round. In each round, the processor P_i also receives the values sent by P_j. In this step, we have used the synchrony assumption. P_i waits for a message from P_j for some fixed predetermined time after which it assumes that P_j has crashed. After $f + 1$ rounds, each process decides on the minimum value in its set V.

The algorithm presented above satisfies termination because each correct process terminates in exactly $f + 1$ rounds. It satisfies validity because the decided value is chosen from the set V, which contains only the proposed values. We show the agreement property: All correct processors decide on the same value.

```
Pᵢ::
  var
      V: set of values initially {vᵢ};

  for k := 1 to f + 1 do
      send {v ∈ V | Pᵢ has not already sent v} to all;
      receive Sⱼ from all processes Pⱼ, j ≠ i;
      V := V ∪ Sⱼ;
  endfor;

  y := min(V);
```

Figure 15.3: Algorithm at P_i for consensus under crash failures

Let V_i denote the set of values at P_i after the round $f + 1$. We show that if any value x is in the set V_i for some correct processor P_i, then it is also in the set V_j for any other correct processor P_j.

First assume that the value x was added to V_i in a round $k < f+1$. Since P_i and P_j are correct processes, P_j will receive that value in round $k + 1$ and will therefore be present in V_j after round $f + 1$.

Now assume that the value x was added to V_i in the last round (round number $f + 1$). This implies that there exists a chain of $f + 1$ distinct processors that transferred the value from one of the processors that had x as its input value to P_i. If all the processors in the chain are faulty, then we contradict the assumption that there are at most f faulty processors. If any processor in the chain is nonfaulty, then it would have succeeded in sending x to all the processors in that round. Hence x was also added to V_j by at most $f + 1$ rounds.

The preceding algorithm requires $O((f + 1)N^2)$ messages because each round requires every process to send a message to all other processes. If each value requires b bits, then the total number of communication bits is $O(bN^3)$ bits because each processor may relay up to N values to all other processors.

The implementation of the above algorithm in Java is given in Figure 15.4. In this implementation we require every process to simply maintain the smallest value that it knows in the variable myValue. The variable changed records whether the minimum value it knows changed in the last round. The process broadcasts its value only if changed is true.

A simple program that calls the Consensus object is shown in Figure 15.5.

```java
import java.util.*;
public class Consensus extends Process {
    int myValue;
    int f; // maximum number of faults
    boolean changed = true;
    boolean hasProposed = false;
    public Consensus(Linker initComm, int f) {
        super(initComm);
        this.f = f;
    }
    public synchronized void propose(int value) {
        myValue = value;
        hasProposed = true;
        notify();
    }
    public int decide() {
        for (int k = 0; k <= f; k++) { // f+1 rounds
            synchronized (this) {
                if (changed) broadcastMsg("proposal", myValue);
            }
            // sleep enough to receive messages for this round
            Util.mySleep(Symbols.roundTime);
        }
        synchronized (this) {
            return myValue;
        }
    }
    public synchronized void handleMsg(Msg m, int src, String tag) {
        while (!hasProposed) myWait();
        if (tag.equals("proposal")) {
            int value = m.getMessageInt();
            if (value < myValue) {
                myValue = value;
                changed = true;
            } else
                changed = false;
        }
    }
}
```

Figure 15.4: Consensus in a synchronous environment

```
public class ConsensusTester {
    public static void main(String[] args) throws Exception {
        String baseName = args[0];
        int myId = Integer.parseInt(args[1]);
        int numProc = Integer.parseInt(args[2]);
        Linker comm = new Linker(baseName, myId, numProc);
        Consensus sp = new Consensus(comm, 3);
        for (int i = 0; i < numProc; i++)
            if (i != myId) (new ListenerThread(i, sp)).start();
        sp.propose(myId);
        System.out.println("The value decided:" + sp.decide());
    }
}
```

Figure 15.5: Consensus tester

15.4.2 Consensus under Byzantine Faults

Byzantine faults allow for malicious behavior by the processes. The consensus problem in this model can be understood in the context of the Byzantine General Agreement problem, which is defined as follows. There were N Byzantine generals who were called out to repel the attack by a Turkish Sultan. These generals camped near the Turkish army. Each of the N Byzantine generals had a preference for whether to *attack* the Turkish army or to *retreat*. The Byzantine armies were strong enough that the loyal generals of the armies knew that if their actions were coordinated (either attack or retreat), then they would be able to resist the Sultan's army. The problem was that some of the generals were treacherous and would try to foil any protocol that loyal generals might devise for the coordination of the attack. They might, for example, send conflicting messages to different generals, and might even collude to mislead loyal generals. The Byzantine General Agreement (BGA) problem requires us to design a protocol by which the loyal generals can coordinate their actions. It is assumed that generals can communicate with each other using reliable messengers.

The BGA problem can easily be seen as the consensus problem in a distributed system under Byzantine faults. We call a protocol f-*resilient* if it can tolerate f Byzantine faulty processors. It has been shown that there is no f-resilient protocol for BGA if $N \leq 3f$.

In this section we give an algorithm that takes $f + 1$ rounds, each round of two phases, to solve the BGA problem. This algorithm uses constant-size messages but requires that $N > 4f$. Each processor has a preference for each round, which is initially its input value.

The algorithm is shown in Figure 15.6. The algorithm is based on the idea of a rotating coordinator (or king). Processor P_i is assumed to be the coordinator or the king for round k. In the first phase of a round, each processor exchanges its value with all other processors. Based on its V vector, it determines its estimate in the variable *myvalue*. In the second phase, the processor receives the value from the coordinator. If it receives no value (because the coordinator has failed), then it assumes $v_\perp$ (a default value) for the king value. Now, it decides whether to use its own value or the *kingvalue*. This decision is based on the multiplicity of *myvalue* in the vector V. If V has more than $N/2 + f$ copies of *myvalue*, then *myvalue* is chosen for $V[i]$; otherwise, *kingvalue* is used.

We first show that agreement persists, that is, if all correct processors prefer a value v at the beginning of a round, then they continue to do so at the end of a round. This property holds because

$$N > 4f$$
$$\equiv N - N/2 > 2f$$
$$\equiv N - f > N/2 + f.$$

Since the number of correct processors is at least $N - f$, each correct processor will receive more than $N/2 + f$ copies of v and hence choose that at the end of second phase.

We now show that the algorithm in Figure 15.6 solves the agreement problem. The validity property follows from the persistence of agreement. If all processors start with the same value v, then v is the value decided. Termination is obvious because the algorithm takes exactly $f + 1$ rounds. We now show the agreement property. Since there are $f + 1$ rounds and at most f faulty processors, at least one of the rounds has a correct king. Each correct processor decides on either the value sent by the king in that round or its own value. It chooses its own value w only if its multiplicity in V is at least $N/2 + f + 1$. Therefore, the king of that round must have at least $N/2 + 1$ multiplicity of w in its vector. Thus the value chosen by the king is also w. Hence, each processor decides on the same value at the end of a round in which the king is nonfaulty. From persistence of agreement, the agreement property at the end of the algorithm follows.

15.5 Knowledge and Common Knowledge

Many problems in a distributed system arise from the lack of global knowledge. By sending and receiving messages, processes increase the knowledge they have about the system. However, there is a limit to the level of knowledge that can be attained. We use the notion of knowledge to prove some fundamental results about distributed systems. In particular, we show that agreement is impossible to achieve

```java
import java.util.*;
public class KingBGA extends Process {
    final static int defaultValue = 0;
    int f; // maximum number of faults
    int V[]; // set of values known
    int kingValue, myValue;
    public KingBGA(Linker initComm, int f) {
        super(initComm);
        this.f = f;
        V = new int[N];
    }
    public synchronized void propose(int val) {
        for (int i = 0; i < N; i++) V[i] = defaultValue;
        V[myId] = val;
    }
    public int decide() {
        for (int k = 0; k <= f; k++) { // f+1 rounds
            broadcastMsg("phase1", V[myId]);
            Util.mySleep(Symbols.roundTime);
            synchronized (this) {
                myValue = getMajority(V);
                if (k == myId)
                    broadcastMsg("king", myValue);
            }
            Util.mySleep(Symbols.roundTime);
            synchronized (this) {
                if (numCopies(V, myValue) > N / 2 + f)
                    V[myId] = myValue;
                else
                    V[myId] = kingValue;
            }
        }
        return V[myId];
    }
    public synchronized void handleMsg(Msg m, int src, String tag) {
        if (tag.equals("phase1")) {
            V[src] = m.getMessageInt();
        } else if (tag.equals("king")) {
            kingValue = m.getMessageInt();
        }
    }
    int getMajority(int V[]) {
        if (numCopies(V, 0) > N / 2)
            return 0;
        else if (numCopies(V, 1) > N / 2)
            return 1;
        else
            return defaultValue;
    }
    int numCopies(int V[], int v) {
        int count = 0;
        for (int i = 0; i < V.length; i++)
            if (V[i] == v) count++;
        return count;
    }
}
```

Figure 15.6: An algorithm for Byzantine General Agreement

in an asynchronous system in the absence of reliable communication.

The notion of knowledge is also useful in proving lower bounds on the message complexity of distributed algorithms. In particular, knowledge about remote processes can be gained in an asynchronous distributed system only by message transfers. For example, consider the mutual exclusion problem. It is clear that if process P_i enters the critical section and later process P_j enters the critical section, then there must be some knowledge gained by process P_j before it can begin eating. This gain of knowledge can happen only through a message transfer. Observe that our assumption of asynchrony is crucial in requiring the message transfer. In a synchronous system with a global clock, the knowledge can indeed be gained simply by passage of time. Thus for a mutual exclusion algorithm, one may have time-division multiplexing in which processes enter the critical section on their preassigned slots. Thus mutual exclusion can be achieved without any message transfers.

Let G be a group of processes in a system. We use $K_i(b)$ to denote that the process i in the group G knows the predicate b. We will assume that a process can know only true predicates:

$$K_i(b) \Rightarrow b$$

The converse may not be true. A predicate b may be true, but it may not be known to process i. For example, let b be that there is a deadlock in the system. It is quite possible that b is true but process i does not know about it.

Now, it is easy to define the meaning of "someone in the group knows b," denoted by $S(b)$, as follows:

$$S(b) \overset{\text{def}}{=} \bigvee_{i \in G} K_i(b)$$

Similarly, we define "everyone in the group knows b," denoted by $E(b)$, as

$$E(b) \overset{\text{def}}{=} \bigwedge_{i \in G} K_i(b)$$

It is important to realize that $S(b)$ and $E(b)$ are also predicates—in any system state they evaluate to true or false. Thus it makes perfect sense to use $E(b)$ or $S(b)$ for a predicate. In particular, $E(E(b))$ means that everyone in the group knows that everyone in the group knows b.

This observation allows us to define $E^k(b)$, for $k \geq 0$, inductively as follows:

$$E^0(b) = b$$

$$E^{k+1}(b) = E(E^k(b))$$

It is important to realize that although

$$\forall k : E^{k+1}(b) \Rightarrow E^k(b)$$

the converse does not hold in general. To appreciate this fact, consider the following scenario. Assume that there are $n \geq 1$ children who have gone out to play. These children were told before they went for play, that they should not get dirty. However, children being children, $k \geq 1$ of the children have dirty foreheads. Now assume that the children stand in a circle such that every child can see everyone else but cannot see his or her own forehead. Now consider the following predicate b:

$$b \stackrel{\text{def}}{=} \text{there is at least one child with a dirty forehead}$$

In this case $E^{k-1}(b)$ is true but $E^k(b)$ is not. For concreteness, let n be 10 and k be 2. It is clear that since k is 2, b is true. Furthermore, since every child can see at least one other child with a dirty forehead, $E(b)$ is also true. Is $E^2(b)$ true? Consider a child, say, child i with a dirty forehead. That child can see exactly one other child, say, child j, with a dirty forehead. So from child i's perspective, there may be just one child, namely, child j, who has a dirty forehead. However, in that case child j would not know that b is true. Thus $K_i(E(b))$ does not hold; therefore, $E^2(b)$ is also false.

The next higher level of knowledge, called *common knowledge* and denoted by $C(b)$, is defined as

$$C(b) \stackrel{\text{def}}{=} \forall k : E^k(b).$$

It is clear that for any k,

$$C(b) \Rightarrow E^k(b).$$

In the example of the children with a dirty forehead, assume that one of the parents walks to the children and announces "At least one of you has a dirty forehead." Every child hears the announcement. Not only that; they also know that everybody else heard the announcement. Furthermore, every child knows that every other child also knows this. We could go on like that. In short, by announcing b, the level of knowledge has become $C(b)$.

Now, assume that the parent repeatedly asks the question: "Can anyone prove that his or her own forehead is dirty?" Assuming that all children can make all logical conclusions and they reply simultaneously, it can be easily shown using induction that all children reply "No" to the first $k-1$ questions and all the children with a dirty forehead reply "Yes" to the kth question (see Problem 15.11).

To understand the role of common knowledge, consider the scenario when $k \geq 2$. At first, it may seem that the statement made by the parent "At least one of you has a dirty forehead." does not add any knowledge because every child can see at least one other child with a dirty forehead and thus already knew b. But this is not true. To appreciate this the reader should also consider a variant in which the parent repeatedly asks: "Can anyone prove that his or her own forehead is dirty?"

without first announcing b. In this case, the children will never answer "Yes." By announcing b, the parent gives common knowledge of b and therefore $E^k(b)$. $E^k(b)$ is required for the children to answer "Yes" in the kth round.

15.6   Application: Two-General Problem

We now prove a fundamental result about common knowledge—it cannot be gained in a distributed system with unreliable messages. We explain the significance of the result in the context of the coordinating general problem under unreliable communication. Assume that there are two generals who need to coordinate an attack on the enemy army. The armies of the generals are camped on the hills surrounding a valley, which has the enemy army. Both the generals would like to attack the enemy army simultaneously because each general's army is outnumbered by the enemy army. They had no agreed-on plan beforehand, and on some night they would like to coordinate with each other so that both attack the enemy the next day. The generals are assumed to behave correctly, but the communication between them is unreliable. Any messenger sent from one general to the other may be caught by the enemy. The question is whether there exists a protocol that allows the generals to agree on a single bit denoting *attack* or *retreat*.

It is clear that in the presence of unreliable messages no protocol can guarantee *agreement* for *all* runs. None of the messages sent by any general may reach the other side. The real question is whether there is some protocol that can guarantee agreement for *some* run (for example, when some messages reach their destination). Unfortunately, even in a simple distributed system with just two processors, P and Q, that communicate with unreliable messages, there is no protocol that allows common knowledge to be gained in any of its run.

If not, let r be a run with the smallest number of messages that achieves common knowledge. Let m be the last message in the run. Assume without loss of generality that the last message was sent from the processor P to processor Q. Since messages are unreliable, processor P does not know whether Q received the message. Thus, if P can assert $C(b)$ after m messages, then it can also do so after $m-1$ messages. But $C(b)$ at P also implies $C(b)$ at Q. Thus $C(b)$ is true after $m-1$ messages, violating minimality of the run r.

In contrast, the lower levels of knowledge are attainable. Indeed, to go from $S(b)$ to $E(b)$, it is sufficient for the processor with the knowledge of b to send messages to all other processors indicating the truthness of b. In the run in which all messages reach their destination, $E(b)$ will hold. The reader should also verify that $E^2(b)$ will not hold for any run after the protocol. The reader is asked to design a protocol that guarantees $E^2(b)$ from $S(b)$ in one of its runs in Problem 15.12.

15.7 Problems

15.1. Why does the following algorithm not work for consensus under FLP assumptions? Give a scenario under which the algorithm fails. It is common knowledge that there are six processes in the system numbered P_0 to P_5. The algorithm is as follows: Every process sends its input bit to all processes (including itself) and waits for five messages. Every process decides on the majority of the five bits received.

15.2. Show that all the following problems are impossible to solve in an asynchronous system in the presence of a single failure.

   (a) *Leader Election*: Show that the special case when the leader can be only from the set $\{P_0, P_1\}$ is equivalent to consensus.

   (b) *Computation of a global function*: Show that a deterministic nontrivial global function such as *min*, *max*, and addition can be used to solve consensus.

15.3. *Atomic broadcast* requires the following properties.

   - *Validity*: If the sender is correct and broadcasts a message m, then all correct processes eventually deliver m.

   - *Agreement*: If a correct process delivers a message m, then all correct processes deliver m.

   - *Integrity*: For any message m, q receives m from p at most once and only if p sent m to q.

   - *Order*: All correct processes receive all broadcast messages in the same order.

   Show that atomic broadcast is impossible to solve in asynchronous systems.

*15.4. (due to Fischer, Lynch and Paterson[FLP85]) Show that if it is known that processes will not die *during* the protocol, then consensus can be reached (despite some initially dead processes).

*15.5. Give a randomized algorithm that achieves consensus in an asynchronous distributed system in the presence of f crash failures under the assumption that $N \geq 2f + 1$.

15.6. Show by an example that if the consensus algorithm decided the final value after f rounds instead of $f + 1$ rounds, then it might violate the agreement property.

15.7. Give an example of an execution of a system with six processes, two of which are faulty in which the Byzantine general agreement algorithm does not work correctly.

15.8. Give an algorithm that solves BGA problem whenever $N \geq 3f + 1$.

*15.9. [due to Dolev and Strong[DS83]] In the Byzantine failure model a faulty process could forward incorrect information about messages received from other processes. A less malevolent model is called *Byzantine failure with mutual authentication*. In this model, we assume that a message can be signed digitally for authentication. There exist many cryptographic algorithms for digital signatures. Give an algorithm for Byzantine General Agreement assuming authentication that is f-resilient for $f < N$, requires only $f + 1$ rounds, and uses a polynomial number of messages.

*15.10. Show that the number of rounds required to solve consensus under the crash model is at least $f + 1$ in the worst case when $f \leq N - 2$.

15.11. Show using induction on k that when the parent repeatedly asks the question all children reply "No" to the first $k - 1$ questions and all the children with a dirty forehead reply "Yes" to the kth question.

15.12. Design a protocol that guarantees $E^2(b)$ from $S(b)$ in one of its runs.

15.13. Consider a game in which two people are asked to guess each other's number. They are told that they have consecutive natural numbers. For example, the person with number 50 can deduce that the other person has either 51 or 49. Now they are repeatedly asked in turn "Can you tell the other person's number?" Will any of them ever be able to answer in the affirmative? If yes, how? If no, why not?

15.8   Bibliographic Remarks

The theory of the consensus problem and its generalizations is quite well developed. We have covered only the very basic ideas from the literature. The reader will find many results in the book by Lynch [Lyn96]. The impossibility of achieving consensus in asynchronous system is due to Fischer, Lynch, and Paterson [FLP85]. The consensus problem with Byzantine faults was first introduced and solved by Lamport, Shostak and Pease [LSP82, PSL80]. The lower bound on the number of bounds needed for solving the problem under Byzantine faults was given by Fischer and Lynch [FL82] and under crash failures by Dolev and Strong [DS83].

The discussion of knowledge and common knowledge is taken from a paper by Halpern and Moses[HM84]. The "two-generals problem" was first described by [Gra78].

Chapter 16

Transactions

16.1 Introduction

The concept of a *transaction* has been very useful in allowing concurrent processing of data with consistent results. A transaction is a sequence of operations such that that entire sequence appears as one indivisible operation. For any observer, it appears as if the entire sequence has been executed or none of the operations in the sequence have been executed. This property of indivisibility is preserved by a transaction despite the presence of concurrency and failures. By *concurrency*, we mean that multiple transactions may be going on at the same time. We are guaranteed that the transactions do not interfere with each other. The concurrent execution of multiple transactions is equivalent to a serial execution of those transactions. Further, if the transaction has not committed and there is *failure*, then everything should be restored to appear as if none of the operations of the transaction happened. If the transaction has committed, then the results of the transaction must become permanent even when there are failures.

As an example of a transaction, consider transfer of money from account A to account B. The transaction, say T_1 can be written as

```
begin_transaction
        withdraw x from account A;
        deposit x to account B;
end_transaction
```

Once the two operations of withdrawing and depositing have been grouped as a transaction, they become atomic to the rest of the world. Assume, for example, that another transaction T_2 is executed concurrently with this transaction. T_2 simply adds the balances in accounts A and B. The semantics of the transaction guarantees that T_2 will not add the balance of account A after the withdrawal and the balance of account B before the deposit. The all-or-nothing property is also guaranteed when there is a failure. If the second operation cannot be performed for some reason (such as account B does not exist), then the effects of the first operation are also not visible, i.e., the balance is restored in account A.

A transaction can be viewed as implementing the following primitives:

1. `begin_transaction`: This denotes the beginning of a transaction.

2. `end_transaction`: This denotes the end of a transaction. All the statements between the beginning and the end of the transaction constitute the transaction. Execution of this primitive results in committing the transaction, and its effects must persist.

3. `abort_transaction`: The user has the ability to call `abort_transaction` in the middle of a transaction. This requires that all values prior to the transaction are restored.

4. `read`: Within a transaction, the program can read objects.

5. `write`: Within a transaction, the program can also write objects.

16.2   ACID Properties

Sometimes the guarantees provided by a transaction are called ACID properties, where ACID stands for atomicity, consistency, isolation, and durability. These terms are explained next.

- *Atomicity*: This property refers to all-or-nothing property explained earlier.

- *Consistency*: A transaction should not violate integrity constraints of the system. A typical example is that of a financial system where the transaction of money transfer from one account to the other should keep the total amount of money in the system constant. It is the responsibility of the programmer writing the transaction to ensure that such constraints are not violated after the transaction has taken place.

- *Isolation*: This means that transactions are isolated from effects of concurrent transactions. Thus, in spite of concurrency, the net effect is that it appears that all transactions executed sequentially in some order.

- *Durability*: This property refers to the aspect of committing a transaction. It says that once a transaction has been committed its effects must become permanent even if there are failures.

16.3   Concurrency Control

The isolation property of transaction is also called the *serializability* condition. A concurrent history H of transactions $T_1, T_2, \ldots, T_n$ is *serializable* if it is equivalent to a serial history. As an example, suppose that there are two transactions: T_1 and T_2. T_1 transfers \$100 from account A to account B and T_2 transfers \$200 from account B to account C. Assuming that each account has \$1000 initially, the final balances for A, B, and C should be \$900, \$900 and \$1200, respectively. T_1 could be implemented as follows:

```
begin_transaction;
  x = read(A);
  x = x-100;
  write x to A;
  x = read(B);
  x = x+100;
  write x to B;
end_transaction;
```

T_2 could be implemented as follows:

```
begin_transaction;
  y = read(B);
  y = y-200;
  write y to B;
  y = read(C);
  y = y+200;
  write y to C;
end_transaction;
```

It is clear that all concurrent histories are not serializable. In the example above, assume that the following history happened:

```
  x = read(A);
  x = x-100;
  write x to A;
  x = read(B);
```

```
        y = read(B);
        y = y-200;
        write y to B;
        y = read(C);
        y = y+200;
        write y to C;
  x = x+100;
  write x to B;
```

In this case, the final values would be $900, 1100$, and 1200, which is clearly wrong. One way to ensure serializability would be by locking the entire database when a transaction is in progress. However, this will allow only serial histories.

A more practical technique frequently employed is called *two-phase locking*. In this technique, a transaction is viewed as consisting of two phases: the locking phase and the unlocking phase. In the locking phase (sometimes called a "growing" phase), a transaction can only lock data items and in the unlocking phase (sometimes called a "shrinking" phase) it can only unlock them. With this technique, the implementation of T_1 would be

```
begin_transaction;
  lock(A);
  x = read(A);
  x = x-100;
  write x to A;
  lock(B);
  x = read(B);
  x = x+100;
  write x to B;
  unlock(A);
  unlock(B);
end_transaction;
```

16.4 Dealing with Failures

There are primarily two techniques used for dealing with failures called *private workspace* and *logging*. In the private workspace approach, a transaction does not change the original primary copy. Any object that is affected by the transaction is kept in a separate copy called a shadow copy. If the transaction aborts, then private or shadow copies are discarded and nothing is lost. If the transaction commits, then all the shadow copies become the primary copies. Note that this technique is different from the technique for nonblocking synchronization, which we studied in Chapter 5. In the private workspace approach, we do not make copy of the entire database before a transaction is started. Instead, a copy of only those objects (or pages) are made that have been updated by the transaction. This technique can be implemented as follows. Assume that objects can be accessed only through pointers in the index table. Let S be primary index table of objects. At the beginning of a transaction, a copy of this table, S', is made and all read and write operations go through S'. Since reads do not change the object, both S and S' point to the same copy, and thus all the read operations still go to the primary copy. For a write, a new copy of that object is made and the pointer in the table S' is changed to the updated version. If the transaction aborts, then the table S' can be discarded; otherwise, S' becomes the primary table. Observe that this scheme requires locking of the objects for transactions to be serializable.

In the logging scheme, all the updates are performed on a single copy. However, a trail of all the writes are kept so that in case of a failure, one can go to the log and undo all the operations. For example, if an operation changed the value of object x from 5 to 3, then in the log it is maintained that x is changed from 5 to 3. If the transaction has to abort, then it is easy to undo this operation.

16.5 Distributed Commit

When a transaction spans multiple sites, we require that either all sites commit the transaction or all abort it. This problem is called the *distributed commit* problem. The problem is, of course, quite simple when there are no failures. In this section, we address how to solve the problem when processes may fail. We assume that links are reliable.

The requirements of the problem are as follows:

- *Agreement*: No two processes (failed or unfailed) decide on different outcome of the transaction.

- *Validity*: If any process starts with *abort*, then *abort* is the only possible final outcome. If all processes start with *commit* and there are no failures, then *commit* is the only possible outcome.

- *Weak termination*: If there are no failures, then all processes eventually decide.

- *Non-blocking*: All nonfaulty processes eventually decide.

We now give a *two-phase commit protocol* that satisfies the first three conditions. The steps in the protocol are:

- The coordinator sends a *request* message to all participants.

- On receiving a request message, each participant replies with either a "yes" or a "no" message. A "yes" message signifies that the participant can commit all the actions performed at its site. This finishes the first phase of the algorithm.

- The coordinator waits to receive messages from all participants. If all of them are "yes," then the coordinator sends the *finalCommit* message. Otherwise, it sends a *finalAbort* message.

- The participant carries out the action associated with the message received from the coordinator.

Thus there are two phases: the voting phase and the decision phase. In the voting phase, the coordinator collects all the votes and in the decision phase it communicates the final decision to all the participants.

The algorithm for the coordinator is shown in Figure 16.1. The coordinator invokes the method `doCoordinator()` to carry out the protocol. In the first phase, the coordinator waits until the flag `donePhase1` becomes true. This flag becomes true if all participants have replied with "yes" messages or when one of the participant has replied with a "no" message. These messages are handled in the method `handleMsg` which make call to `notify()` appropriately.

The algorithm for a participant is shown in Figure 16.2. A participant implements the consensus interface with the methods `propose` and `decide`. When a participant invokes `decide`, it is blocked until it gets a *finalCommit* or a *finalAbort* message from the coordinator. We have not shown the actions that the coordinator and participants need to take when they timeout waiting for messages. We have also not shown the actions that processes need to take on recovering from a crash. This part is left as an exercise for the reader (see Problem 16.6).

Let us now analyze the protocol from the perspective of the coordinator. If it does not hear from any of the participants in the first phase, then it can abort the entire transaction. Therefore, if a participant fails before it sends out its vote in the first phase, the failure is easily handled. What if the participant fails after it has sent out its vote as commit? Since the transaction may have committed, when the process recovers, it must find out the state of the transaction and commit all the changes. This observation implies that a participant can send a "yes" message only if it can make all the changes for committing a transaction despite a fault. In other words, the participant must have logged onto its stable storage the necessary information required to commit the transaction.

Let us now analyze the protocol from the perspective of a participant. Initially it is expecting a *request* message that may not arrive for the predetermined timeout

```
public class TwoPhaseCoord extends Process {
    boolean globalCommit = false ;
    boolean donePhase1 = false ;
    boolean noReceived = false ;
    int numParticipants ;
    int numReplies = 0;
    public TwoPhaseCoord( Linker initComm ) {
        super(initComm );
        numParticipants = N - 1;
    }
    public synchronized  void doCoordinator () {
        // Phase 1
        broadcastMsg ("request", myId );
        while (! donePhase1 )
            myWait ();

        // Phase 2
        if ( noReceived )
            broadcastMsg ("finalAbort", myId );
        else {
            globalCommit = true;
            broadcastMsg ("finalCommit", myId );
        }
    }
    public synchronized void handleMsg (Msg m, int src , String tag ) {
        if ( tag . equals ("yes")) {
            numReplies++;
            if ( numReplies == numParticipants ) {
                donePhase1 = true ;
                notify ();
            }
        } else if ( tag . equals ("no")) {
            noReceived = true ;
            donePhase1 = true ;
            notify ();
        }
    }
}
```

Figure 16.1: Algorithm for the coordinator of the two-phase commit protocol

```java
public class TwoPhaseParticipant extends Process {
    boolean localCommit;
    boolean globalCommit;
    boolean done = false;
    boolean hasProposed = false;
    public TwoPhaseParticipant(Linker initComm) {
        super(initComm);
    }
    public synchronized void propose(boolean vote) {
        localCommit = vote;
        hasProposed = true;
        notify();
    }
    public synchronized boolean decide() {
        while (!done) myWait();
        return globalCommit;
    }
    public synchronized void handleMsg(Msg m, int src, String tag) {
        while (!hasProposed) myWait();
        if (tag.equals("request")) {
            if (localCommit)
                sendMsg(src, "yes");
            else
                sendMsg(src, "no");
        } else if (tag.equals("finalCommit")) {
            globalCommit = true;
            done = true;
            notify();
        } else if (tag.equals("finalAbort")) {
            globalCommit = false;
            done = true;
            notify();
        }
    }
}
```

Figure 16.2: Algorithm for the participants in the two-phase commit protocol

interval. In this case, the participant can simply send a "no" message to the coordinator and can assume that the global transaction had aborted. The coordinator can also crash in the second phase. What if the participant has replied with a "yes" message in the first phase and does not hear from the coordinator in the second phase? In this case, it does not know whether the coordinator had committed the global transaction. In this case, the participant should inquire other participants about the final decision. If the coordinator crashed after sending *finalCommit* or *finalAbort* message to any participant who does not crash, then all participants will learn about the final decision. However, this still leaves out the case when the coordinator crashed before informing any participant (or the participants that it informed also crashed). In this case, all the participants have no choice but to wait for the coordinator to recover. This is the reason why two-phase commit protocol is called *blocking*.

16.6 Problems

16.1. A contracted two-phase locking scheme is one in which the second phase is contracted, that is, all locks are unlocked at the same time. What are the advantages and disadvantages of this scheme compared with the ordinary two-phase locking scheme ?

16.2. Write a class that provides the following services:(a) `lock(String varname; int pid)`; returns 1 if allowed by two-phase locking scheme, returns 0 otherwise, and (b) `unlock(String varname, int pid)`; returns 1 if locked by the process, returns 0 otherwise. Assume that the processor never crashes.

16.3. Which of the following schedules are serializable ?
   (a) $r_1(a, b); w_1(b); r_2(a); w_1(a); w_2(a)$.
   (b) $r_1(a, b); w_1(a); r_2(a); w_2(a); r_1(b)$.
   (c) $r_2(a); r_1(a, b); w_2(c); w_1(a); w_1(c)$.
   (d) $r_1(a), r_2(b), w_1(a), w_2(b), r_1(b), w_1(b), r_2(c), w_2(c)$

   For each of the serializable schedules, show a possible two-phase locking history.

16.4. Assume that you have two floats representing checking balance and savings balance stored on disk. Write a program that transfers \$100 from the checking account to the savings account. Assume that the processor can crash at anytime but disks are error-free. This means that you will also have to write a crash recovery procedure. You are given the following primitives:

```
class Stable {
 float val;
// to copy disk object val to memory object x, use
  synchronized void get(float x)
// to copy memory object x to disk object val, use
  synchronized void set(float x)
}
```

16.5. Explain why the two-phase commit protocol does not violate the FLP impossibility result.

16.6. Complete the code for the participants (Figure 16.2) and the coordinator (Figure 16.1) by specifying actions on timeout and crash recovery.

16.7   Bibliographic Remarks

The reader is referred to the book by Gray and Reuter [GR93] for a comprehensive treatment of transactions.

Chapter 17

Recovery

17.1   Introduction

In this chapter, we study methods for fault tolerance using checkpointing. A checkpoint can be *local* to a process or *global* in the system. A *global checkpoint* is simply a global state that is stored on the stable storage so that in the event of a failure the entire system can be rolled back to the global checkpoint and restarted. To record a global state, one could employ methods presented in Chapter 9. These methods, called coordinated checkpointing, can be efficiently implemented. However, there are two major disadvantages of using coordinated checkpoints:

1. There is the overhead of computing a global snapshot. When a *coordinated* checkpoint is taken, processes are forced to take their local checkpoints whenever the algorithm for coordinated checkpoint requires it. It is better for this decision to be local because then a process is free to take its local checkpoint whenever it is idle or the size of its state is small.

2. In case of a failure, the entire system is required to roll back. In particular, even those processes that never communicated with the process that failed are also required to roll back. This results in wasted computation and slow recovery.

   An alternative method is to let processes take their local checkpoints at their will. During a *failure-free* mode of computation, this will result in an overhead on computation lower than that for coordinated checkpointing. In case of a failure, a suitable set of local checkpoints is chosen to form a global checkpoint. Observe that processes that have not failed have their current states available, and those states can also serve as checkpoints. There are some disadvantages of uncoordinated checkpointing compared with coordinated checkpointing schemes. First, for coordinated checkpointing it is sufficient to keep just the most recent global snapshot in the stable storage. For uncoordinated checkpoints a more complex garbage collection scheme is required. Moreover, in the case of a failure the recovery method for coordinated checkpointing is simpler. There is no need to compute a consistent global checkpoint. Finally, but most importantly, simple uncoordinated checkpointing does not guarantee any progress. If local checkpoints are taken at inopportune times, the only consistent global state may be the initial one. This problem is called the *domino effect*, and an example is shown in Figure 17.1. Assume that process P_1 crashes and therefore must roll back to $c_{1,1}$, its last checkpoint. Because a message was sent between $c_{1,1}$ and $c_{1,2}$ that is received before $c_{2,2}$, process P_2 is in an inconsistent state at $c_{2,2}$ with respect to $c_{1,1}$. Therefore, P_2 rolls back to $c_{2,1}$. But this forces P_3 to roll back. Continuing in this manner, we find that the only consistent global checkpoint is the initial one. Rolling back to the initial global checkpoint results in wasting the entire computation.

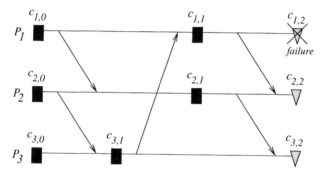

Figure 17.1: An example of the domino effect

A hybrid of the completely coordinated and the completely uncoordinated schemes is called *communication-induced checkpointing*. In this method, processes are free to take their local checkpoints whenever desired, but on the basis of the communication pattern, they may be forced to take additional local checkpoints. These methods guarantee that recovery will not suffer from the domino effect.

The characteristics of the application, the probability of failures, and technological factors may dictate which of the above mentioned choices of checkpointing is best for a given situation. In this chapter, we will study issues in uncoordinated checkpointing and communication-induced checkpointing.

17.2   Zigzag Relation

Consider any distributed computation with N processes $P_1, \ldots, P_N$. Each process P_i checkpoints its local state at some intermittent interval, giving rise to a sequence of local checkpoints denoted by S_i. We will assume that the initial state and the final state in any process are checkpointed. For any checkpoint c we denote by $pred.c$, the predecessor of the checkpoint c in the sequence S_i whenever it exists, that is, when c is not the initial checkpoint. Similarly, we use $succ.c$ for the successor of the checkpoint c.

Given a set of local checkpoints, X, we say that X is consistent iff $\forall c, d \in X : c || d$. A set of local checkpoints is called global if it contains N checkpoints, one from each process.

Let the set of all local checkpoints be S:

$$S = \bigcup_i S_i.$$

We first tackle the problem of finding a global checkpoint that contains a given set of checkpoints $X \subseteq S$. A relation called *zigzag precedes*, which is weaker (bigger) than $\rightarrow$, is useful in analysis of such problems.

Definition 17.1 *The relation zigzag precedes, denoted by* $\xrightarrow{z}$, *is the smallest relation that satisfies*

(Z1) $\qquad\qquad\qquad c \rightarrow d$ *implies* $c \xrightarrow{z} d$.

(Z2) $\qquad\qquad\qquad \exists e \in S : (c \rightarrow e) \wedge (pred.e \xrightarrow{z} d)$ *implies* $c \xrightarrow{z} d$.

The following property of the *zigzag* relation is easy to show:

(Z3) $\qquad\qquad\qquad (c \xrightarrow{z} e) \wedge (pred.e \xrightarrow{z} d)$ *implies* $(c \xrightarrow{z} d)$.

On the basis of this relation, we say that a set of local checkpoints X is *z-consistent* iff $\forall c, d \in X : c \xcancel{\xrightarrow{z}} d$.

Observe that all initial local checkpoints c satisfy

$$\forall s \in S : s \xcancel{\xrightarrow{z}} c.$$

Similarly, if c is a final local checkpoint, then

$$\forall s \in S : c \xcancel{\xrightarrow{z}} s.$$

Alternatively, a zigzag path between two checkpoints c and d is defined as follows. There is a zigzag path from c to d iff

1. Both c and d are in the same process and $c \prec d$; or,

2. there is a sequence of messages $m_1, \ldots, m_t$ such that

   (a) m_1 is sent after the checkpoint c.

   (b) If m_k is received by process r, then m_{k+1} is sent by process r in the same or a later checkpoint interval. Note that the message m_{k+1} may be sent before m_k.

   (c) m_t is received before the checkpoint d.

In Figure 17.2, there is a zigzag path from $c_{1,1}$ to $c_{3,1}$ even though there is no happened-before path. This path corresponds to the messages m_3 and m_4 in the diagram. The message m_4 is sent in the same checkpoint interval in which m_3 is received. Also note that there is a zigzag path from $c_{2,2}$ to itself because of messages m_5 and m_3. Such a path is called a *zigzag cycle*.

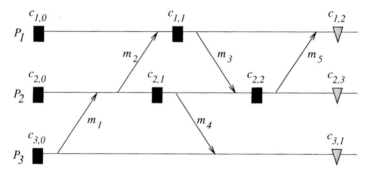

Figure 17.2: Examples of zigzag paths

We leave it as an exercise for the reader to show that $c \xrightarrow{z} d$ iff there is a zigzag path from c to d.

We now show that given a set of local checkpoints X, there exists a consistent global checkpoint G containing X iff X is z-consistent.

We prove the contrapositive. Given c and d in X (possibly $c = d$), we show that $c \xrightarrow{z} d$ implies that there is no consistent global state G containing c and d. We prove a slightly stronger claim. We show that $c \xrightarrow{z} d$ implies that there is no consistent global state G containing c or any checkpoint preceding it and d.

The proof is based on induction on k, the minimum number of applications of rule (Z2) to derive that $c \xrightarrow{z} d$. When $k = 0$, we have $c \rightarrow d$. Thus c or any checkpoint preceding c and d cannot be part of a consistent state by the definition of consistency. Now consider the case when $c \xrightarrow{z} d$ because $\exists e : (c \rightarrow e) \wedge (pred.e \xrightarrow{z} d)$. We show that any consistent set of states Y containing c and d cannot have any checkpoint from the process containing the checkpoint e. Y cannot contain e or any state following e because $c \to e$ would imply that c happened before that state. Furthermore, Y cannot contain any checkpoint previous to e because $pred.e \overset{z}{\to} d$ and the induction hypothesis would imply that Y is inconsistent. The induction hypothesis is applicable because $pred.e \overset{z}{\to} d$ must have fewer applications of (Z2) rule. Since any consistent set of checkpoints cannot contain any checkpoint from the process $e.p$, we conclude that there is no global checkpoint containing c and d.

Conversely, it is sufficient to show that if X is not global, then there exists Y strictly containing X that is z-consistent. By repeating the process, the set can be made global. Furthermore, the set is always consistent because $x \overset{z}{\nrightarrow} y$ implies $x \nrightarrow y$. For any process P_i, which does not have a checkpoint in X, we define

$$e = min\{f \in P_i \mid \forall x \in X : f \overset{z}{\nrightarrow} x\}$$

where min is taken over the relation $\prec$. Note that the set over which min is taken is nonempty because the final checkpoint on process P_i cannot zigzag precede any other checkpoint. We show that $Y = X \cup \{e\}$ is z-consistent. It is sufficient to show that $e \overset{z}{\nrightarrow} e$ and $c \overset{z}{\nrightarrow} e$ for any c in X. If e is an initial local checkpoint, then $e \overset{z}{\nrightarrow} e$ and $c \overset{z}{\nrightarrow} e$ for any c in X clearly hold. Otherwise, $pred.e$ exists. Since e is the minimum event for which $\forall x \in X : e \nrightarrow x$ we see that there exists an event, say, $d \in X$, such that $pred.e \overset{z}{\to} d$. Since $e \overset{z}{\to} e$ and $pred.e \overset{z}{\to} d$ imply that $e \overset{z}{\to} d$, we know that $e \overset{z}{\to} e$ is not possible. Similarly, $c \overset{z}{\to} e$ and $pred.e \overset{z}{\to} d$ imply $c \overset{z}{\to} d$, which is false because X is z-consistent.

This result implies that if a checkpoint is part of a zigzag cycle, then it cannot be part of any global checkpoint. Such checkpoints are called *useless* checkpoints.

17.3 Communication-Induced Checkpointing

If a computation satisfies a condition called rollback-dependency trackability (RDT), then for every zigzag path there is also a causal path. In other words, rollback dependency is then trackable by tracking causality. Formally,

Definition 17.2 (RDT) *A computation with checkpoints satisfies rollback-dependency trackability if for all checkpoints c, d: $c \to d \equiv c \overset{z}{\to} d$.*

Because there are no cycles in the happened-before relation, it follows that if a computation satisfies RDT, then it does not have any zigzag cycles. This implies that no checkpoint is useless in a computation that satisfies RDT. We now develop an algorithm for checkpointing to ensure RDT.

The algorithm takes additional checkpoints before receiving some of the messages to ensure that the overall computation is RDT. The intuition behind the algorithm is that for every zigzag path there should be a causal path. The difficulty arises when in a checkpoint interval a message is sent before another message is received. For example, in Figure 17.2 m_4 is sent before m_3 is received. When m_3 is received, a zigzag path is formed from $c_{1,1}$ to $c_{3,1}$. The message m_3 had dependency on $c_{1,1}$, which was not sent as part of m_4. To avoid this situation, we use the following rule:

Fixed dependency after send (FDAS): A process takes additional checkpoints to guarantee that the transitive dependency vector remains unchanged after any send event (until the next checkpoint).

Thus a process takes a checkpoint before a receive of a message if it has sent a message in that checkpoint interval and the vector clock changes when the message is received.

A computation that uses FDAS is guaranteed to satisfy RDT because any zigzag path from checkpoints c to d implies the existence of a causal path from c to d. There are two main advantages for a computation to be RDT: (1) it allows us to calculate efficiently the maximum recoverable global state containing a given set of checkpoints (see Problem 17.2), and (2) every zigzag path implies the existence of a happened-before path. Since there are no cycles in the happened-before relation, it follows that the RDT graph does not have any zigzag cycles. Hence, using FDAS we can guarantee that there are no *useless* checkpoints in the computation.

17.4   Optimistic Message Logging: Main Ideas

In *checkpointing*-based methods for recovery, after a process fails, some or all of the processes roll back to their last checkpoints such that the resulting system state is consistent. For large systems, the cost of this synchronization is prohibitive. Furthermore, these protocols may not restore the maximum recoverable state.

If along with checkpoints, messages are logged to the stable storage, then the maximum recoverable state can always be restored. Theoretically, message logging alone is sufficient (assuming deterministic processes), but checkpointing speeds up the recovery. Messages can be logged by either the sender or the receiver. In *pessimistic logging*, messages are logged either as soon as they are received or before the receiver sends a new message. When a process fails, its last checkpoint is restored and the logged messages that were received after the checkpointed state are replayed in the order they were received. Pessimism in logging ensures that no other process needs to be rolled back. Although this recovery mechanism is simple, it reduces the speed of the computation. Therefore, it is not a desirable scheme in an environment where failures are rare and message activity is high.

In *optimistic logging*, it is assumed that failures are rare. A process stores the received messages in volatile memory and logs them to stable storage at infrequent intervals. Since volatile memory is lost in a failure, some of the messages cannot be replayed after the failure. Thus some of the process states are *lost* in the failure. States in other processes that depend on these lost states become *orphans*. A recovery protocol must roll back these orphan states to *nonorphan* states. The following properties are desirable for an optimistic recovery protocol:

- *Asynchronous recovery*: A process should be able to restart immediately after a failure. It should not have to wait for messages from other processes.

- *Minimal amount of rollback*: In some algorithms, processes that causally depend on the lost computation might roll back more than once. In the worst case, they may roll back an exponential number of times. A process should roll back at most once in response to each failure.

- *No assumptions about the ordering of messages*: If assumptions are made about the ordering of messages such as FIFO, then we lose the asynchronous character of the computation. A recovery protocol should make as weak assumptions as possible about the ordering of messages.

- *Handle concurrent failures*: It is possible that two or more processes fail concurrently in a distributed computation. A recovery protocol should handle this situation correctly and efficiently.

- *Recover maximum recoverable state*: No computation should be needlessly rolled back.

We present an optimistic recovery protocol that has all these features. Our protocol is based on two mechanisms—a *fault-tolerant vector clock* and a *version end-table* mechanism. The fault-tolerant vector clock is used to maintain causality information despite failures. The version end-table mechanism is used to detect orphan states and obsolete messages. In this chapter, we present necessary and sufficient conditions for a message to be obsolete and for a state to be orphan in terms of the version end-table data structure.

17.4.1 Model

In our model, processes are assumed to be *piecewise deterministic*. This means that when a process receives a message, it performs some internal computation, sends some messages, and then blocks itself to receive a message. All these actions are completely deterministic, that is, actions performed after a message receive and before blocking for another message receive are determined completely by the contents of the message received and the state of the process at the time of message receive. A nondeterministic action can be modeled by treating it as a message receive.

The receiver of a message depends on the content of the message and therefore on the sender of the message. This dependency relation is transitive. The receiver becomes dependent only after the received message is delivered. From now on, unless otherwise stated, receive of a message will imply its delivery.

A process periodically takes its checkpoint. It also asynchronously logs to the stable storage all messages received in the order they are received. At the time of checkpointing, all unlogged messages are also logged.

A failed process *restarts* by creating a new version of itself. It restores its last checkpoint and replays the logged messages that were received after the restored state. Because some of the messages might not have been logged at the time of the failure, some of the old states, called *lost* states, cannot be recreated. Now, consider the states in other processes that depend on the lost states. These states, called *orphan* states, must be rolled back. Other processes have not failed, so before rolling back, they can log all the unlogged messages and save their states. Thus no information is lost in rollback. Note the distinction between restart and rollback. A failed process restarts, whereas an orphan process rolls back. Some information is lost in restart but not in rollback. A process creates a new version of itself on restart but not on rollback. A message sent by a lost or an orphan state is called an *obsolete* message. A process receiving an *obsolete* message must discard it. Otherwise, the receiver becomes an *orphan*.

In Figure 17.3, a distributed computation is shown. Process P_1 fails at state f_{10}, restores state s_{11}, takes some actions needed for recovery, and restarts from state r_{10}. States s_{12} and f_{10} are lost. Being dependent on s_{12}, state s_{22} of P_2 is an *orphan*. P_2 rolls back, restores state s_{21}, takes actions needed for recovery, and restarts from state r_{20}. Dashed lines show the lost computation. Solid lines show the useful computation at the current point.

17.4.2   Fault-Tolerant Vector Clock

Recall that a vector clock is a vector whose number of components equals the number of processes. Each entry is the timestamp of the corresponding process. To maintain causality despite failures, we extend each entry by a *version number*. The extended vector clock is referred to as the *fault-tolerant vector clock* (FTVC). We use the term "clock" and the acronym FTVC interchangeably. Let us consider the FTVC of a process P_i. The version number in the ith entry of its FTVC (its own version number) is equal to the number of times it has rolled back. The version number

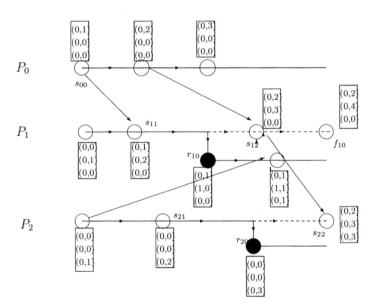

Figure 17.3: A distributed computation

in the jth entry is equal to the highest version number of P_j on which P_i depends. Let entry e correspond to a tuple(version v, timestamp ts). Then, $e_1 < e_2 \equiv (v_1 < v_2) \vee [(v_1 = v_2) \wedge (ts_1 < ts_2)]$.

A process P_i sends its FTVC along with every outgoing message. After sending a message, P_i increments its timestamp. On receiving a message, it updates its FTVC with the message's FTVC by taking the componentwise maximum of entries and incrementing its own timestamp. To take the maximum, the entry with the higher version number is chosen. If both entries have the same version number, then the entry with the higher timestamp value is chosen.

When a process restarts after a failure or rolls back because of failure of some other process, it increments its version number and sets its timestamp to zero. Note that this operation does not require access to previous timestamps that may be lost on a failure. It requires only its previous version number. As explained in Section 17.5.2, the version number is not lost in a failure. A formal description of the FTVC algorithm is given in Figure 17.4.

An example of FTVC is shown in Figure 17.3. The FTVC of each state is shown in a rectangular box near it.

17.4.3 Version End Table

Orphan states and resulting obsolete messages are detected with the version end-table mechanism. This method requires that, after recovering from a failure, a process notify other processes by broadcasting a *token*. The token contains the version number that failed and the timestamp of that version at the point of restoration. We do not make any assumption about the ordering of tokens among themselves or with respect to the messages. We assume that tokens are delivered reliably.

Every process maintains some information, called *vtable*, about other processes in its stable storage. In *vtable* of P_i, there is a record for every *known* version of processes that ended in a failure. If P_i has received a token about kth version of P_j, then it keeps that token's timestamp in the corresponding record in *vtable*. The routine *insert*(*vtable*[j], *token*) inserts the *token* in that part of the *vtable* of P_i that keeps track of P_j.

A formal description of the version end-table manipulation algorithm is given in Figure 17.5.

17.5 An Asynchronous Recovery Protocol

Our protocol for asynchronous recovery is shown in Figure 17.6. We describe the actions taken by a process, say, P_i, on the occurrence of different events. We assume that each action taken by a process is atomic. This means that any failure during

```
P_i::
  type entry = (integer ver, integer ts); // version, timestamp
  var clock : array [1..N] of entry initially
      ∀j : clock[j].ver = 0 ;
      ∀j : j ≠ i : clock[j].ts = 0; clock[i].ts = 1;

  To send message :
    send (data, clock) ;
    clock[i].ts := clock[i].ts + 1;

  Upon receive of a message (data, mclock) :
    // P_i receives vector clock 'mclock' in incoming message
    ∀j : clock[j] = max(clock[j], mclock[j]);
    clock[i].ts := clock[i].ts + 1;

  Upon Restart (state s restored) :
    clock = s.clock;
    clock[i].ver := clock[i].ver + 1;
    clock[i].ts = 0;

  Upon Rollback(state s restored) :
    clock = s.clock;
```

Figure 17.4: Formal description of the fault-tolerant vector clock

```
P_i::
  var
      vtable : array[1..N] of set of entry initially empty;
      token : entry;
  Receive_token (v_1, t_1) from P_j :
      insert(vtable[j], (v_1, t_1)) ;
  Upon Restart
      insert(vtable[i], (v, clock[i].ts)) ;
```

Figure 17.5: Formal description of the version end-table mechanism

the execution of any action may be viewed as a failure before or after the execution of the entire action.

17.5.1   Message Receive

On receiving a message, P_i first checks whether the message is obsolete. This is done as follows. Let e_j refer to the jth entry in the message's FTVC. Recall that each entry is of the form (v, t), where v is the version number and t is the timestamp. If there exists an entry e_j, such that e_j is (v, t) and (v, t') belongs to $vtable[j]$ of P_i and $t > t'$, then the message is obsolete. This is proved later.

If the message is obsolete, then it is discarded. Otherwise, P_i checks whether the message is deliverable. The message is not deliverable if its FTVC contains a version number k for any process P_j, such that P_i has not received all the tokens from P_j with the version number l less than k. In this case, delivery of the message is postponed. Since we assume failures to be rare, this should not affect the speed of the computation.

If the message is delivered, then the vector clock and the version end-table are updated. P_i updates its FTVC with the message's FTVC as explained in Section 17.4.2. The message and its FTVC are logged in the volatile storage. Asynchronously, the volatile log is flushed to the stable storage. The version end-table is updated as explained in Section 17.4.3.

17.5.2   On Restart after a Failure

After a failure, P_i restores its last checkpoint from the stable storage (including the version end-table). Then it replays all the logged messages received after the restored state, in the receipt order. To inform other processes about its failure, it broadcasts a token containing its current version number and timestamp. After that, it increments its own version number and resets its own timestamp to zero. Finally, it updates its version end-table, takes a new checkpoint, and starts computing in a normal fashion. The new checkpoint is needed to avoid the loss of the current version number in another failure. Note that the recovery is unaffected by a failure during this checkpointing. The entire event must appear atomic despite a failure. If the failure occurs before the new checkpoint is finished, then it should appear that the restart never happened and the restart event can be executed again.

17.5.3   On Receiving a Token

We require all tokens to be logged synchronously, that is, the process is not allowed to compute further until the information about the token is in stable storage. This prevents the process from losing the information about the token if it fails after

---

P_i::

  Receive_message (data, mclock) :

    // Check whether message is obsolete

    $\forall j$:**if** $((mclock[j].ver, t) \in vtable[j])$ **and** $(t < mclock[j].ts)$ **then**

        discard message ;

    if $\exists j, l$ s.t. $l < mclock[j].ver \wedge P_i$ has no token about lth version of P_j **then**

        postpone the delivery of the message until that token arrives;

  Restart (after failure) :

    restore last checkpoint;

    replay all the logged messages that follow the restored state;

    $insert(vtable[i], (v, clock[i].ts))$;

    $broadcast\_token(clock[i])$;

  Receive_token (v,t) from P_j :

    synchronously log the token to the stable storage;

    if FTVC depends on version v of P_j with timestamp t'

        and $(t < t')$ **then** Rollback;

    // Regardless of rollback, following actions are taken

    update $vtable$;

    deliver messages that were held for this token;

  Rollback (due to token (v, t) from P_j) :

    log all the unlogged messages to the stable storage;

    restore the maximum checkpoint such that

        it does not depend upon any timestamp $t' > t$ of version v for P_j..(I)

    discard the checkpoints that follow;

    replay the messages logged after this checkpoint

        until condition (I) holds;

    discard the logged messages that follow;

Figure 17.6: An optimistic protocol for asynchronous recovery

acting on it. Since we expect the number of failures to be small, this would incur only a small overhead.

The token enables a process to discover whether it has become an orphan. To check whether it has become an orphan, it proceeds as follows. Assume that it received the token (v, t) from P_j. It checks whether its vector clock indicates that it depends on a state (v, t') such that $t < t'$. If so, then P_i is an orphan and it needs to roll back.

Regardless of the rollback, P_i enters the record (v, t) in version end-table $[j]$. Finally, messages that were held for this token are delivered.

17.5.4   On Rollback

On a rollback due to token (v, t) from P_j, P_i first logs all the unlogged messages to the stable storage. Then it restores the maximum checkpoint s such that s does not depend on any state on P_j with version number v and timestamp greater than t. Then logged messages that were received after s are replayed as long as messages are not obsolete. It discards the checkpoints and logged messages that follow this state. Now the FTVC is updated by incrementing its timestamp. Note that it does not increment its version number. After this step, P_i restarts computing as normal.

This protocol has the following properties:

- *Asynchronous recovery*: After a failure, a process restores itself and starts computing. It broadcasts a token about its failure, but it does not require any response.

- *Minimal rollback*: In response to the failure of a given version of a given process, other processes roll back at most once. This rollback occurs on receiving the corresponding token.

- *Handling concurrent failures*: In response to multiple failures, a process rolls back in the order in which it receives information about different failures. Concurrent failures have the same effect as that of multiple nonconcurrent failures.

- *Recovering maximum recoverable state*: Only orphan states are rolled back.

We now do the overhead analysis of the protocol. Except for application messages, the protocol causes no extra messages to be sent during failure-free run. It tags a FTVC to every application message. Let the maximum number of failures of any process be f. The protocol adds $\log f$ bits to each timestamp in the vector clock. Since we expect the number of failures to be small, $\log f$ should be small.

Thus the total overhead is $O(N \log f)$ bits per message in addition to the vector clock.

A token is broadcast only when a process fails. The size of a token is equal to just one entry of the vector clock.

Let the number of processes in the system be n. There are at most f versions of a process, and there is one entry for each version of a process in the version end-table.

17.6 Problems

17.1. Show that the following rules are special cases of FDAS.

  (a) A process takes a checkpoint before every receive of a message.

  (b) A process takes a checkpoint after every send of a message.

  (c) A process takes a checkpoint before any receive after any send of a message.

17.2. Assume that a computation satisfies RDT. Given a set of checkpoints X from this computation, show how you will determine whether there exists a global checkpoint containing X. If there exists one, then give an efficient algorithm to determine the least and the greatest global checkpoints containing X.

17.3. (due to Helary et al. [HMNR97]) Assume that all processes maintain a variant of logical clocks defined as follows: The logical clock is incremented on any checkpointing event. The clock value is piggybacked on every message. On receiving a message, the logical clock is computed as the maximum of the local clock and the value received with the message. Processes are free to take their local checkpoints whenever desired. In addition, a process is forced to take a local checkpoint on receiving a message if (a) it has sent out a message since its last checkpoint, and (b) the value of its logical clock will change on receiving the message. Show that this algorithm guarantees that there are no *useless* checkpoints. Will this protocol force more checkpoints or fewer checkpoints than the FDAS protocol?

17.4. In many applications, the distributed program may output to the external environment such that the output message cannot be revoked (or the environment cannot be rolled back). This is called the *output commit* problem. What changes will you make to the algorithm to take care of such messages?

17.5. Give a scheme for garbage collection of obsolete local checkpoints and message logs.

17.7 Bibliographic Remarks

The *zigzag* relation was first defined by Netzer and Xu [NX95]. The definition we have used in this chapter is different from but equivalent to their definition. The notion of the R-graph, RDT computation, and the fixed-dependency-after-send rule was introduced by Wang [Wan97].

Strom and Yemini [SY85] initiated the area of optimistic message logging. Their scheme, however, suffers from the *exponential rollback* problem, where a single failure of a process can roll back another process an exponential number of times. The algorithm discussed in this chapter is taken from a paper by Damani and Garg [DG96].

Chapter 18

Self-Stabilization

18.1 Introduction

In this chapter we discuss a class of algorithms, called *self-stabilizing* algorithms, that can tolerate many kinds of "data" faults. A "data" fault corresponds to change in value of one or more variable of a program because of some unforeseen error. For example, a spanning tree is usually implemented using *parent* variables. Every node in the computer network maintains the *parent* pointer that points to the parent in the spanning tree. What if one or more of the *parent* pointers get corrupted? Now, the *parent* pointers may not form a valid spanning tree. Such errors will be called "data" faults. We will assume that the code of the program does not get corrupted. Because the code of the program does not change with time, it can be periodically checked for correctness using a copy stored in the secondary storage.

We assume that the system states can be divided into legal and illegal states. The definition of the legal state is dependent on the application. Usually, system and algorithm designers are very careful about transitions from the legal states, but illegal states of the system are ignored. When a fault occurs, the system moves to an illegal state and if the system is not designed properly, it may continue to execute in illegal states. A system is called *self-stabilizing* if regardless of the initial state, the system is guaranteed to reach a legal state after a finite number of moves.

We will illustrate the concept of self-stabilizing algorithms for two problems: mutual exclusion and spanning tree construction.

18.2   Mutual Exclusion with K-State Machines

We will model the mutual exclusion problem as follows. A machine can enter the critical section only if it has a *privilege*. Therefore, in the case of mutual exclusion, legal states are those global states in which exactly one machine has a privilege. The goal of the self-stabilizing mutual exclusion algorithm is to determine who has the privilege and how the privileges move in the network.

> Bottom:
>   **if** $(L = S)$ **then** $S := S + 1\ mod\ K$;
>
> For other machines:
>   **if** $(L \neq S)$ **then** $S := L$;

Figure 18.1: K-state self-stabilizing algorithm

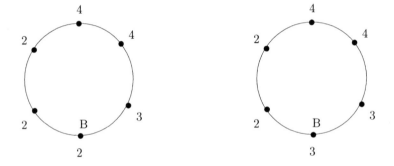

Figure 18.2: A move by the bottom machine in the K-state algorithm

We assume that there are N machines numbered $0 \ldots N - 1$. The state of any machine is determined by its *label* from the set $\{0 \ldots K - 1\}$. We use L, S, and R to denote the labels of the left neighbor, itself, and the right neighbor for any machine. Machine 0, also called the *bottom* machine, is treated differently from all other machines. The program is given in Figure 18.1, and a sample execution of the algorithm is shown in Figure 18.2. The bottom machine has a privilege if its label has the same value as its left neighbor, (i.e., $L = S$). In Figure 18.2, the bottom machine and its left neighbor have labels 2, and therefore the bottom machine has a privilege. Once a machine possessing a privilege executes its critical section, it should execute the transition given by the program. In Figure 18.2, on exiting from the critical section, the bottom machine executes the statement $S := S + 1 \ mod \ K$ and acquires the label 3.

A normal machine has a privilege only when $L \neq S$. On exiting the critical section, it executes $S := L$ and thus loses its privilege. In Figure 18.3, P_5 moves and makes it label as 4.

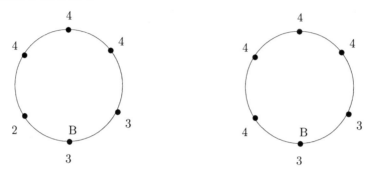

Figure 18.3: A move by a normal machine in the K-state algorithm

In this algorithm, the system is in a legal state if exactly one machine has the privilege. It is easy to verify that $(x_0, x_1, \ldots, x_{N-1})$ is legal if and only if either all x_i values are equal or there exists $m < N - 1$ such that all x_i values with $i \leq m$ are equal to some value and all other x_i values are equal to some other value. In the first case, the bottom machine has the privilege. In the second case the machine P_{m+1} has the privilege. It is easy to verify that if the system is in a legal state, then it will stay legal.

It is also easy to verify that in any configuration, at least one move is possible. Now we consider any unbounded sequence of moves. We claim that a sequence of moves in which the bottom machine does not move is at most $O(N^2)$. This is because machine 1 can move at most once if the bottom machine does not move. This implies that the machine 2 can move at most twice and so on. Thus, the total number of moves is bounded by $O(N^2)$.

We now show that given any configuration of the ring, either (1) no other machine has the same label as the bottom, or (2) there exists a label that is different from all machines. We show that if condition (1) does not hold, then condition (2) is true. If there exists a machine that has the same label as that of bottom, then there are now $K - 1$ labels left to be distributed among $N - 2$ machines. Since $K \geq N$, we see that there is some label which is not used.

Furthermore, within a finite number of moves, condition (1) will be true. Note that if some label is missing from the network, it can be generated only by the bottom machine. Moreover, the bottom machine simply cycles among all labels. Since the bottom machine moves after some finite number of moves by normal machines, the bottom machine will eventually get the missing label.

We now show that if the system is in an illegal state, then within $O(N^2)$ moves, it reaches a legal state. It is easy to see that once the bottom machine gets the unique label, the system stabilizes in $O(N^2)$ moves. The bottom machine can move at most N times before it acquires the missing label. Machine 1 therefore can move at most $N + 1$ times before the bottom acquires the label. Similarly, machine i can move at most $N + i$ times before the bottom gets the label. By adding up all the moves, we get $N + (N + 1) + \ldots + (N + N - 1) = O(N^2)$ moves.

In this algorithm, the processes could read the state of their left neighbors. How do we implement this in a distributed system? One possibility is for a machine to periodically query its left neighbor. However, this may generate a lot of messages in the network. A more message-efficient solution is for a token to go around the system. The token carries with it the state of the last machine that it visited. But now we have to worry about the token getting lost and the presence of multiple tokens in the system. To guard against the token getting lost, we will require the bottom machine to generate a new token if it does not see a token in a certain timeout interval. To accomplish this, we use the following Java object as a periodic task. On invocation, this task sends a *restart* message to the bottom machine. To handle this message, the bottom machine calls the `sendToken` method.

```
import java.util.TimerTask;
public class RestartTask extends TimerTask {
    MsgHandler app;
    public RestartTask(MsgHandler app) {
        this.app = app;
    }
    public void run() {
        app.handleMsg(null, 0, "restart");
    }
}
```

We use a boolean `tokenSent` to record if the token has been sent by the bottom machine in the last timeout interval. If not, a token is sent out.

Multiple tokens do not pose any problem in this scheme because that only means that multiple processes will read the state of their left neighbors. The algorithm is shown in Figure 18.4 for the bottom machine and in Figure 18.5 for the normal machine.

```
import java.util.Timer;
public class StableBottom extends Process implements Lock {
    int myState = 0;
    int leftState = 0;
    int next;
    Timer t = new Timer();
    boolean tokenSent = false;
    public StableBottom(Linker initComm) {
        super(initComm);
        next = (myId + 1) % N;
    }
    public synchronized void initiate() {
        t.schedule(new RestartTask(this), 1000, 1000);
    }
    public synchronized void requestCS() {
        while (leftState != myState) myWait();
    }
    public synchronized void releaseCS() {
        myState = (leftState + 1) % N;
    }
    public synchronized void sendToken() {
        if (!tokenSent) {
            sendMsg(next, "token", myState);
            tokenSent = true;
        } else tokenSent = false;
    }
    public synchronized void handleMsg(Msg m, int src, String tag) {
        if (tag.equals("token"))
        {
            leftState = m.getMessageInt();
            notify();
            Util.mySleep(1000);
            sendMsg(next, "token", myState);
            tokenSent = true;
        } else if (tag.equals("restart"))
            sendToken();
    }
}
```

Figure 18.4: Self-stabilizing algorithm for mutual exclusion in a ring for the bottom machine

```java
import java.util.Timer;
public class StableNormal extends Process implements Lock {
    int myState = 0;
    int leftState = 0;
    public StableNormal(Linker initComm) {
        super(initComm);
    }
    public synchronized void requestCS() {
        while (leftState == myState) myWait();
    }
    public synchronized void releaseCS() {
        myState = leftState;
        sendToken();
    }
    public synchronized void sendToken() {
        int next = (myId + 1) % N;
        sendMsg(next, "token", myState);
    }
    public synchronized void handleMsg(Msg m, int src, String tag) {
        if (tag.equals("token")) {
            leftState = m.getMessageInt();
            notify();
            Util.mySleep(1000);
            sendToken();
        }
    }
}
```

Figure 18.5: Self-stabilizing algorithm for mutual exclusion in a ring for a normal machine

18.3   Self-Stabilizing Spanning Tree Construction

Assume that the underlying topology of a communication network is a connected undirected graph. Furthermore, one of the node is a distinguished node called *root*. Our task is to design a self-stabilizing algorithm to maintain a spanning tree rooted at the given node. Note that determining *parent* pointers of the spanning tree once is not enough. Any data fault can corrupt these pointers. We would need to recalculate parent pointers periodically. To calculate the parent pointers, we also use a variable `dist` that indicates the distance of that node from the root.

Root: (execute periodically)
  $dist := 0;$
  $parent := -1;$

For other node: (execute periodically)
  read *dist* of all neighbors;
  Let j be the neighbor with a minimum distance $dist_j$;
  $parent := j;$
  $dist := dist_j + 1;$

Figure 18.6: Self-stabilizing algorithm for (BFS) spanning tree

The algorithm shown in Figure 18.6 is quite simple. In this version, we assume that a node can read the value of variables of its neighbors. Later, we will translate this program into a distributed program. Each node maintains only two variables— `parent` and `dist`. The root node periodically sets `parent` to -1 and `dist` to 0. If any of these values get corrupted, the root node will reset it to the correct value by this mechanism. A nonroot node periodically reads the variable `dist` of all its neighbors. It chooses the neighbor with the least distance and makes that neighbor its parent. It also sets its own distance to one more than the distance of that neighbor.

It is easy to verify that no matter what the values of *parent* and *dist* initially are, the program eventually converges to valid values of `parent` and `dist`.

Let us now translate this program into a distributed program. The program for the root node shown in Figure 18.7 is identical to that in Figure 18.6. For periodic recalculation we use a timer that schedules `RestartTask` after a fixed time interval.

The algorithm for a nonroot node is shown in Figure 18.8. A nonroot node reads the values of the neighboring nodes by sending them a query message of type $Q.dist$. Whenever a node receives a message of type $Q.dist$ it responds with a message of type *A.dist* with the value of its `dist` variable. The variable `numReports` indicate the number of *A.dist* messages that node is expecting. Whenever `numReports` become 0, it knows that it has heard from all its neighbors and therefore it knows the neighbor with the least distance. The variable `newDist` is used for recalculation of the distance.

The main program that invokes `StableSpanRoot` and `StableSpanNonroot` is shown in Figure 18.9.

```java
import java.util.Timer;
public class StableSpanRoot extends Process {
    int parent = -1;
    int dist = 0;
    Timer t = new Timer();
    public StableSpanRoot(Linker initComm) {
        super(initComm);
        t.schedule(new RestartTask(this), 1000, 1000);
    }
    public synchronized void recalculate(){
        parent = -1;
        dist = 0;
        System.out.println("parent of " + myId + " is " + parent);
        System.out.println("dist of " + myId + " is " + dist);
    }
    public synchronized void handleMsg(Msg m, int src, String tag) {
        if (tag.equals("Q.dist")) {
            sendMsg(src, "A.dist", 0);
        } else if (tag.equals("restart")) {
            recalculate();
        }
    }
}
```

Figure 18.7: Self-stabilizing spanning tree algorithm for the root

18.4 Problems

18.1. Show that a system with four machines may not stabilize if it uses the K-state machine algorithm with $K = 2$.

18.2. Show that the K-state machine algorithm converges to a legal state in at most $O(N^2)$ moves by providing a norm function on the configuration of the ring that is at most $O(N^2)$, decreases by at least 1 for each move, and is always nonnegative.

```
import java . util . Timer;
public class StableSpanNonroot extends Process {
    int parent = −1;
    int dist = 0;
    int newDist = 0; //distance after recalculation
    Timer t = new Timer ();
    int numReports;
    public StableSpanNonroot (Linker initComm) {
        super (initComm);
        t . schedule (new RestartTask (this), 1000, 1000);
    }
    public synchronized void recalculate (){
        newDist = N; //init newDist to max possible
        sendToNeighbors ("Q. dist" ,0); //query neighbors for their dist
        numReports = comm. neighbors . size ();
        while (numReports > 0) myWait (); //wait for all responses
        dist = newDist;
        System . out . println ("parent of " + myId + " is " + parent);
        System . out . println ("dist of " + myId + " is " + dist);
    }
    public synchronized void handleMsg (Msg m, int src, String tag) {
        if (tag . equals ("Q. dist")) {
                sendMsg (src, "A. dist", dist); //reply with my dist
        } else if (tag . equals ("A. dist")) {
            int hisDist = m. getMessageInt ();
            if (( hisDist >= 0) && (newDist > hisDist )) {
                newDist = hisDist +1;
                parent = src;
            }
            numReports−−;
            notifyAll ();
        } else if (tag . equals ("restart")) {
            recalculate ();
        }
    }
}
```

Figure 18.8: Self-stabilizing spanning tree algorithm for nonroot nodes

```
public class StableTreeTester {
    public static void main(String [] args) throws Exception {
        String baseName = args [0];
        int myId = Integer.parseInt(args [1]);
        int numProc = Integer.parseInt(args [2]);
        Linker comm = new Linker(baseName, myId, numProc);
        if ( myId==0) {
            StableSpanRoot bot = new StableSpanRoot(comm);
            for (int i = 0; i < numProc; i++)
                if (i != myId)
                    (new ListenerThread(i, bot)).start();
        } else {
            StableSpanNonroot normal = new StableSpanNonroot(comm);
            for (int i = 0; i < numProc; i++)
                if (i != myId)
                    (new ListenerThread(i, normal)).start();
        }
    }
}
```

Figure 18.9: A Java program for spanning tree

18.3. In our K-state machine algorithm we have assumed that a machine can *read* the value of the state of its left machine and *write* its own state in one atomic action. Give a self-stabilizing algorithm in which a processor can only *read* a remote value or *write* a local value in one step, but not both.

*18.4. (due to Dijkstra [Dij74]) Show that the following four-state machine algorithm is self-stabilizing. The state of each machine is represented by two booleans xS and upS. For the bottom machine $upS = true$ and for the top machine $upS = false$ always hold.

Bottom:
    if $(xS = xR)$ and $\neg upR$ **then** $xS := \neg xS$;

Normal:
    if $xS \neq xL$ **then** $xS := \neg xS; upS := true$;
    if $xS = xR$ and upS and $\neg upR$ **then** $upS := false$;

Top:
    if $(xS \neq xL)$ **then** $xS := \neg xS$;

*18.5. Assume that each process P_i has a pointer that is either null or points to one of its neighbors. Give a self-stabilizing, distributed algorithm on a network of processes that guarantees that the system reaches a configuration where (a) if P_i points to P_j, then P_j points to P_i, and (b) there are no two neighboring processes such that both have null pointers.

18.5   Bibliographic Remarks

The idea of self-stabilizing algorithms first appeared in a paper by Dijkstra [Dij74], where three self-stabilizing algorithms were presented for mutual exclusion in a ring.

Appendix A

Various Utility Classes

Algorithms for several utility classes are shown in Figures A.1–A.6.

```java
import java.util.*;
public class Util {
    public static int max(int a, int b) {
        if (a > b) return a;
        return b;
    }
    public static void mySleep(int time) {
        try {
            Thread.sleep(time);
        } catch (InterruptedException e) {
        }
    }
    public static void myWait(Object obj) {
        println("waiting");
        try {
            obj.wait();
        } catch (InterruptedException e) {
        }
    }
    public static boolean lessThan(int A[], int B[]) {
        for (int j = 0; j < A.length; j++)
            if (A[j] > B[j]) return false;
        for (int j = 0; j < A.length; j++)
            if (A[j] < B[j]) return true;
        return false;
    }
    public static int maxArray(int A[]) {
        int v = A[0];
        for (int i =0; i<A.length; i++)
            if (A[i] > v) v = A[i];
        return v;
    }
    public static String writeArray(int A[]){
        StringBuffer s = new StringBuffer();
        for (int j = 0; j < A.length; j++)
            s.append(String.valueOf(A[j]) + " ");
        return new String(s.toString());
    }
    public static void readArray(String s, int A[]) {
        StringTokenizer st = new StringTokenizer(s);
        for (int j = 0; j < A.length; j++)
            A[j] = Integer.parseInt(st.nextToken());
    }
    public static int searchArray(int A[], int x) {
        for (int i = 0; i < A.length; i++)
            if (A[i] == x) return i;
        return -1;
    }
    public static void println(String s){
        if (Symbols.debugFlag) {
            System.out.println(s);
            System.out.flush();
        }
    }
}
```

Figure A.1: Util.java

```java
public class Symbols {
    public static final int Infinity = -1;
    // internet related
    public static final String nameServer =
                            "linux02.ece.utexas.edu";
    public static final int ServerPort = 7033;
    public static final int coordinator = 0;
    // time bounds on messages for synchronous algorithms
    public static final int roundTime = 500; // ms
    public static final boolean debugFlag = true;
}
```

Figure A.2: Symbols.java

```java
import java.util.*;
public class Matrix {
    public static String write(int A[][]){
        StringBuffer s = new StringBuffer();
        for (int j = 0; j < A.length; j++)
            s.append(Util.writeArray(A[j]) + " ");
        return new String(s.toString());
    }
    public static void read(String s, int A[][]) {
        StringTokenizer st = new StringTokenizer(s);
        for (int i = 0; i < A.length; i++)
            for (int j = 0; j < A[i].length; j++)
                A[i][j] = Integer.parseInt(st.nextToken());
    }
    public static void setZero(int A[][]) {
        for (int i = 0; i < A.length; i++)
            for (int j = 0; j < A[i].length; j++)
                A[i][j] = 0;
    }
    public static void setMax(int A[][], int B[][]) {
        for (int i = 0; i < A.length; i++)
            for (int j = 0; j < A[i].length; j++)
                A[i][j] = Util.max(A[i][j], B[i][j]);
    }
}
```

Figure A.3: Matrix.java

```java
import java.util.*;
public class MsgList extends LinkedList {
    public Msg removeM(int seqNo) {
        SeqMessage sm;
        ListIterator iter = super.listIterator(0);
        while (iter.hasNext()) {
            sm = (SeqMessage) iter.next();
            if (sm.getSeqNo() == seqNo) {
                iter.remove();
                return sm.getMessage();
            }
        }
        return null;
    }
}
```

Figure A.4: MsgList.java

```java
import java.util.LinkedList;
public class IntLinkedList extends LinkedList {
    public void add(int i) {
        super.add(new Integer(i));
    }
    public boolean contains(int i) {
        return super.contains(new Integer(i));
    }
    public int removeHead() {
        Integer j = (Integer) super.removeFirst();
        return j.intValue();
    }
    public boolean removeObject(int i) {
        return super.remove(new Integer(i));
    }
    public int getEntry(int index) {
        Integer j = (Integer) super.get(index);
        return j.intValue();
    }
}
```

Figure A.5: IntLinkedList.java

```java
public class PortAddr {
    String hostname;
    int portnum;
    public PortAddr(String s, int i) {
        hostname = new String(s);
        portnum = i;
    }
    public String getHostName() {
        return hostname;
    }
    public int getPort() {
        return portnum;
    }
}
```

Figure A.6: PortAddr.java

Bibliography

[AEA91]   D. Agrawal and A. El-Abbadi. An efficient and fault-tolerant solution for distributed mutual exclusion. *ACM Trans. Comput. Syst.*, 9(1):1–20, February 1991.

[AMG03]   R. Atreya, N. Mittal, and V. K. Garg. Detecting locally stable predicates without modifying application messages. In *Proc. Intnatl. Conf. on Principles of Distributed Systems*, La Martinique, France, December 2003.

[Ang80]   D. Angluin. Local and global properties in networks of processors. In *Proc. of the 12th ACM Symp. on Theory of Computing*, pages 82 – 93, 1980.

[AW98]   H. Attiya and J. Welch. *Distributed Computing - Fundamentals, Simulations and Advanced Topics*. McGraw Hill, Berkshire, SL6 2QL, England, 1998.

[Awe85]   B. Awerbuch. Complexity of network synchronization. *Journal of the ACM*, 32(4):804–823, October 1985.

[Bar96]   V. Barbosa. *An Introduction to Distributed Algorithms*. The MIT Press, Cambridge, MA, 1996.

[BJ87]   K. P. Birman and T. A. Joseph. Reliable communication in the presence of failures. *ACM Trans. Comput. Syst.*, 5(1):47–76, 1987.

[BN84]   A. D. Birrell and B. J. Nelson. Implementing remote procedure calls. *ACM Trans. Comput. Syst.*, 2(1):39–59, February 1984.

[Bou87]   L. Bouge. Repeated snapshots in distributed systems with synchronous communication and their implementation in CSP. *Theoretical Computer Science*, 49:145–169, 1987.

[Bur80]   J. Burns. A formal model for message passing systems. Technical Report TR–91, Indiana University, 1980. Department of Computer Science.

[CDK94]   G. Couloris, J. Dollimore, and T. Kindberg. *Distributed Systems: Concepts and Design.* Addison-Wesley, Reading, MA, 1994.

[CJ97]   R. Chow and T. Johnson. *Distributed Operating Systems and Algorithms.* Addison-Wesley Longman, Reading, MA, 1997.

[CL85]   K. M. Chandy and L. Lamport. Distributed snapshots: Determining global states of distributed systems. *ACM Trans. Comput. Syst.*, 3(1):63–75, February 1985.

[CM89]   K. M. Chandy and J. Misra. *Parallel Program Design: A Foundation.* Addison-Wesley, Reading, MA, 1989.

[Com00]   D. E. Comer. *Internetworking with TCP/IP: Volume 1. Principles, Protocols, and Architectures.* Prentice-Hall, Upper Saddle River, NJ 07458, USA, fourth edition, 2000.

[CR79]   E. J. H. Chang and R. Roberts. An improved algorithm for decentralized extrema-finding in circular configurations of processes. *Commun. of the ACM*, 22(5):281–283, 1979.

[DG96]   O. P. Damani and V. K. Garg. How to recover efficiently and asynchronously when optimism fails. In *ICDCS '96; Proc. of the 16th Intnatl. Conf. on Distributed Computing Systems; Hong Kong*, pages 108–115. IEEE, May 1996.

[Dij65a]   E. W. Dijkstra. Co-operating Sequential Processes. In F. Genuys, editor, *Programming Languages.* Academic Press, London, 1965.

[Dij65b]   E. W. Dijkstra. Solution of a problem in concurrent programming control. *Commun. of the ACM*, 8(9):569, September 1965.

[Dij74]   E. W. Dijkstra. Self-stabilizing systems in spite of distributed control. *Commun. of the ACM*, 17:643–644, 1974.

[Dij85]   E. W. Dijkstra. The distributed snapshot of K.M. Chandy and L. Lamport. In M. Broy, editor, *Control Flow and Data Flow: Concepts of Distributed Programming*, volume F14. NATO ASI Series, Springer-Verlag, New York, NY, 1985.

[Dij87]   E. W. Dijkstra. Shmuel Safra's version of termination detection. Report EWD998-0, University of Texas at Austin, January 1987.

[DKR82]   D. Dolev, M. Klawe, and M. Rodeh. An $O(n \log n)$ unidirectional distributed algorithm for extrema finding in a circle. *Journal of Algorithms, 3:245–260,* 1982.

[DS80]   E. W. Dijkstra and C. S Scholten. Termination detection for diffusing computations. *Information Processing Letters,* 11(4):1–4, August 1980.

[DS83]   D. Dolev and H. R. Strong. Authenticated algorithms for Byzantine agreement. *SIAM Journal on Computing,* 12(4):656–666, 1983.

[Far98]   J. Farley. *Java Distributed Computing.* O'Reilly, Sebastopol, CA, 1998.

[Fid89]   C. J. Fidge. Partial orders for parallel debugging. *Proc. of the ACM SIGPLAN/SIGOPS Workshop on Parallel and Distributed Debugging, (ACM SIGPLAN Notices),* 24(1):183–194, January 1989.

[FL82]   M. J. Fischer and N. A. Lynch. A lower bound on the time to assure interactive consistency. *Information Processing Letters,* 14(4):183–186, 1982.

[FLP85]   M. J. Fischer, N. Lynch, and M. Paterson. Impossibility of distributed consensus with one faulty process. *Journal of the ACM,* 32(2):374–382, April 1985.

[Gar92]   V. K. Garg. Some optimal algorithms for decomposed partially ordered sets. *Information Processing Letters,* 44:39–43, November 1992.

[Gar96]   V. K. Garg. *Principles of Distributed Systems.* Kluwer Academic Publishers, Boston, MA, 1996.

[Gar02]   V. K. Garg. *Elements of Distributed Computing.* Wiley, New York, NY, 2002.

[GC95]   V. K. Garg and C. Chase. Distributed algorithms for detecting conjunctive predicates. In *Proc. of the IEEE Intnatl. Conf. on Distributed Computing Systems,* pages 423–430, Vancouver, Canada, June 1995.

[Gif79]   D. K. Gifford. Weighted voting for replicated data. *Proc. 7th Symp. on Operating Syst. Principles,,* 13(5):150–162, December, 1979.

[Gos91]   A. Goscinski. *Distributed Operating Systems, The Logical Design.* Addison-Wesley, Reading, MA, 1991.

[GR93]   J. Gray and A. Reuter. *Transaction Processing.* Morgan Kaufmann Publishers, San Mateo, CA, 1993.

[Gra78]   J. N. Gray. Notes on database operating systems. In G. Goos and
           J. Hartmanis, editors, *Operating Systems: An Advance Course*, vol-
           ume 60 of *Lecture Notes in Computer Science*, pages 393–481. Springer-
           Verlag, 1978.

[GW92]   V. K. Garg and B. Waldecker. Detection of unstable predicates in
           distributed programs. In *Proc. of 12th Conf. on the Foundations of
           Software Technology & Theoretical Computer Science*, pages 253–264.
           Springer Verlag, December 1992. Lecture Notes in Computer Science
           652.

[HA90]   P. Hutto and M. Ahamad. Slow memory : Weakening consistency to
           enhance concurreny in distributed shared memories. *Proc. of Tenth
           Intnatl. Conf. on Distributed Computing Systems*, May 1990.

[Han72]   P. Brinch Hansen. Structured multi-programming. *CACM*, 15(7):574–
           578, July 1972.

[Har98]   S. J. Hartley. *Concurent Programming: The Java Programming Lan-
           guage*. Oxford, New York, NY, 1998.

[Hel89]   J. Helary. Observing global states of asynchronous distributed applica-
           tions. In *Workshop on Distributed Algorithms*, pages 124–135. Springer
           Verlag, LNCS 392, 1989.

[Her88]   M. Herlihy. Impossibility and universality results for wait-free synchro-
           nization. Technical Report TR-CS-8, Carnegie-Mellon University (Pitts-
           burg PA),, May 1988.

[HM84]   J.Y. Halpern and Y. Moses. Knowledge and common knowledge in a
           distributed environment. In *Proc. of the ACM Symp. on Principles of
           Distributed Computing*, pages 50 – 61, Vancouver, B.C., Canada, 1984.

[HMNR97]   J. Helary, A. Mostefaoui, R. H. B. Netzer, and M. Raynal. Preventing
           useless checkpoints in distributed computations. In *Symp. on Reliable
           Distributed Systems*, pages 183–190, Durham, NC, 1997.

[HMRS95]   M. Hurfin, M. Mizuno, M. Raynal, and M. Singhal. Efficient distributed
           detection of conjunction of local predicates. Technical Report 2731,
           IRISA, Rennes, France, November 1995.

[Hoa74]   C. A. R. Hoare. Monitors: An operating system structuring concept.
           Commun. of the ACM, 17(10):549–557, October 1974. Erratum in *Com-
           mun. of the ACM*, Vol. 18, No. 2 (February), p. 95, 1975.

[HR82]   G. S. Ho and C. V. Ramamoorthy. Protocols for deadlock detection in distributed database systems. *IEEE Trans. on Software Engineering*, 8(6):554–557, November 1982.

[HS80]   D. S. Hirschberg and J. B. Sinclair. Decentralized extrema-finding in circular configurations of processors. *Commun. of the ACM*, 23(11):627–628, 1980.

[HW90]   M. P. Herlihy and J. M. Wing. Linerizability: A correctness condition for atomic objects. *ACM Trans. Prog. Lang. Syst.*, 12(3):463–492, July 1990.

[Lam74]   L. Lamport. A new solution of dijkstra's concurrent programming program. *Commun. of the ACM*, 17(8), August 1974.

[Lam78]   L. Lamport. Time, clocks, and the ordering of events in a distributed system. *Commun. of the ACM*, 21(7):558–565, July 1978.

[Lam79]   L. Lamport. How to make a correct multiprocess program execute correctly on a multiprocessor. *IEEE Trans. on Computers*, 28(9):690–691, 1979.

[Lam86]   L. Lamport. On interprocess communication, part II: Algorithms. *Distributed Computing*, 1:86–101, 1986.

[Lea99]   D. Lea. *Concurrent Programming in Java: Design principles and Patterns*. The Java Series. Addison Wesley, Reading, MA, 2nd edition, 1999.

[Lov73]   L. Lovasz. Coverings and colorings of hypergraphs. In *4th Southeastern Conf. on Combinatorics, Graph Theory, and Computing*, pages 3–12, 1973.

[LSP82]   L. Lamport, R. Shostak, and M. Pease. The Byzantine generals problem. *ACM Trans. on Programming Languages and Systems*, 4(3):382–401, July 1982.

[Lub85]   M. Luby. A simple parallel algorithm for the maximal independent set problem. In ACM, editor, *Proc. of the 17th annual ACM Symp. on Theory of Computing, Providence, RI*, pages 1–10, May 1985.

[LY87]   T. H. Lai and T. H. Yang. On distributed snapshots. *Information Processing Letters*, pages 153–158, May 1987.

[Lyn96] N. A. Lynch. *Distributed Algorithms.* Morgan Kaufmann series in data management systems. Morgan Kaufmann Publishers, Los Altos, CA 94022, USA, 1996.

[Mae85] M. Maekawa. A square root N algorithm for mutual exclusion in decentralized systems. *ACM Trans. Comput. Syst.*, 3(2):145–159, May 1985.

[Mat89] F. Mattern. Virtual time and global states of distributed systems. In *Parallel and Distributed Algorithms: Proc. of the Intnatl. Workshop on Parallel and Distributed Algorithms*, pages 215–226. Elsevier Science Publishers B.V. (North-Holland), 1989.

[Mat93] F. Mattern. Efficient algorithms for distributed snapshots and global virtual time approximation. *Journal of Parallel and Distributed Computing*, pages 423–434, August 1993.

[MG95] V. V. Murty and V. K. Garg. An algorithm to guarantee synchronous ordering of messages. In *Proc. of Second Intnatl. Symp. on Autonomous Decentralized Systems*, pages 208–214. IEEE Computer Society Press, 1995.

[MG98] N. Mittal and V. K. Garg. Consistency conditions for multi-object distributed operations. In *Proc. of the 18th Int'l Conf. on Distributed Computing Systems (ICDCS-18)*, pages 582–589, May 1998.

[MS94] K. Marzullo and L. S. Sabel. Efficient detection of a class of stable properties. *Distributed Computing*, 8(2):81–91, 1994.

[NX95] R. H. B. Netzer and J. Xu. Necessary and sufficent conditions for consistent global snapshots. *IEEE Trans. on Parallel and Distributed Systems*, 6(2):165–169, February 1995.

[Pet81] G. L. Peterson. Myths about the mutual exclusion problem. *Information Processing Letters*, 12(3):115–116, June 1981.

[Pet82] G. Peterson. unidirectional algorithm for the circular extrema problem. *ACM Trans. on Programming Languages and Systems, 4:758–762*, 1982.

[PKR82] J. K. Pachl, E. Korach, and D. Rotem. A technique for proving lower bounds for distributed maximum-finding algorithms. In *ACM Symp. on Theory of Computing*, pages 378–382, 1982.

[PSL80]   M. Pease, R. Shostak, and L. Lamport. Reaching agreements in the presence of faults. *Journal of the ACM*, 27(2):228–234, April 1980.

[PW95]   D. Peleg and A. Wool. Crumbling walls: a class of practical and efficient quorum systems. In *Proc. of the 14th Annual ACM Symp. on Principles of Distributed Computing (PODC '95)*, pages 120–129, New York, August 1995. ACM.

[RA81]   G. Ricart and A. K. Agrawala. An optimal algorithm for mutual exclusion in computer networks. *Commun. of the ACM*, 24(1):9 – 17, 1981.

[Ray88]   M. Raynal. *Distributed Algorithms and Protocols*. John Wiley & Sons, 1988.

[Ray89]   K. Raymond. A tree-based algorithm for distributed mutual exclusion. *ACM Trans. Comput. Syst.*, 7(1):61–77, February 1989.

[RH90]   M. Raynal and J. M. Helary. *Synchronization and Control of Distributed Systems and Programs*. Wiley, Chichester, UK, 1990.

[RST91]   M. Raynal, A. Schiper, and S. Toueg. The causal ordering abstraction and a simple way to implement it. *Information Processing Letters*, 39(6):343–350, July 1991.

[SK85]   I. Suzuki and T. Kasami. A distributed mutual exclusion algorithm. *ACM Trans. Comput. Syst.*, 3(4):344–349, November 1985.

[SK86]   M. Spezialetti and P. Kearns. Efficient distributed snapshots. In *Proc. of the 6th Intnatl. Conf. on Distributed Computing Systems*, pages 382–388, 1986.

[Ske82]   D. Skeen. *Crash Recovery in Distributed Database System*. PhD Dissertation, EECS Department, University of California at Berkeley, 1982.

[SL87]   S. Sarin and N. A. Lynch. Discarding obsolete information in a replicated database system. *IEEE Trans. on Software Engineering*, SE-13(1):39–47, January 1987.

[SM94]   ed. S. Mullender. *Distributed Systems*. Addison-Wesley, Reading, MA, 1994.

[SS94]   M. Singhal and N. G. Shivaratri. *Advanced Concepts in Operating Systems*. McGraw Hill, New York, NY, 1994.

[SS95]   S. D. Stoller and F. B. Schneider. Faster possibility detection by combin-
           ing two approaches. In *Proc. of the 9th Intnatl. Workshop on Distributed
           Algorithms*, pages 318–332, France, September 1995. Springer-Verlag.

[SY85]   R. E. Strom and S. Yemeni. Optimistic recovery in distributed systems.
           ACM Trans. Comput. Syst., 3(3):204–226, 1985.

[Tay83]   R. N. Taylor. Complexity of analyzing the synchronization structure of
           concurrent programs. *Acta Informatica*, 19(1):57–84, April 1983.

[Tay89]   K. Taylor. The role of inhibition in asynchronous consistent-cut proto-
           cols. In *Workshop on Distributed Algorithms*, pages 280–291. Springer
           Verlag, LNCS 392, 1989.

[Tel94]   G. Tel. *Introduction to Distributed Algorithms*. Cambridge University
           Press, Cambridge, England, 1994.

[TG93]   A. I. Tomlinson and V. K. Garg. Detecting relational global predicates
           in distributed systems. In *Proc. of the Workshop on Parallel and Dis-
           tributed Debugging*, pages 21–31, San Diego, CA, May 1993.

[Tho79]   R. H. Thomas. A majority consensus approach to concurrency con-
           trol for multiple copy databases. *ACM Trans. on Database Systems*,
           4(2):180–209, June 1979.

[TvS02]   A. S. Tanenbaum and M. van Steen. *Distributed systems: principles and
           paradigms*. Prentice Hall, 2002.

[VD92]   S. Venkatesan and B. Dathan. Testing and debugging distributed pro-
           grams using global predicates. In *30th Annual Allerton Conf. on Com-
           mun., Control and Computing*, pages 137–146, Allerton, Illinois, Octo-
           ber 1992.

[Wan97]   Y. M. Wang. Consistent global checkpoints that contain a given set of
           local checkpoints. *IEEE Transactions on Computers*, 46(4), April 1997.

[YM94]   Z. Yang and T. A. Marsland. Introduction. In Z. Yang and T. A.
           Marsland, editors, *Global State and Time in Distributed Systems*. IEEE
           Computer Society Press, 1994.

Index

α synchronizer, 226
β synchronizer, 230
γ synchronizer, 230

abort, 233
ACID properties, 254
agreement, 240, 248
AlphaSynch.java, 229
anonymous ring, 210
asynchronous recovery, 272
asynchrony of events, 235
atomic, 66
atomic snapshots, 76
atomicity, 254
Attempt1.java, 20
Attempt2.java, 21
Attempt3.java, 21

bakery algorithm, 24
Bakery.java, 25
barrier synchronization, 187
BCell.java, 49
binary semaphore, 31
BinarySemaphore.java, 32
bivalent, 236
bivalent state, 79
BoundedBuffer.java, 35
BoundedBufferMonitor.java, 45
broadcast, 213, 215
busy wait, 31
Byzantine failure, 239
Byzantine General Agreement, 243

Camera.java, 152
CameraLinker.java, 158
CameraTester.java, 160
CamUser.java, 152
causal consistency, 60
causal ordering, 192, 193
causal total order, 203
CausalLinker.java, 195
CausalMessage.java, 194
Cell.java, 50
CentMutex.java, 134
centralized algorithm, 203
CentSensor.java, 167
Chang–Roberts algorithm, 210
Chat.java, 197
checker process, 166
checkpoint, 263
checkpointing, 268
CircToken.java, 145
clocks, 111, 115
clustering, 230
commit, 233
common knowledge, 247
communication-induced checkpointing,
        264, 267
commute property, 235
CompSwap.java, 82
CompSwapConsensus.java, 83
concurrent, 115
concurrent object, 53
concurrent queue, 86
concurrent system, 54

condition variables, 42
conditional synchronization, 33
conflict graph, 140
Connector.java, 102
consensus, 78, 233, 239
consensus number, 79
Consensus.java, 78, 242
ConsensusTester.java, 243
consistency, 254
consistent cut, 166
consistent interval, 185
convergecast, 215
coordinated checkpoints, 263
coordinating general problem, 248
counting semaphores, 32
CountingSemaphore.java, 33
CQueue.java, 86
crash, 239
critical region, 18
critical section, 18, 130
critical state, 79
crumbling wall, 144

DatagramClient.java, 95
datagrams, 92
DatagramServer.java, 93
DatagramSocket, 90
deadlock, 49, 209
deadlocks, 188
debugging, 164
Dekker.java, 29
diffusing computation, 180
Dijkstra and Scholten's algorithm, 180
dining philosopher, 39
DiningMonitor.java, 47
DiningPhilosopher.java, 41
DinMutex.java, 143
direct-dependency clocks, 122
DirectClock.java, 122
directly precedes, 123

disjunctive normal form, 164
disjunctive predicate, 165
distributed commit, 257
distributed computation, 111, 114
distributed database, 233
distributed objects, 196
distributed systems, 1
DistSensor.java, 174
domain name system, 89
domino effect, 264
DSTerm.java, 183
durability, 255

Election.java, 209
events, 114

failure detection, 112
fairness, 130
fault-tolerant vector clock, 270
Fibonacci.java, 14
FIFO consistency, 62
Fixed dependency after send, 268
flooding algorithm, 213
FooBar.java, 12
fork, 9
FuncUser.java, 217

global checkpoint, 263
global functions, 215
global properties, 164
global snapshot, 151
global snapshot algorithm, 149
global state, 150
GlobalFunc.java, 218
GlobalFuncTester.java, 219
GlobalService.java, 216
grid quorum system, 146

happened-before diagrams, 115
happened-before model, 150
happened-before relation, 114

HelloWorldThread.java, 11
history, 54
HWMutex.java, 28

InetAddress, 89
initial independence, 234
interface definition language, 8
interleaving model, 114
invocation, 54
isolation, 254

KingBGA.java, 245
knowledge, 244

Lamport's Algorithm for Total Order,
    204
LamportClock.java, 117
LamportMutex.java, 137
leader election, 209
legal, 54
lightweight processes, 9
linearizable, 57
Linker, 100
Linker.java, 104
ListenerThread.java, 132
ListQueue.java, 48
liveness, 130
LLSC.java, 84
locally stable, 185
location transparency, 101
lock-free, 65
Lock.java, 18, 130
LockFreeSnapshot.java, 77
LockTester.java, 131
logging, 256
logical clock, 116

majority voting system, 144
marker, 152
matrix clock, 125
MatrixClock.java, 124

maximum recoverable state, 276
message ordering, 191
minimal rollback, 276
monitor, 42
MRMW Register, 74
MRSW Register, 73, 74
MRSW.java, 75
Msg.java, 103
MsgHandler.java, 130
multicast messages, 203
MultiValued.java, 72
MultiWriter.j, 76
mutual exclusion, 18, 129, 203, 280
MyThread.java, 19

name server, 96
Name.java, 99
NameRmiClient.java, 109
NameServer.java, 98
NameService.java, 105
NameServiceImpl.java, 106
NameTable.java, 97
nondeterminism, 191
normal, 62

object serialization, 107
ObjPointer.java, 83
occurred before, 54
omission model, 239
optimistic logging, 269
orphan, 270

parallel system, 1
pessimistic logging, 268
Peterson's algorithm, 21
PetersonAlgorithm.java, 22
Philosopher.java, 40
pointer-swinging, 84
private workspace, 256
process, 8
process-time diagrams, 115

Process.java, 133
producer-consumer problem, 33
ProducerConsumer.java, 37
progress, 22
pulse, 221

quorum, 144

RAMutex.java, 139
reader-writer problem, 36
ReaderWriter.java, 38
receive omission, 239
RecvCamera.java, 155
regular, 66
Regular SRSW Register, 70
RegularBoolean.java, 71
reliable communication, 246
remote method invocations, 101
remote procedure calls, 101
replicated state machines, 205
Resource.java, 41
response, 54
restarts, 270
RestartTask.java, 282
Ricart and Agrawala's algorithm, 136
ring, 209
RingLeader.java, 211
rmiregistry, 107
rollback, 270
rollback-dependency trackability, 267
run, 115

safe, 66
Safe SRSW Register, 70
SafeBoolean.java, 70
safety, 130
self-stabilizing, 279
semaphore, 31
send omission, 239
SenderCamera.java, 159
Sensor.java, 165

SensorCircToken.java, 170
SensorTester.java, 171
SensorUser.java, 165
SeqMessage.java, 156
SeqQueue.java, 85
sequential consistency, 55
sequential history, 54
serializability, 255
shared clock, 112
shared memory, 112
ShortestPath.java, 179
simple synchronizer, 223
SimpleSynch.java, 224
Skeen's algorithm, 204
space-time diagrams, 115
spanning tree, 181, 216, 285
SpanTree.java, 214
SRSW Boolean Register, 71
SRSW Multivalued Register, 71
SRSW Register, 73
stable predicate, 163
StableBottom.java, 283
StableNormal.java, 284
StableSpanNonroot.java, 287
StableSpanRoot.java, 286
StableTreeTester.java, 288
starvation-freedom, 22
symmetry, 210
Synch.java, 28
SynchBfsTree.java, 227
SynchLinker.java, 202
synchronizer, 221
Synchronizer.java, 222
synchronous ordering, 196

TermDetector.java, 179
terminating reliable broadcast, 238
termination, 181, 240
TermShortestPath.java, 184
TermToken.java, 186

TestAndSet.java, 27, 81
TestSetConsensus.java, 82
threads, 9
time-based model, 150
Topology.java, 100
total order, 203
transaction, 233, 253
Transmission Control Protocol, 90
tree-based quorum system, 147
Tree.java, 226
triangular quorum system, 146
two-phase commit, 257
two-phase locking, 256
TwoPhaseCoord.java, 259
TwoPhaseParticipant.java, 260

universal, 78
universal construction, 84
Universal Datagram Protocol, 90
universal object, 79

validity, 240
VCLinker.java, 120
vector clock, 118
VectorClock.java, 119
version end-table, 272

wait, 9
wait-for graph, 188
wait-free, 65
weak conjunctive predicate, 166
wheel coterie, 146

z-consistent, 265
zigzag relation, 265